PARLIAMENTS
AND
ASSEMBLIES
OF THE
UNITED KINGDOM

ISBN 0 9525777 6 3

PUBLISHED BY

DYSON BELL MARTIN

IN ASSOCIATION WITH

PARLIAMENTARY MONITORING SERVICES LTD

Editors	*Paul Thompson*
	Jonathan Bracken
Managing Editor	*Lionel Zetter*
Associate Editors	*Thomas P McLaughlin*
	Peter Stoker

© Text : Dyson Bell Martin

© Format and Appendices :

Parliamentary Monitoring Services Ltd
19 Douglas Street
Westminster
LONDON
SW1P 4PA

Price : £20 in UK

Dyson Bell Martin

Is the parliamentary, legislative and public law practice of Bircham & Co, solicitors and parliamentary agents. The firm is one of a handful of law firms authorised to promote and oppose private legislation before the UK Parliament and has been providing parliamentary and related services for over 150 years. The firm has its principal office in Westminster and representative offices in Edinburgh, Cardiff and Brussels.

Counting major companies, trade, professional and amenity bodies, public and local authorities, regulators and charities amongst its clients, the firm provides specialist advice and support on all aspects of the governmental, policy-making, legislative and regulatory process in the UK and EU, often working in conjunction with in-house government relations and legal teams and other professional advisers. In particular, the firm's services include policy research and analysis, strategic and procedural advice, case preparation and legislative drafting.

Parliamentary Monitoring Services Ltd

Is an independent company dealing in all aspects of political intelligence, research, monitoring and publishing. The company is based in Westminster and has been established for twenty years. Clients include national and specialist publications, public relations companies, multi-national corporations, trade associations, diplomatic missions and charities.

The company has a multi-disciplinary staff comprised of politics graduates, former House of Commons and House of Lords researchers, ex-employees of the main political parties, former civil servants, and journalists. Together they provide a unique blend of political skills, and an unparalleled service to clients.

Foreword

 THE FIRST MINISTER

Scottish Executive

Parliament Headquarters Building
George IV Bridge
EDINBURGH
EH99 1SP

Devolution is not just about improving the arrangements for handling issues distinctly Scottish. For example, as many of the devolved competences have a distinct EU dimension, it is important that we have in place a close relationship both with Westminster and Brussels. Such a relationship will ensure that Scotland's voice is heard in Westminster and at the heart of Europe.

I am sure that the book will enlighten you on the new constitutional arrangements. Happy reading.

DONALD DEWAR

Parliaments and Assemblies
of the
United Kingdom

Contents:

Chapter 1

Introduction

1 Introduction

The purpose of this guide is to provide a simple reference work for those who need a detailed understanding of the nature and workings of the Parliaments and Assemblies of the United Kingdom and, so far as they relate to the UK, the institutions of the European Community. Necessarily, this first edition is somewhat experimental and the publishers would welcome readers' comments, corrections and suggestions for future editions.

To ease understanding and facilitate cross reference all the main chapters have a common format.

The guide states the position as at 1st June 1999 and, for that purpose, anticipates the official opening of the Scottish Parliament and the National Assembly for Wales on 1st July 1999. In doing so, it takes as its basis a number of official documents which are or may be subject to change, in particular:-

+ The Scotland Act 1998 (Transitory and Transitional Provisions) (Standing Orders and Parliamentary Publications) Order 1999;

+ The National Assembly for Wales (Transfer of Functions) Order 1999; and

+ The Standing Orders of the National Assembly for Wales, made by the Secretary of State on 8th April 1999.

Chapter 2

Arrangements Between Institutions

2 Arrangements Between Institutions

2.1 Common Membership

There is no statutory bar on a person being a member of more than one of the Parliaments and Assemblies but a political party may prohibit the holding of such dual mandates and require a sitting member of one body who is elected to another body to stand down from the first body at the next election.

The Secretary of State for Wales, who will normally be a member of the House of Commons but not necessarily a member of the National Assembly, is entitled to attend and participate in any proceedings of the National Assembly for Wales. No equivalent provision is made in relation to the Scottish Parliament or Northern Ireland Assembly.

2.2 Legislative Overlap

The UK Government has announced that it expects a convention to be adopted that the UK Parliament would not normally legislate with regard to devolved matters without the consent of the relevant devolved body.

No specific procedures have been put in place in relation to this to date.

As respects subordinate legislation, in some cases procedures need to be undertaken both at Westminster and in the Scottish Parliament or one of the Assemblies. No specific arrangements for co-ordination have yet been announced.

For powers of intervention in relation to devolved legislation, see 3.3 in particular.

2.3 **European Legislation**

Ministers will not ordinarily agree in the EC Council of Ministers to any proposal for Community legislation until it has been considered by the Commons' European Legislation Committee and, where the proposal is to be debated in the House or considered by a standing committee, the House of Commons has passed a resolution upon it. A similar arrangement applies to the House of Lords' European Communities Committee. A proposal will only be agreed in the Lords once there is to be no further scrutiny or debate, any government response has been received or, where there has been correspondence with ministers, once that correspondence is closed.

2.4 **Concordats**

No concordats are yet in existence but guidance was issued by the UK Government on 27th February 1999 as to the principles which will govern the non-statutory concordats which are intended to regulate the administrative working relationships between the UK Government, the Scottish Executive and the Welsh Assembly. The principles include publication of all formally agreed concordats which are expected to be issued after 1st July 1999.

2.5 **Joint Ministerial Committee**

During the passage of the Scotland Bill it was announced that the UK Government would establish a joint ministerial committee as a non-statutory standing consultative body to consider reserved matters that impinge on devolved responsibilities. The committee is expected to be created after 1st July 1999.

2.6   British-Irish Council

Under the "Good Friday" or Belfast Agreement of 10th April 1998 provision is made for the establishment of a British-Irish Council to "promote the harmonious and mutually beneficial development of the totality of relationships amongst the peoples of the islands". The Council is to comprise representatives of the British and Irish Governments, devolved institutions in Northern Ireland, Scotland and Wales and, if appropriate, elsewhere in the United Kingdom, together with representatives of the Isle of Man and the Channel Islands. The Council is not yet in existence.

2.7   Devolution Issues

Questions concerning the lawful exercise of powers devolved under the Scotland Act, the Government of Wales Act and the Northern Ireland Act are categorised in those Acts as "devolution issues" (see also 6.1.4, 7.1.5 and 8.1.4).

Each of the Acts specifies which higher courts are to take references or appeals from lower courts on devolution issues and provides for all such issues ultimately to be referred to the Judicial Committee of the Privy Council except, where on an appeal before the House of Lords, that House considers that it should determine the issue.

The relevant law officers within their jurisdictions, the Lord Advocate in relation to Scottish matters, the National Assembly for Wales in relation to Welsh matters, the Attorney General for Northern Ireland and, acting jointly, the First and deputy First Minister in relation to Northern Ireland matters, must be notified of any relevant devolution issue proceedings to which they are not a party and can instigate proceedings for the determination of such issues.

Each of the relevant law officers may institute devolution issue proceedings as may the Lord Advocate in relation to Scottish matters in Scotland, the National Assembly for Wales in relation to Welsh matters generally and the Attorney General in relation to Northern Ireland matters in Northern Ireland. In addition, the Lord Advocate in relation to Scottish matters, the National Assembly for Wales in relation to Welsh matters and the Attorney General for Northern Ireland or the First and deputy First Minister acting jointly in relation to Northern Ireland matters may defend devolution proceedings anywhere in the UK. The Attorney General may also do so in Northern Ireland.

Any of the above may also require any devolution proceedings to which they are a party to be referred to the Judicial Committee. In addition, the Lord Advocate in relation to Scottish matters, the National Assembly for Wales in relation to Welsh matters and the First and deputy First Minister acting jointly in relation to Northern Ireland matters, as well as each of the three law officers in relation to Scottish or Northern Ireland matters and the Attorney General in relation to Welsh matters, may refer to the Judicial Committee any devolution issue which is not the subject of proceedings. If such a reference is made relating to the proposed exercise of a function by a member of the Scottish Executive, the National Assembly for Wales or a Northern Ireland Minister or Department, as the case may be, the function must not be exercised following notification to them of the reference.

Where a court or tribunal decides that a provision of an Act of the Scottish Parliament or of the Northern Ireland Assembly is outside its legislative competence or that a member of the Scottish Executive or the National Assembly for Wales or a Minister or Department in Northern Ireland does not have the power to make, confer or approve subordinate legislation, it may make an order negating any retrospective effect of its decision or suspending its effect to allow the defect to be corrected.

2.8   *Human Rights*

The main provisions of the Human Rights Act 1998, which will enable breaches of Convention rights as formulated in the European Convention on Human Rights to be pursued in the UK courts, are not expected to be brought into force in the UK until 2nd October 2000. However, by virtue of the devolution legislation, the Convention rights already apply in relation to action by the Scottish Parliament and the Northern Ireland Assembly and to the exercise of powers by the Scottish

Executive, the National Assembly for Wales and a Northern Ireland Minister or Department.

Human rights questions can only be raised in legal proceedings by the Attorney General, the Advocate General and the Attorney General for Northern Ireland, by the Lord Advocate in relation to Scottish or Northern Ireland matters, the National Assembly for Wales in relation to Welsh matters or by "a victim" (i.e. an individual or body directly affected, rather than a public body or pressure group).

In relation to human rights and legislation generally see also 3.3.

2.9   *International Obligations*

Each of the Secretaries of State in relation to Scotland and Northern Ireland and any Minister of the Crown in relation to Wales has power to direct a relevant executive body (i.e. the Scottish Executive, a Minister or Northern Ireland department or the Assembly) to take action required to give effect to any international obligations or to refrain from action incompatible with such obligations. They also have certain powers to revoke subordinate legislation which is incompatible with international obligations: see 3.3.

Chapter 3

Forms of Legislation

3   Forms of Legislation

3.1   Types of Legislation

✦ European Regulations
laws of the EC which are directly applicable and do not require any national implementation to have effect.

✦ European Directives
laws of the EC which provide a framework that requires national implementation to have effect but, in default of national implementation, are liable to be construed by the courts as directly effective.

✦ Acts of Parliament
laws applicable to the UK or parts of it derived from bills passed by the UK Parliament.

✦ Acts of the Scottish Parliament
laws applicable to Scotland derived from bills passed by the Scottish Parliament established under the Scotland Act 1998.

✦ Acts of the Northern Ireland Assembly
laws applicable to Northern Ireland derived from bills passed by the Northern Ireland Assembly established under the Northern Ireland Act 1998.

+ Orders in Council, Orders, Rules, Regulations, Schemes, warrants, byelaws and other instruments made under any Act

> laws made by the Crown, UK Ministers, Scottish Ministers, the Welsh Assembly and others by way of subordinate legislation under the authority of Acts of Parliament or, in the case of Scottish Ministers, Acts of the Scottish Parliament.

3.2 *Format*

+ EC Regulations and Directives

These have a descriptive title and document number, a preamble and a series of numbered articles with numbered paragraphs, the articles often being arranged in parts or titles culminating in an article describing the commencement arrangements. A series of annexes may follow the articles.

+ UK Bills

These have a sessional number, short title (with "H.L." appended for bills commencing in the House of Lords), long title, a table of contents where justified, a formal enacting formula ("Be it enacted ....."), numbered clauses (which become "sections" when enacted and which may be divided into subsections, paragraphs and sub-paragraphs) and, very often, schedules expanding on the clauses. The back sheet includes the name of the member in charge and, in the Commons, the principal supporters.

+ Scottish and Northern Ireland Bills

It is expected that bills before the Scottish Parliament and the Northern Ireland Assembly will follow a similar format to UK bills.

+ Subordinate legislation

All forms of subordinate legislation have a similar format. Each begins with a title, the date when it was laid and will come into force, normally a preamble setting out the authority for making it and then numbered clauses, sub-divided into paragraphs, the clauses being known as articles, rules or regulations depending upon whether the instrument is entitled an order or rules or regulations. The instrument may also have a number of schedules.

3.3   *Legitimacy*

Acts of the Scottish Parliament and of the Northern Ireland Assembly and all forms of subordinate legislation must fall within the ambit of the primary legislation conferring the power to make them and are thus liable to be overturned by the courts if found to be outside the ambit of the relevant powers (i.e. *ultra vires*). In addition, the following general constraints apply to various forms of legislation.

✦ Incompatibility with Community law

There is no bar as such on the UK Parliament passing legislation contrary to EC law (as comprised in treaties, regulations and directives) but such legislation is liable to be challenged, suspended and possibly rendered void by rulings of the European Court of Justice or the domestic courts (in line with the House of Lords judgment in the Factortame cases concerning the fisheries "quota hopping" restrictions in the Merchant Shipping Act 1986).

In accordance with EC Directive 83/189, proposals for certain technical standards and regulations must also first be notified in draft to the European Commission and the process of their adoption is then suspended to allow the Commission and other member states to propose amendments eliminating or reducing any potential barriers to trade.

The Scottish Parliament and the Assemblies for Wales and Northern Ireland are all precluded from passing legislation incompatible with Community law (see 6.1.3, 7.1.4 and 8.1.3).

✦ Devolution

As noted elsewhere, there are constraints upon what the UK Parliament and the devolved bodies can do by way of legislation (see 2.2, 6.1, 7.1 and 8.1).

The Advocate General, the Lord Advocate and the Attorney General in relation to Scotland and the Attorney General for Northern Ireland in relation to Northern Ireland are entitled to refer the question of whether a bill before the Scottish Parliament or the Assembly, as the case may be, is within legislative competence to the Judicial Committee of the Privy Council (see 2.7).

As respects bills before the Scottish Parliament, the Secretary of State has a power in certain circumstances to make an order stopping the passage of a bill. Provision is also made to preclude the Presiding Officer submitting a bill for Royal Assent where it is subject to devolution proceedings: see 6.12.4. In Northern Ireland, the role of the Secretary of State in submitting bills for Royal Assent will achieve a similar effect (see 8.12).

As respects subordinate legislation in Scotland, provision is made to enable the relevant Secretary of State by order to revoke an instrument if he believes that it modifies the law as it applies to reserved matters and, in doing so, has an adverse effect on the law as it applies to reserved matters.

+ International Obligations

Each of the Secretaries of State in relation to Scotland and Northern Ireland and a Minister of the Crown in relation to Wales may revoke any subordinate legislation made by (or which could be revoked by) a devolved body if it contains provisions which he has reasonable grounds for believing are incompatible with any international obligations or the interests of defence or national security.

+ Human Rights

As the UK is a signatory to the European Convention on Human Rights, the power to legislate should be exercised subject to the fundamental rights set out in the Convention and legislation which is incompatible with the Convention may be challenged before the European Court of Human Rights in Strasbourg.

The Human Rights Act 1998, the main provisions of which are expected to be brought into force in the UK on 2nd October 2000, provides for the application of Convention rights as part of domestic law. Under that Act, the Minister responsible for a Government bill before the UK Parliament must make a statement of compatibility before Second Reading of the bill. Once enacted, Acts of Parliament may be the subject of a declaration of incompatibility by the courts. Such declarations do not set aside the legislation in question but provide the basis for

Ministers to make any necessary amendment or repeal by subordinate legislation under a "fast track" procedure provided by the Act.

A general statement of legislative competence encompassing Human Rights is required from a member of the Scottish Executive in relation to a bill before the Scottish Parliament and from the Minister in charge of a bill before the Northern Ireland Assembly.

As noted (see 2.8), the requirements of the Convention, so far as they are to be applied by the Human Rights Act, are applied directly by the Scotland Act 1998, the Government of Wales Act 1998 and the Northern Ireland Act 1998 so as to have effect immediately rather than awaiting the coming into force of the Human Rights Act (see also 3.4 below as to interpretation). In addition, they are all specifically precluded from passing legislation incompatible with Convention rights (see 6.1.3, 7.1.4 and 8.1.3).

3.4   *Interpretation*

+ Community legislation

All versions of Community legislation in any of the official languages of the Community are regarded as equally authoritative.

The European Court of Justice (and the UK courts when construing Community legislation) takes a purposive or teleological approach to legislative interpretation which may include examination of relevant preparatory papers ("travaux preparatoire").

+ UK and devolved legislation

The UK courts tend to take a more literal approach to statutory interpretation but, following the House of Lords' decision in Pepper v Hart (1993), the courts are prepared now to take account of Hansard in the interpretation of Acts of Parliament, at least in cases of ambiguity.

The Interpretation Act 1978 provides a number of standard interpretative rules for legislation generally. However, it is only partly applicable to Acts of the Scottish Parliament, to instruments made under such Acts and to Northern Ireland.

Once fully in force, the Human Rights Act 1998 will require all primary and subordinate legislation - irrespective of when it was enacted - to be interpreted, so far as it is possible to do so, in a way which is compatible with Convention rights.

✦ Acts of the Scottish Parliament etc.

Acts of the Scottish Parliament and subordinate legislation brought forward by the Scottish Executive which could be read to be outside competence are required to be construed as narrowly as is required for them to be within competence, if such a reading is possible, and are to have effect accordingly. For this purpose, "competence" means legislative competence in the case of Acts and bills leading to Acts (see 6.1.3) and, in relation to subordinate legislation, means the powers conferred by the Scotland Act.

Standard interpretative rules for Acts of the Scottish Parliament have been made by a statutory instrument under the Scotland Act 1998.

✦ Acts of the Northern Ireland Assembly etc.

Similar provisions respecting competence apply in relation to legislation authorised by the Northern Ireland Act 1998.

✦ Welsh subordinate legislation

The texts of any subordinate legislation which is in both English and Welsh when made by the Assembly are required to be treated for all purposes as of equal standing.

Chapter 4

The House of Commons

4.11 Committees

4.12 Parliamentary Bills

4.13 Subordinate Legislation

4.14 European Legislation

4.15 Finance and Taxation

4.1   Form and Functions

4.1.1   Overview

The House of Commons, together with the House of Lords and the Sovereign, form the UK Parliament:

+ The Commons is the elected assembly (659 members) from whose members the Sovereign invites one member to form and preside as Prime Minister over a UK Government.

+ It provides democratic legitimacy to the UK government of the day, most notably by virtue of the convention that, upon losing a vote of confidence, the Prime Minister must resign and advise the Sovereign to dissolve Parliament.

+ It has the power (shared in part with the House of Lords) to initiate and enact primary legislation for all or any part of the UK.

+ It has the sole power to sanction the Government's proposals for taxation and public expenditure except to the extent devolved to the Scottish Parliament.

+ It provides (together with the House of Lords and, in certain respects, the Scottish Parliament and the National Assembly for Wales) a degree of supervision over subordinate legislation.

+ It operates as a national debating forum and investigative body, both through its plenary sessions and by its committee system, in relation to matters of general public interest. More specifically, it holds the UK Government and others to account, scrutinises legislation and, pursuant to particular enactments, reviews the activities of certain public bodies.

4.1.2   *Jurisdiction*

The House of Commons, together with the Sovereign and the House of Lords, operate as a Parliament for England, Scotland, Wales and Northern Ireland but subject now to powers devolved to the Scottish Parliament, the National Assembly for Wales and the Northern Ireland Assembly.

So far as legislation is concerned, Parliament's territorial authority extends to all areas beyond the UK over which the Crown asserts sovereignty and, in addition, legislation can be interpreted as having extra-territorial effect. Whilst its legislative authority used to extend to a large number of UK dependencies, by virtue of the Statute of Westminster and later enactments, Parliament's legislative authority outside of the UK has been greatly confined and now extends to no more than the Channel Islands, the Isle of Man and a few dependencies. Legislation is not, however, automatically applied outside the UK and, in the case of the Channel Islands and the Isle of Man, a limited number of UK Acts will contain an enabling power allowing their application, if necessary with modifications, by Order in Council.

4.1.3   Legislative Competence

See 3.3 and 4.1.2.

4.2   Electoral Arrangements

4.2.1   Composition and Electoral System

The House of Commons comprises 659 members of Parliament elected to represent single member constituencies on a simple majority ("first past the post") basis. 529 members represent constituencies in England, 40 in Wales, 72 in Scotland and 18 in Northern Ireland. Parliamentary constituencies are kept under review by four national Boundary Commissions pursuant to the Parliamentary Constituencies Act 1986.

4.2.2   Franchise

Those eligible to vote are all British, other Commonwealth and Irish citizens resident in the UK aged 18 or over other than peers, detained mental patients, convicted prisoners in detention or unlawfully at large and those convicted of corrupt or illegal practices at elections. British citizens resident overseas may also be registered as voters for 20 years after leaving the UK and are permitted to vote at elections in the last UK constituency in which they resided.

4.2.3 Candidacy and Election Rules

To be eligible for election as a member of Parliament a person must be a British, other Commonwealth or Irish citizen of at least 21 years of age and not disqualified by the House of Commons Disqualification Act 1975 (holders of judicial or public office etc.) or be under any other disability (e.g. peers, bankrupts, convicted prisoners: see 4.9.11).

4.2.4 Vacancies

A by-election will be held following the death, resignation (by acceptance of a disqualifying office: see 4.9.11) or disqualification of a member. The date of the election will be set by the relevant returning officer after receipt of the writ issued following a motion before the House which is normally moved by the chief whip of the vacating member's party.

4.3 Opening and Dissolution

4.3.1 Duration

A Parliament is a period not exceeding five years which begins and ends with a proclamation made by the Sovereign. The proclamation dissolves an existing Parliament and orders the issue of writs for the election of a new Parliament and appoints the day and place for its meeting. A Parliament is divided into sessions (which usually run from November to the following October). During the course of a session the House may adjourn to such a date as it pleases.

4.3.2 Opening

✦ Meeting of a new Parliament

Parliament may only be assembled by authority of the Sovereign which is issued by proclamation. On the day appointed, the Commons go up to the Lords, where both Houses are addressed by the Lord Chancellor, who reads the Royal Commission. The following day, members are again summoned to the Lords where the Speaker-elect acquaints the Lords with his or her election, which is confirmed on behalf of the Sovereign by the Lord Chancellor who promises that the Commons will receive 'all their ancient and undoubted rights'. On returning from the Lords, members are called to take the oath in order of seniority, the Speaker doing so first.

+ Opening of new session

In every session (in the case of the first of a Parliament after the initial meetings) the session is opened with the Queen's Speech given by the Sovereign in the House of Lords. The speech is written by the government and outlines its programme for the session ahead. The session then begins with a debate lasting six days in the Commons and four days in the Lords on that programme, which is known as the debate on the Address.

4.3.3 *Dissolution*

A Parliament ends with a dissolution which is followed in turn by a general election. Dissolution takes place by royal proclamation after the Sovereign has been advised by the Prime Minister of the latter's wish to call an election. Under the Parliament Act 1911, a Parliament would automatically be dissolved five years after the date on which it had first met.

4.4 The Role of the UK Government

4.4.1 *Appointment*

The Sovereign will ordinarily invite the leader of the majority party in the House following a general election to form the Government and act as Prime Minister. If no party commands a majority on its own, then the person who appears most likely to command a working majority will be invited to do so.

4.4.2 *Cabinet and Departments*

The Prime Minister appoints the head of each department of State - generally known as Secretaries of State, although the Lord Chancellor and the Minister of Agriculture, Fisheries and Food also head departments. The heads of the principal departments, together with a number of other senior ministers (but not the Attorney General), form the Cabinet. The Cabinet usually comprises about 20 people, who are invariably made Privy Councillors, which involves swearing an oath of secrecy and allegiance to the Crown. The Cabinet determines major issues of policy and the broad economic policy within which the Chancellor of the Exchequer sets the budget.

The principal departments of State are:

+ Ministry of Agriculture, Fisheries and Food;

+ Cabinet Office;

+ Department of Culture, Media and Sport;

+ Ministry of Defence;

+ Department for Education and Employment;

+ Department of the Environment, Transport and the Regions;

+ Foreign and Commonwealth Office;

+ Department of Health;

+ HM Treasury;

+ Home Office;

+ Department for International Development;

+ Lord Chancellor's Department;

+ Law Officers' Department;

+ Northern Ireland Office;

+ Privy Council Office;

+ Office of the Secretary of State for Scotland;

+ Department of Social Security;

+ Department of Trade and Industry;

+ Office of the Secretary of State for Wales.

The Prime Minister also appoints Ministers of State and Parliamentary Under Secretaries of State to each department and the Government whips. It is now normal practice for most ministers to be appointed from the ranks of the majority party's members of Parliament, although the Lord Chancellor is a cabinet minister and each department is also represented in the House of Lords.

4.4.3   The Crown - Sovereign and Government

The Sovereign is nominally the head of the Government as well as head of the armed forces and the judiciary; and all foreign affairs are conducted in her name. The Sovereign also retains certain prerogative powers. Further, primary legislation must be assented to by the Sovereign after being passed by both Houses of Parliament although this has never been declined in modern times. The Sovereign's powers are generally exercised on the advice of her ministers and, in many cases, by the Government in the name of the Crown, the Government therefore effectively exercising sovereign powers.

4.4.4 Power in House

Whilst the Government and its supporters command a majority in the House it is able to control the business programme and secure the passage of its business notwithstanding that the maximum number of paid Government ministers (including the whips) who may sit and vote in the House is only 95 of the 659 members. The Government also has the sole right to move financial resolutions (see 4.15).

4.4.5 Votes of Confidence

The House may resolve by a simple majority that it has no confidence in the Government or to censure individual ministers. An adverse vote in the House is likely to be followed by a resignation or, in the case of a vote against the Government, a general election.

4.5 Officials

4.5.1 The Speaker

The Speaker is elected by the whole House at the beginning of each Parliament, or after the death or retirement of the previous Speaker. The Speaker chairs debates in the chamber, taking the chair for about half the time that business is being discussed - otherwise, one of the three deputies presides. The Speaker also represents the House in a number of capacities and is *ex officio* the chair of the House of Commons Commission. The Speaker does not vote, except to exercise a casting vote.

4.5.2 The Leader of the House, the Whips and "the usual channels"

The Leader of the House is a Government minister, currently the Lord President of the Council. In addition to having responsibilities for members' pensions, the Leader of the House makes the weekly business statement and, in conjunction with the Government Chief Whip, is responsible for the arrangement and details of that business. The Government and Opposition Chief Whips are together known as "the usual channels".

4.5.3 The Chairman of Ways and Means

The Chairman of Ways and Means presides over committees of the whole House and deputises for the Speaker when the Speaker is absent. He also has specific powers in relation to the passage of private legislation through the House. The Chairman is elected by the House on a motion of the Leader of the House.

4.5.4 The House of Commons' Service

The permanent staff of the House are not civil servants but are almost all employed by the House of Commons' Commission which is made up of the Speaker, the Leader of the House and four other members. It has wide powers over the staffing and expenditure of the six House Departments, i.e. those of the Clerk of the House, the Serjeant at Arms, the Library, Finance and Administration, the Official Report and the Refreshment Department.

4.5.5 Clerks

The Clerk of the House is the principal permanent officer and is appointed by the Sovereign for life. Within his department will be found the Clerk of Committees in charge of the Committee Office, the Clerk of Legislation in charge of the Clerk of Bills, the Public and Private Bill Office and the Clerk of Delegated Legislation, the Clerk of the Journals in charge of the Journal Office (i.e. records), the Table Office (order paper and daily business) and the Vote Office (documentation).

4.5.6 The Serjeant at Arms

The Serjeant at Arms is appointed by the Sovereign and carries out the rules of the House and orders of the Speaker concerning the maintenance of order. He may arrest and hold persons who are to be imprisoned for breaches of privilege. The police in the House are under his direction and he also has charge of all the committee rooms and buildings of the House.

4.5.7 *The Comptroller and Auditor General*

The Comptroller and Auditor General is appointed by Letters Patent following an address presented by the House (see 4.15.5).

4.5.8 *The Commissioner for Public Standards*

The Commissioner is appointed by the House and has certain responsibilities relating to the conduct of members (see 4.9.8).

4.5.9 *The Parliamentary Commissioner for Administration*

The Commissioner is appointed by Letters Patent and may only be removed on an address of both Houses of Parliament. She investigates complaints made to members and referred to her in relation to alleged maladministration by government departments or particular non-departmental public bodies. If she thinks fit after investigating a case, the Commissioner may lay a special report before both Houses.

4.6 Sittings

4.6.1 *Annual Programme*

Parliament follows an annual programme (in the UK Parliament known as "a session"). When a session ends with a few limited exceptions, any outstanding business lapses.

The pattern of the year's sittings is usually as follows:

November	Queen's Speech
Late December/ early January	Christmas Recess
March	The Budget
Spring	Easter Recess (usually the Bank Holiday and the following week)
Whitsun	Recess (approximately ten days)
Summer	Recess (usually from the third or fourth week of July until mid-October)
Autumn	Usually a "spill-over" sitting of 1-2 weeks, followed by Prorogation.

4.6.2 Sitting Times

The current sitting times for the House of Commons are 2.30pm to 10.30pm on Mondays and Tuesdays, 9.30am to 10.30pm on Wednesdays (with a half hour break from 2.00pm to 2.30pm), 11.30am to 7.30pm on Thursdays and 9.30am to 3.00pm on Fridays (but see 4.7.2 as to the "Westminster Hall" experimental sittings).

From Monday to Wednesday the "moment of interruption" is at 10.00pm and normally the House only sits for a further 30 minutes after that time. However, a motion "to suspend the 10 o'clock rule" for certain business allows the House to sit until any hour, to a specified hour, or for a specified time depending upon the nature of the business.

If the House sits through the night and beyond the time at which it would normally convene the next day, the business for that next day is lost.

4.6.3 Adjournments and Prorogation

The House adjourns from day to day, over weekends and for longer periods known as recesses. Recesses are agreed by resolution on a business motion, the Leader of the House usually announcing the intended recess dates approximately two weeks in advance, at the same time as making a weekly business statement. Parliament may be recalled during an adjournment, either by royal proclamation or at the request of ministers, by notice from the Speaker.

Prorogation marks the end of a session of Parliament. Both Houses are prorogued at the same time and all unfinished business (other than bills which are specifically "carried over" to the next session and House of Lords judicial business) lapses on prorogation. The Commons are summoned to attend the House of Lords where the Lord Chancellor, sitting with four other Lords Commissioners, outlines the session's achievements before he announces the prorogation.

4.7   Business

4.7.1   *Arrangement of Business*

The Government effectively controls the timetable in that government business normally has precedence and it can arrange such business as it sees fit. The main exceptions to government business taking precedence are the 13 Fridays devoted to Private Members' Bills, 20 Opposition Days, three days allotted for consideration of estimates, adjournment debates on Wednesday mornings and the half-hour adjournment debates at the end of each day's sitting.

The Government Whips' Office is responsible for arranging the business in consultation, where appropriate, through the "usual channels" with the whips of other parties.

4.7.2   *Daily Programme*

The usual daily programme is set out in the accompanying table. On an experimental basis, for the 1999-2000 session, the House will operate a parallel chamber in the Grand Committee Room to be known as "Westminster Hall" which will debate matters for which time cannot be found on the floor of the House (e.g. select committee reports). This will replace Wednesday morning sittings.

THE DAILY PROGRAMME				
TIME	MONDAY& TUESDAY	WEDNESDAY	THURSDAY	FRIDAY
9.30		Prayers Adjournment Debates (subject to Westminster Hall sittings)		Prayers Private business, petitions and motions for unopposed returns Orders of the Day and Motions
11.00				Interruption : PNQs etc. Orders of the Day and Motions
11.30			Prayers Business after Prayers Question Time	

12.30			Business after Questions Public Business at commencement Orders of the Day etc.	
2.00		Suspension		
2.30	Prayers Business after Prayers Question Time	Business after Prayers Question Time	Public Business cont.	Interruption / Excepted business House Adjourned
3.30	Business after Questions Public Business - at commencement - Orders of the Day etc.	Business after Questions Public Business - at commencement - Orders of the Day etc.	Public Business cont.	
4.00			[Opposed Private Business]	
7.00	[Opposed Private Business]	[Opposed Private Business]	Interruption / Excepted business Adjournment Debate	
7.30			House Adjourned	
10.00	Interruption / Excepted business Adjournment Debate	Interruption / Excepted business Adjournment Debate		
10.30	House Adjourned	House Adjourned		

✦ Prayers

Five minutes each day with no strangers admitted.

✦ Business after Prayers

Possibly ten to fifteen minutes devoted to any report of a response by the Sovereign to an Address, formal communications by the Speaker, motions for new writs, private business and motions for unopposed returns (e.g. receipt of a departmental report). Private business, which must end by 2.45pm (11.45am on Thursdays), comprises in particular the stages of private bills which are taken as read unless any Member shouts "object".

✦ Question Time

Oral Questions to Ministers (and at 3.00pm on Wednesdays to the Prime Minister) conclude at 3.30pm (12.30pm on Thursdays).

Business for the coming week is usually announced by the Leader of the House as an oral answer on Thursdays at 12.30pm.

+ Business after Questions

Ministerial statements, introduction of new members, motions to adjourn for an emergency debate, ceremonial speeches and personal statements.

+ Public Business - at commencement

Presentation of public bills under government motions relating to committees and regulating business and for bringing in public bills or nominating select committees.

+ Public Business - main

The ordinary public business of the day comprising orders of the day (e.g. stage of a bill) and notices of motion.

+ Opposed Private Business

Debates on private bills may be set down for 7.00pm to 10.00pm (4.00pm to 7.00pm on Thursdays).

+ Interruption/Excepted Business

The "ten o'clock rule" requires business to be interrupted at ten o'clock (7.00pm on Thursdays) with the exception of "exempted business" (e.g. finance and other taxation bills), proceedings under specific Acts or on European Union documents, negative resolutions on statutory instruments, debates on deregulation orders and debates on petitions complaining of urgent personal grievance.

+ Public Petitions and Adjournment Debate

Public petitions may be presented formally once the motion to adjourn is signified (other than on Fridays when they are taken at the commencement of public business).

The last half hour is allocated to an adjournment debate allowing one member to raise a matter and a Minister to respond without there being a vote. Members may participate in a ballot each week for the purpose but the Speaker chooses the subject for the Thursday adjournment debate.

Wednesdays, Thursdays and Fridays

On Wednesdays, two one and a half hour followed by three half hour adjournment debates take place after prayers at 9.30am with business then being suspended from 2.00pm to 2.30pm.

On Thursdays, the normal Monday to Tuesday programme applies but has been advanced on an experimental basis so as to commence at 11.30am.

On Fridays, except for the ten Fridays when the House does not sit, after prayers at 9.30am, public petitions and motions for unopposed returns (which on other days are taken as business after prayers) are taken first and the Speaker may interrupt proceedings at 11.00am for private notice questions, ministerial statements and personal explanations. The moment of interruption takes place at 2.30pm.

4.7.3   *Questions and Answers*

✦ Question for Oral Answer

Notice of a question for oral answer by a Minister (or certain others, e.g. the chairman of the Public Accounts Commission) may be tabled not earlier then 10 days in advance and, after random shuffling, those successful in the quota are placed on the Notice Paper. Each department is allocated a particular day for oral questions ("the question rota") the Prime Minister now taking questions at 3.00pm on Wednesdays. A supplementary question may be asked and specific rules apply to the manner in which questions and answers may be given. Question time concludes at 3.30pm.

Some questions may be asked after 3.30pm, particularly Private Notice Questions. These are questions submitted to the Speaker by 12.00 noon or 10.00am on a Friday and which, in the Speaker's opinion, are of an urgent character and relate to a matter of public importance or to the arrangement of business.

✦ Written Answers

Questions may be tabled for written answer in due course or on a particular day and oral questions which are not reached by 3.30pm will also be given a written answer. Answers are prepared in accordance with official guidance.

4.7.4   *Orders of the Day and Motions*

The ordinary public business of the House consists of orders of the day (i.e. items of business set down by order of the House such as a stage of a bill) and notices of motion put down by individual members which permit that member a right of reply.

Orders of the day are liable to involve ancillary motions such as "That the Bill be read a Second Time" but do not provide the proponent with a right of reply.

Notices of motion include substantive motions (which express an opinion about something) and motions for the adjournment of the House. A substantive motion can only be 'moved' or proposed by a member giving notice of it, except a motion standing in the name of a member of the Government, which can be moved by any other Minister. The majority require notice. After a speech from the proponent, the Chair calls members to speak, usually alternating between those in favour and those against the motion. A motion can only be withdrawn by leave of the House. The Chair may also select an amendment to the motion, which one of the supporters of the amendment will move. When the time for the debate runs out, or earlier if a member moves that the question be now put and the Chair accepts this, the Chair asks the House to decide, by voting if necessary, whether any amendment should be made to the motion, and then whether the motion, as amended if it has been, should be agreed to or not. If the motion is agreed to, it becomes a resolution or an order of the House.

Motions for the adjournment of the House, unlike substantive motions, do not lead to a decision being taken. In addition to the adjournment debates at the end of each sitting and on Wednesdays, which provide backbenchers with an opportunity to raise matters and obtain a ministerial reply, the Government may also initiate an adjournment debate for the consideration of some major matter of public importance.

A particular form of motion which will not ordinarily be debated is the Early Day Motion (EDM). An EDM may be tabled by any member and is then printed with an indication each day for 10 days, and thereafter every Thursday, of how many supporters it has attracted. With the exception of EDMs in the name of the Leader of the Opposition (e.g. in relation to an instrument subject to negative resolution), time for debate of EDMs is not normally found.

4.7.5   Rules of Debate

Members may normally only speak once in any debate. The Speaker has a discretion to limit individual speeches (other than by the main front bench spokespersons) to a length of up to a minimum of eight minutes. Members who wish to intervene in a speech must call 'give way'. It is for the member who is speaking to decide whether to allow his speech to be interrupted. Members may not refer to a case which may prejudice a court trial (the sub judice rule). Members must refrain from 'unparliamentary language' when alluding to other members. All speeches must be relevant and not unduly repetitive. Members who are not speaking must not walk around the Chamber or in front of a member who is addressing the House. They must not heckle or disrupt other speakers. All members bow to the Speaker's Chair on entering and leaving.

4.7.6   Voting and Decisions

The motion that a question be now proposed may be proposed by any member as may a motion that the question be now put. If accepted by the Chair such "closure" motions can be the subject of a division and require 100 members in the majority to be decided in the affirmative.

When a motion is put to the vote, the Chair says "The Question is, that ...". The Chair takes the sense of the House by asking "As many as are of that opinion say 'Aye'" and "As many as are of the contrary opinion say 'No'". He or she then indicates "I think the 'Ayes' (or 'Noes') have it". The House may acquiesce to this or members may dispute it by exclaiming 'No'. The Chair will then say 'Clear the lobby' in order to start the process of voting which is termed a division. Bells ring throughout the precincts. Not more than two minutes later, the Chair again puts the question, and if then challenged again, there is a division. Should the further question not be challenged, the Chair announces 'The Ayes (or Noes) have it' and the division is called off.

Members vote on a division by going through the Aye or No lobby to each side of the chamber before the doors to them are locked on direction of the Chair (minimum eight minutes). On returning to the chamber, one of the tellers for the majority reports the vote and declares the numbers. Any vote must be either for or against. There is no formal way in which an abstention can be recorded. Members may vote in a division although they did not hear the question put. A system, known as 'pairing', enables a member to absent himself or herself by agreeing with a member of an opposing party not to vote in a particular division.

4.8 Public Access & Information

4.8.1 *Access to Sittings*

Public access to the House is through St. Stephen's Entrance, opposite the east end of Westminster Abbey. The Strangers' Gallery is open to the public when the House is sitting. UK residents may apply in advance to their constituency MP for tickets (which are obtained from the Admissions Order Office) or may join the public queue outside St. Stephen's Entrance.

4.8.2 *Access to Committees*

There is no system of tickets or advance booking for select and standing committees.

4.8.3 *Tours*

Members of the public are not admitted for tours of the building unless they have arranged a "line of route" permit through their MP. Permits are restricted to groups of 16 or less.

4.8.4 *Information*

The Public Information Office acts as a central answering point for enquiries from the public:

Telephone:	0171 219 4272
Fax:	0171 219 5839
Email:	pio@parliament.uk

A recorded message on 0171 219 5532 details the forthcoming business in the House (normally available within 20 minutes of the Business Statement).

The Parliamentary Education Unit acts for both Houses in providing services for schools etc.:

Telephone:	0171 219 2105
Fax:	0171 219 0818
Email:	edunit@parliament.uk

Information about both Houses and Parliamentary documentation can also be found on the Parliament's website http://www.parliament.uk. Items available include Hansard (Commons Official Report by 12.30pm on the following day) and Order Paper (by 9.30am on sitting days).

4.8.5 **Documentation**

The working papers of the Commons are commonly called 'the Vote'. The Order Paper lists the business for the day, notices of amendments etc. The Votes and Proceedings is the official record of what happens in the chamber and includes such matters as all votes taken. It provides the basis for the sessional Journal (the legal record of proceedings). The Notice Paper contains notices of questions and motions tabled the previous day and is where early day motions are recorded. The Remaining Orders is a list of outstanding Government business.

Hansard is the verbatim record of proceedings in the chamber and is published daily. Hansard also contains the texts of answers to written questions. Verbatim records are also produced of standing and select committee proceedings.

4.8.6 **The Media**

The Parliamentary Channel, which is provided by the BBC via cable, shows continuous unedited coverage of the Commons. BBC2's "Despatch Box" has recorded highlights, from Mondays to Thursdays, at midnight. BBC2 also transmit "Westminster" on Tuesdays, Wednesdays and Thursdays 2.45pm - 3.30pm, with regional reviews on "Around Westminster" on Sundays at 1.00pm.

On BBC Radio 4 "Today in Parliament" broadcasts a daily account of proceedings from Mondays to Fridays (11.30pm-12.00pm) [long wave]. "Yesterday in Parliament" is an edited version of "Today in Parliament" broadcast from Tuesdays to Saturdays at 8.35am. The "Westminster Hour" on Sundays at 10.00pm looks forward to the forthcoming week's events in Parliament.

Overall control of televised proceedings rests with both Houses and is exercised by the Supervisor of Broadcasting who reports to the Select Committee on Broadcasting.

The leading national and provincial newspapers and the broadcasting media each have a lobby correspondent who has privileged access to the facilities of Parliament. Lobby journalists have access to the Members' Lobby, the press gallery and certain other areas of the Palace of Westminster.

4.9 Conduct and Ethics

4.9.1 *Oaths of Allegiance*

Members may not sit or vote in the House or exercise any of the other privileges of a member until they have taken the oath of allegiance or affirmed.

Members may take the oath in the form it would be taken in Scotland. The oath must be taken in English although the Speaker has permitted members to recite the oath in Welsh or Gaelic in addition to the English version.

4.9.2 *Language*

All speeches must be in English and, whilst the Chair will permit limited quotation from other languages, the member concerned is expected to provide a translation.

4.9.3 *Forms of Address*

Members must address the Chair as "Madam Speaker" or "Mr Deputy Speaker" as appropriate except during a committee of the whole House when the Chair is referred to by name. Members may not refer to one another by name in debate but may describe another member as the Honourable (or, in the case of a Privy Councillor, Right Honourable) gentleman or lady or where confusion may arise to refer to the "Honourable (or Right Honourable) member for ...." and refer to that member's constituency. In referring to a member of the same party the phrase "Honourable (or Right Honourable) friend" may be used. A member who is a Queen's Counsel is referred to as "Honourable and Learned" and a member who has served in HM forces may be referred to as "Honourable and gallant".

4.9.4   Dress Code

By convention members may not wear decorations, military insignia or military uniforms in the chamber and, as recently as the 1987/88 session, the Speaker has ruled that it is customary "for members to wear jackets and ties". No such ruling has been made in relation to the dress of women members.

4.9.5   Calling of Speakers

The decision as to who is to speak in a debate is entirely within the discretion of the Chair (with the obvious exception of the mover of an amendment or proposer of a question which has been selected for debate). Conventionally preference is given to maiden speakers and to Privy Councillors. Members therefore 'try to catch the Speaker's eye' by standing up as other members finish their speeches. In calling members to speak the Chair attempts to strike a fair balance of opinion and also to ensure that each member is given adequate opportunity to speak during the session. It is common practice for members to write to the Speaker in advance of a debate, drawing attention to their interest in the subject and their particular wish to be called. Members who do so are more likely to be called than those who simply seek to "catch the Speaker's eye".

4.9.6   Order in the Chamber

The standing orders provide the Chair with summary powers of dealing with disorder. The action which the Chair takes, which will depend on the nature of the infringement, may range from simply asking a member to return to the point of the debate to ordering the withdrawal of particular remarks, requiring a member to resume their seat, ordering a member to withdraw from the chamber or "naming" a member (see 4.9.10).

When the Speaker rises from her chair all members in the House are required to resume their seat and to hear her in silence.

4.9.7 *Sub judice*

No reference may be made in debate (or in motions, questions etc.) to:

+ any matter which is before (or awaiting adjudication) by the criminal court: from the time a charge is made to the time when a verdict and sentence is announced or, where an appeal is lodged, until the appeal is decided;

+ any matter before (or awaiting adjudication in) the civil courts: from the time that the case is set down for trial or otherwise put before the court and from the time when any notice of appeal is lodged until judgment is given;

+ any matter awaiting or under adjudication by the courts martial from the time when the charge is made until the sentence of the court has been confirmed and promulgated and from the time when any petition is made to the Army Council, Air Council or Board of Admiralty until the case is decided.

In relation to matters before the civil courts, the Speaker or, in committee, the chairman, may permit discussion of cases which relate to ministerial decisions, provided there is no real or substantial danger of prejudice to the proceedings.

4.9.8 *Members' Interests*

Members are required to provide details of registerable interests to the Registrar of Members' Interests. Such interests fall into ten categories:

+ Directorships;

+ Remunerated employment, office, profession etc.;

+ Clients;

+ Sponsorship;

+ Gifts, benefits and hospitality (UK);

+ Overseas visits;

+ Overseas benefits and gifts;

+ Land and property;

+ Shareholdings;

+ Miscellaneous.

In addition, members are required to deposit with the Parliamentary Commissioner for Standards copies of any agreement which they enter into relating to the provision of services by them in their capacity as a member. Where a member has such a paid interest, he or she is precluded from initiating or taking part in any delegation where the problem in issue affects only the body from which he or she has a paid interest.

As well as being obliged to register their interests, members must also declare an interest when they participate in any proceedings relating to such interests and, in accordance with the resolution of the House of 6th November 1995 ("the advocacy rule"), members may not advance a cause by means of a debate, question, motion, bill etc., where they have some form of pecuniary interest in the matter.

Guidance to members on conduct is provided by the Parliamentary Commissioner for Standards who also investigates complaints from other members or the public and may refer such complaints to the Committee on Standards and Privileges.

4.9.9   *Investigation of Conduct*

Complaints about the conduct of a member must be made in writing to the Parliamentary Commissioner for Standards accompanied by the necessary supporting evidence. The Committee on Standards and Privileges follows the practice of the former Select Committee on Members' Interests and will not entertain anonymous complaints or unsubstantiated allegations which are not supported by evidence, for example complaints which are simply founded upon newspaper or television reports. Complaints are initially investigated by the Commissioner and, where she is satisfied that there is sufficient evidence to justify taking the complaint further, she will conduct a preliminary investigation, providing the member concerned with the opportunity to respond to the complaint. The Commissioner then reports to the Committee on Standards and Privileges. That committee like other Select Committees, has the power to summon witnesses and demand the production of documents and may investigate matters further or simply act on the recommendations of the Commissioner. Normally, the committee meets in private. Any report by the committee is then put before the House.

4.9.10 Exclusion

As part of the Chair's powers for enforcing order, the Chair may order a member who persists in disorderly conduct to withdraw from the House. Where any member refuses to do so, the Chair may "name" that member by means of a motion stating "that [name of member] be suspended from the service of the House" and the matter is put to a vote forthwith. A member who is named is suspended for five sitting days on the first occasion and twenty sitting days on the second occasion. A member who refuses to withdraw from the chamber once named may be removed forcibly by the Serjeant at Arms on the order of the Speaker and, in that event, the member is suspended from the service of the House for the remainder of the session.

4.9.11 Disqualification

A member will become disqualified from membership of the House of Commons if he or she:

+ is convicted of treason or an election offence (corrupt or illegal practice) or imprisoned for any offence for more than one year;

+ is detained as a mental patient;

+ is adjudged bankrupt;

+ succeeds to a peerage (but this can be disclaimed for life within one month of succession under the Peerage Act 1963);

+ accepts a disqualifying office such as a judicial or civil service post, membership of a legislature outside the Commonwealth or membership of a public body or other office which is specifically mentioned in Schedule 1 to the House of Commons Disqualification Act 1975;

+ becomes a member of the clergy of the Church of England, Church of Scotland or Roman Catholic Church.

It is a settled principle of parliamentary law that members cannot relinquish their seats. Therefore, two crown offices are specifically reserved to which a member may be appointed for the purpose of disqualifying that member from the House. Those two offices are the steward or bailiff of Her Majesty's three Chiltern Hundreds of Stoke, Desborough and Burnham or the steward of the manor of Northstead. Appointment is colloquially known as "taking the Chiltern Hundreds".

4.9.12 Public Disturbance

Any disturbance of the proceedings of the House by members of the public (strangers) is a contempt of the House and it is open to the House to punish such behaviour. In practice minor disturbances are often dealt with by no more than ejecting the individuals concerned from the strangers' gallery. Where the disturbance is more serious and involves criminal conduct, offenders are passed into the custody of the police for appropriate action to be taken.

4.10 Powers and Privileges of Members

4.10.1 Defamation

Anything which is said in proceedings in Parliament is absolutely privileged and article IX of the Bill of Rights 1689 provides that "freedom of speech and debates or proceedings in Parliament ought not to be impeached or questioned in any court". The publication of debates and proceedings, whether or not with the authority of the House, is also privileged but only to the extent that the publication is a fair and accurate account of what took place (similar to the privilege which attaches to reports of court proceedings). The protection of privilege does not extend to publication by an individual member and a member who publishes a defamatory speech, or repeats outside Parliament defamatory comments which were made in the House, may be sued in the normal way.

4.10.2 Witnesses and Documents

The House has the power to compel witnesses to attend before it and to produce documentary evidence. Typically, the power to send for "persons, papers and records" is exercised by select committees. A person who fails to appear, to answer questions or to produce documents may be punished by the House for contempt.

The power to call for persons, papers and records enjoyed by the House is extensive and witnesses can be required to answer self-incriminating questions and to disclose matters which are subject to legal privilege.

Prior publication of proceedings or documents submitted to Parliament is a contempt of Parliament but the Commons will ordinarily take no action unless the proceedings took place in private or publication was expressly prohibited. The Commons has also resolved that, whilst a member may be reprimanded for leaking material to the press prior to publication, it would normally be inappropriate to proceed against the journalists concerned.

Any obstruction or molestation of a person who is summoned to appear before the House as a witness is a contempt of Parliament and may be punished as such. The Witnesses (Public Inquiries) Protection Act 1892 makes it an offence to "punish, damnify or injure" a witness before the committee of the House on account of the evidence that they give. For this purpose, "molestation" includes assaults upon witnesses in the precincts of the House or the use of threatening or abusive language towards them.

4.10.3 *Sanctions*

The House has powers which are similar to inherent powers of the superior courts to punish contempts and this includes the detention of contemnors, either in the custody of the Serjeant at Arms or in prison. Warrants of committal issued by the Speaker are executed by the Serjeant at Arms who may forcibly enter premises and call upon the civil powers for assistance in the execution of that warrant. The power to imprison for contempt has not been exercised since the turn of the century except for detention for very brief periods (for example, the detention until the rising of the House of persons causing a disturbance in the gallery).

4.11 Committees

4.11.1 *Committees of the Whole House*

For certain proceedings, the House sits as a Committee of the Whole House which all members are entitled to attend. The main difference from normal procedure is that it is not chaired by the Speaker and members may speak more than once on the same issue.

4.11.2 Standing Committees

There are seven types of standing committee :

✦ Public Bills

These committees consider public bills referred to them. There are usually six or seven of these standing committees with different members (between 16 and 50, reflecting the political balance in the House) for each bill.

✦ Second Reading/Report

A Second Reading Committee considers the second reading of a bill in certain instances before it is taken formally on the floor of the House. The report stage may also then be taken by standing committee.

✦ Special

These are committees appointed to call for and hear evidence on a public bill.

✦ Grand

Scottish, Welsh and Northern Ireland grand committees exist, each consisting of all members for that part of the UK, plus five others in the case of the Welsh and 25 others in the case of the Northern Ireland Grand Committee nominated by the committee of selection. The committees consider relevant bills and instruments and other matters referred to them and take questions to Ministers.

✦ Delegated Legislation

These committees consider instruments referred to them, each committee having different membership for each instrument.

✦ European

Three committees (A, B and C) exist, each having 13 members appointed for the whole session: see 4.14.3.

✦ Regional Affairs

This committee comprises all English members plus five others nominated by the committee of selection - to consider matters referred to it on a motion by a Minister.

4.11.3 *Select Committees*

These committees can be divided into four categories : departmental, legislative, procedural and administrative.

Select committees are ordinarily appointed for a Parliament, with power to sit at any time including during adjournments. They are able to sit in public or private. Individual select committees have particular powers to appoint sub-committees. Each committee also has a specific quorum which includes the chairman.

+ Departmental select committees etc.

There are currently 16 departmental select committees which examine the expenditure, administration and policy of government departments and related matters of interest. These are -

- Agriculture
- Culture, Sports and Media
- Defence
- Education and Employment
- Environment, Transport and Regional Affairs
- Foreign Affairs
- Health
- Home Affairs
- International Development
- Northern Ireland Affairs
- Science and Technology
- Scottish Affairs
- Social Security
- Trade and Industry
- Treasury
- Welsh Affairs

In addition, there are three subject committees having much in common with the Departmental Committees -

- Public Administration

To consider reports of the Parliamentary Commissioner for Administration or the Health Services Commission.

- Public Accounts

To consider public expenditure - see 4.15.5.

- Environmental Audit

To consider the contribution of government and public bodies to environmental protection and sustainable development.

All these committees have power to call for and receive evidence ("to send for persons, papers and records": see 4.10.2), to appoint special advisers and to make reports. In relation to evidence from civil servants, this is given on behalf of Ministers and in accordance with published guidance (known as "the Osmotherly rules"). Evidence given before select committees is privileged (i.e. a defence to action for defamation) and may be published but only on the direction of the committee or the Speaker.

+ Legislative

There are 6 types of legislative select committees -

- Consolidation &c. Bills

A joint committee with the Lords - see 5.12.4.

- Deregulation

To consider deregulation orders - see 4.13.6.

- European Legislation/Scrutiny

To examine European documents - see 4.14.2.

- Statutory Instruments

To consider the propriety of statutory instruments, jointly with the Lords - see 4.13.1.

- Public Bill

To consider a particular public bill. Such committees are now infrequent.

- Local

There are a number of select committees for local legislation, the Unopposed Bills Committee and Court of Referees appointed for the Parliament and individual hybrid bill and private bill committees for particular bills.

+ Procedural

There are six procedural committees -

- Liaison

To consider the work of select committees and recommend reports to be debated.

- Procedure

To consider the practice and procedure of the House.

- Standards and Privileges

To consider matters of privilege, the work of the Parliamentary Commissioner for Standards and the conduct of members.

- Modernisation
To consider modernising the procedures of the House.

- Parliamentary privilege
A new joint committee to consider parliamentary privilege.

- Selection
To select members for particular committees, including private bill and grand committees.

In this context, the Chairmen's Panel, consisting of 10 members nominated by the Speaker to act as chairmen of standing committees, and with powers to meet to consider matters of procedure, should also be noted.

✦ Administrative
There are currently five administrative committees concerned with internal organisation of the House, namely the Broadcasting Select Committees, four domestic committees concerned with accommodation and works, administration, catering and information and one concerned with expenditure (finance and services).

4.11.4 *Joint Committees*

A number of joint committees have been appointed to consider particular bills or matters, e.g. the Joint Committee on Parliamentary Privilege referred to above. Such committees are dependent for their authority on the particular powers conferred upon them by the two Houses concurrently. Typically, such committees have the same number of members from each House.

In addition, a number of committees comprising members of each House exist by virtue of statute. These include the Ecclesiastical Committee which considers Church Measures pursuant to the Church of England (Assembly) Powers Act 1919 and the Intelligence and Security Committee appointed by the then Prime Minister under the Intelligence Services Act 1994.

4.12   Parliamentary Bills

4.12.1   Types of Bill

Primary legislation in the form of bills which become Acts is categorised by the manner of its treatment in Parliament as follows:-

✦ Public Bills

- Government Bills

  General

  Special (Finance/Hybrid etc.)

- Private Members' Bills

  Ballot Bills

  10 minute rule Bills

  Others

✦ Private Bills

- Local Bills
- Personal Bills

4.12.2   Format

See 3.2 above.

4.12.3   Accompanying documentation for Public Bills

At least in the case of Government bills, this should include -

✦ Explanatory and financial memorandum - a general description of each provision together with its effects on public expenditure and public sector manpower;

✦ Statement of compatibility with Convention Rights;

✦ Regulatory impact assessment - a summary of the cost implications for the private sector;

✦ Notes on clauses - a fuller non-technical description of the provisions.

4.12.4   Stages of a Government Bill

The Government may, in advance of the normal stages of a bill, publish a draft and the draft may then be referred to a joint committee.

Each bill must pass through both Houses of Parliament and, in the Commons, will usually have a debate in principle on second reading, the opportunity for detailed scrutiny and amendment at committee stage and, thereafter, further review and amendment at report and third reading.

The normal convention is that a bill which does not complete all stages in a single session is lost. However, it is open to the House to resolve to carry a bill over to the next session and the Modernisation Committee has recommended that this be done in certain limited circumstances.

The usual steps in the passage of a bill, together with an indication of the main variations, are shown on the accompanying table.

Ordinary Steps	Special Steps	Comments
	Queen's Speech	Normally November
	Publication of draft and referral to joint committee	e.g. Financial Services & Markets Bill
	National Assembly for Wales Consultation	Required under the Government of Wales Act 1998
FIRST READING		Purely formal
Printing		Includes explanatory memo etc.
	Reference to Examiners and S.O. Committee	If bill is hybrid
	Second Reading Committee	Special procedure in lieu of a Second Reading Debate on the floor of the House for certain (usually non-controversial) bills
	Scottish, Welsh or Northern Ireland Grand Committee	Second Reading Committee procedure for bills relating to these parts of the UK
SECOND READING		Decision in principle
	Financial Resolutions	
	Timetabling Resolutions	i.e. guillotines
	Instructions	Motion to instruct a committee to act in a particular way e.g. to permit particular amendments
	Hybrid Bill Committee	To hear petitions against bill
Amendments tabled		
STANDING COMMITTEE		Consideration of detail and possible amendment.
	Committee of whole House (whole or part)	Procedure for Finance Bills, constitutional bills etc.
	Joint Committee	For bills such as tax simplification bills.
Reprint		
Amendments tabled		

REPORT & CONSIDERATION		Possible further amendment. Third reading may also be taken simultaneously
Reprint		
Amendments tabled		Corrective amendments only
THIRD READING		
HOUSE OF LORDS: all stages/approval HC amendments		A Commons Bill must pass through all stages in the Lords and then be subject to approval in the Commons of Lords' amendments; and vice versa.
ROYAL ASSENT		Notified by Speaker under Royal Assent Act 1967 or declared by the Lords Commissioners at prorogation.

4.12.5 Special Forms of Public Bill

✦ Finance bills

See 4.15.3. The committee stage of such bills is ordinarily taken in part on the floor of the House.

✦ Consolidated fund and appropriation bills

See 4.15.4. Such bills are taken without debate or any committee stage.

✦ Tax simplification bills

Such bills are referred to a second reading committee and the Joint Committee on Tax Simplification Bills.

✦ Consolidation bills

See 5.12.4.

✦ Law Commission bills

Such bills are normally referred to a second reading committee.

✦ Hybrid bills

These are bills (such as the Channel Tunnel Rail Link Bill) which have the characteristics of a private bill (typically a bill affecting any one locality) and, whilst stillpublic bills, are subject to similar procedures to private bills. As with private bills, some of those affected may petition against the bill and give evidence or make representations at a specially constituted select committee.

✦ Provisional Order Confirmation Bills

These are bills to confirm provisional orders of local application and are usually taken formally although, when opposed, they can be referred to a joint committee.

✦ Private Members' Bills

Bills introduced (or taken up from the Lords) by a member who is not a Minister are known as Private Members' Bills and, unless the Government otherwise allows, can normally only make progress on the floor of the House on the 13 days allocated to them each session. In addition, only one standing committee (Standing Committee C) is allocated to them.

Priority is given on the first seven available days to the Second Reading of the bills chosen by the members successful in a ballot held on the second Thursday of each session. Thereafter, priority is determined by the stage each bill has reached.

Stages can be taken formally "on the nod" and, if no one objects, one after the other. However, any member can object at any stage necessitating a debate and, if no time is then available, the bill will fall back to the end of the list for a future day.

In addition to the ballot, a Private Members' Bill can be introduced at any time without debate and also ("the 10 minute rule bill") by way of a short speech immediately after Question Time on a Tuesday or Wednesday by one member only who secures that opportunity by notice to the Public Bill Office. This must normally be given three weeks prior to the day in question or, following a recess, immediately after its announcement.

4.12.6 *Scrutiny of Public Bills*

Public Bills can be amended at the committee stage, on consideration and, in a technical rather than substantive manner, at third reading.

✦ Tabling and Printing of Amendments

Amendments, which can be tabled by any member, are given a number and printed the day after they are tabled. Starred amendments (from the previous sitting day) will not normally be called (at least at the committee stage).

A marshalled list of amendments is published immediately preceding the first sitting of a committee (the blue list) and on report and on each sitting day thereafter.

✦ Admissibility

The rules concerning admissibility of amendments are complex. By way of summary of the main points, amendments must -

- Be within the "scope" of the bill (germane to the subject matter and objects of the bill) and relevant to the clause to which they relate.
- Be consistent with the principle of the bill established at second reading and, in committee, with previous decisions of the committee.
- Be intelligible either on their own or with other amendments already tabled.
- Not impose or increase a public charge unless supported by the appropriate financial resolution.
- Be proposed at an appropriate place in the bill.
- Not negate or provide for the deletion of a clause in committee (the correct procedure being to oppose the motion that the clause "stand part").

✦ Selection

In standing committee, the Chair has the power of selection and grouping of amendments and will publish a provisional list before each sitting. There is a presumption in favour of amendments tabled by a Minister or the Minister in charge and, typically, amendments which are wrecking amendments, out of order, nonsensical or repetitive will not be selected.

On report, the Speaker has the power of selection and grouping and will publish a list on the day. In general, amendments on subjects fully debated in committee or which seek to undo decisions already taken will not be selected.

✦ Order of Consideration

Subject to any motion to the contrary (at standing committee, taken at the beginning), the bill and amendments are debated and considered in the following order:

Standing Committee	Report
Clauses in Order	New Clauses
New Clauses	Amendments to Clauses
Schedules in Order	New Schedules
New Schedules	Amendments to Schedules
Amendments to Long Title	

In standing committee, decisions are by simple majority of members present voting in their places. After debate on any amendments to a clause or schedule, the decision on the provision itself is taken on the motion that the clause or schedule (as amended) "stand part" of the bill. In relation to new clauses and schedules, the main debate is on a motion that the clause or schedule be read a second time, with any amendments then being moved formally. Finally, the motion that the clause or schedule be added to the bill is taken without debate.

On report, once all provisions have been disposed of, third reading is normally taken straightaway at the same sitting. However, third reading can be set down for a future day and the bill reprinted in advance of that day.

4.12.7 *Approval of Lords' Amendments*

Commons bills amended in the Lords and Lords bills amended in the Commons require, as an additional stage, the approval of the original House to the amendments.

Commons bills amended in the Lords are returned with a message inviting agreement to the amendments which are printed separately. Likewise, Lords' bills which have been amended by the Commons are returned with a message inviting concurrence. Amendments to the Lords' amendments or amendments in lieu of amendments made by the Second House (necessitating disagreement with the original amendments) and consequential amendments may be tabled.

In the Commons, the Speaker has the power of selection but the member in charge is responsible for grouping amendments. The Lords' amendments are then taken in the order in which they are printed.

If the Commons disagrees with any Lords' amendment without offering an amendment in lieu, reasons are given as settled by a select committee which sits immediately, having been appointed by motion at the end of the debate.

The Lords can accept the Commons' message, reject it or offer alternative amendments. Once the two Houses are agreed, the bill proceeds to Royal Assent. If, however, at any stage in the process, proposals put forward by one House are rejected by the other; and the initiating House then insists on its own original proposals, the bill is lost unless the other House then concurs.

4.12.8 *The Parliament Acts 1911 and 1949*

Provision is made by these Acts to bypass the House of Lords. Where a bill which the Lords fail to agree and which was passed by the Commons at least one month before the end of a session is passed by the Commons in the next session in exactly the same form and with at least one year having expired since its original second reading. In these circumstances, it may be presented by the Commons for Royal Assent within one month if the Lords have not by then concurred with it in the form sent to them.

4.12.9 *Private Bills*

These are bills of a local or personal nature ordinarily introduced on 27th November only by outside interests ("promoters") using a Parliamentary Agent. Such bills have their own procedure. This involves complex notification arrangements and the opportunity for some of those affected to petition against the bill and, together with the promoters, to give evidence and make representations before a select committee constituted from members having no constituency interest in the subject matter. The need for such bills has now been largely replaced, most recently by the Transport and Works order-making procedure for rail and navigation projects. A small number of local bills (e.g. for university mergers and special local authority powers) and personal bills (to enable marriage between relations) are, however, still promoted.

4.13   Subordinate Legislation

4.13.1   *Scrutiny Committees*

In addition to the other procedures described below, all general instruments (i.e. ones which are not only of local application) other than Orders in Council made under the Northern Ireland Act 1974, deregulation orders and Church of England measures, whether required to be laid before the House or not, are referred to the Joint Committee on Delegated Legislation consisting of seven members of each House or, in the case of instruments only required to be laid before the Commons, to the Commons' Select Committee on Statutory Instruments which consists of the Commons' members of the Joint Committee.   Both committees can appoint a sub-committee and sit during adjournments.

The role of the committees is not to consider the merits of an instrument or the policy behind it but rather its technical correctness.   Each committee has the power to issue a report in certain specified cases, for example where it considers the drafting defective or that provisions require further elucidation or may be beyond the powers conferred (ultra vires).   First, however, the committee will give the department concerned an opportunity to make explanations orally or in writing.   The issue of a committee report does not trigger any further procedure but, in the Lords at least, is a pre-requisite for moving an affirmative resolution on the instrument in question.

4.13.2   *Laying before Parliament*

Whilst some instruments are subject to no form of Parliamentary procedure, all that are so subject are required by their parent Act in the first instance to be laid, either in draft or in final form, before the House of Commons or both Houses.   Drafts may only be laid on a day when the House is sitting but made instruments can be laid on any day during the Parliament.   The process of laying is governed by the Laying of Documents before Parliament (Interpretation) Act 1948 and Standing Orders.   Those instruments which have been laid are notified in the Vote the next sitting day with a full list being published for each week.

4.13.3 Standing Committees on Statutory Instruments

Standing committees consider instruments subject to affirmative resolution procedure unless a non-referral motion is moved and, where notice of a motion to annul the instrument has been given, those subject to negative resolution procedure but only if a motion is moved by a Minister for that purpose. Proceedings before such a committee last no more than one and a half hours and, in addition to its appointed members, any member may attend and speak but may not vote. The motion before the committee is that "the Committee has considered the [draft] instrument" and, even if negative, the instrument is still reported back to the House.

4.13.4 Affirmative Resolution Procedure

Depending upon the enabling Act, an affirmative resolution may be required in one or both Houses either -

(a) to give effect to a draft instrument which has been laid; or

(b) to ratify within a specified period (usually 40 days) an instrument already made, the instrument nevertheless having immediate effect.

A few enabling Acts enable instruments to be modified but, in most cases, this is not so and the instrument is either approved or fails as it stands.

Where the instrument is referred to a standing committee, the motion to approve is still taken on the floor of the House but the question is put forthwith without debate. If the instrument is not referred to a standing committee, but is considered on the floor of the House, debate is limited to one and a half hours after which the question on the motion is put.

4.13.5 Negative Resolution Procedure

This is very much more common than affirmative resolution procedure and any legislation stipulating that an instrument "shall be subject to annulment in pursuance of a resolution of either House of Parliament" (other than where the functions have been devolved) attracts this procedure.

Such instruments may have immediate effect but are revoked if a resolution is successful. In some cases, however, a draft of the instrument is required to be laid.

By virtue of the Statutory Instruments Act 1946, there is a standard time limit of 40 days for all negative resolutions (any period during which Parliament is dissolved or prorogued or, if in excess of four days, adjourned being discounted). Any member may table a motion (a "prayer") even after the expiry of the 40 day period. There is however no obligation upon the Government to provide time for debate and, unless the Government agrees to refer the instrument to a standing committee or provide time for debate on the floor of the House, a prayer to annul will not be considered. Only the tabling of a prayer by the leader of the opposition is normally found time. It would also be possible for the opposition to table a prayer for one of their "opposition days".

4.13.6 *Deregulation Orders*

Deregulation Orders are made under the Deregulation and Contracting Out Act 1994 and provide a means of removing burdens on business contained in primary legislation. A proposal for such an order in the form of a draft is laid before Parliament by the relevant Minister following which 60 days must elapse (ignoring periods when Parliament is dissolved or prorogued or, if in excess of four days, adjourned) before the Minister can lay the final draft order before Parliament for approval. During the 60 day period, the proposal is referred to the Deregulation Committee, which has similar powers to a select committee in respect of hearing evidence etc., the committee being required by the Act and Standing Orders to consider the proposal against certain specified criteria. At the end of the 60 day period, the Minister can proceed to lay the draft order and must accompany it with a statement concerning the committee's report (and any equivalent report by the Lords) giving details of other representations received and any changes made from the original proposal. The committee must then report to the House within 15 sitting days. The motion to approve a deregulation order is taken on the floor of the House and, if the committee recommended approval without a division, the question is put forthwith. If the committee divided on the question, the debate can continue for one and a half hours and, if the committee recommended against the order, three hours is allowed for a debate on a motion to disagree with the committee's recommendation whereafter, if the House agrees that motion, the motion on the draft order is put forthwith.

4.13.7 Church Measures

Church measures are made under the Church of England (Assembly) Powers Act 1919 by the General Synod of the Church of England. Measures agreed by the Synod are submitted to the Statutory Ecclesiastical Committee comprising members of both Houses who make a report which is referred to the Legislative Committee of the Synod. If the Synod agrees, the measure and the report are laid before Parliament, in the Commons by the second Church Estates Commissioner. A motion is then required to agree that the measure should be presented for Royal Assent.

4.13.8 Special Parliamentary Procedure

This procedure is now rare but it does apply, for example, to compulsory purchase orders affecting public open space where no equivalent exchange land has been provided. Those affected have the opportunity to petition and those petitions which are not successfully challenged may be referred to a joint committee. The order can then be brought into force in accordance with the joint committee's recommendation. If the joint committee has rejected the order, the Minister may bring in a confirmation bill to confirm the order. Such bills normally require only a report and third reading stage in each House.

4.14 European Legislation

4.14.1 Documentation

Draft regulations and directives are deposited in Parliament by the relevant UK Department of State which will also produce and deposit an explanatory memorandum setting out the Government's position on the legislation and the programme anticipated for its approval. See 2.3 as to delay in adoption of documentation in the Council of Ministers.

4.14.2 *The European Legislation Committee*

This Committee, which will be replaced in the 1999-2000 session by the European Scrutiny Committee, has all the ordinary powers of a Select Committee, considers European Community documents deposited in Parliament and issues a report either recommending no further action or that the document be referred to a European Standing Committee or be debated on the floor of the House. Three of its members are also delegates to the Conference of European Affairs Committees (COSAC) which meets twice a year in the country holding the EU presidency.

4.14.3 *European Standing Committees*

The European Standing Committees consider documents referred by the European Legislation Committee (unless a Minister has successfully moved a motion for the document to be debated on the floor of the House) and do so in accordance with motions moved by the Government who determine the committees' programmes. Proceedings before such a committee commence with an explanatory statement by the Minister, followed by questions by any member (whether or not on the committee) and then consideration of the motion before the committee and any amendments selected by the chairman to it. At the conclusion of the proceedings (maximum two and a half hours) the question is put on any amendments moved and on the substantive motion.

4.14.4 *Debate on the floor of the House*

A debate on the floor of the House will occur if the relevant Minister moves a motion for this purpose either following a report from a European Standing Committee or following a motion that a document be not referred to such a committee. The question on a motion in relation to a document upon which a European Standing Committee has reported and the question on any amendment to such a motion (if selected) are put forthwith. Debates on a motion in relation to a document which has not been considered by a European Standing Committee lasts for up to one and a half hours.

4.15 Finance and Taxation

The basic principle governing financial issues in the UK Parliament is that the Crown (represented by Ministers) and not the House of Commons demands money and proposes expenditure, the House of Commons grants money and agrees to expenditure and the House of Lords assents.   Both taxation and expenditure require legislative authorisation.   Proposals for public expenditure are contained in estimates presented to the House of Commons. Once the estimates have been approved Parliament passes an Appropriation Act allowing the Government to make use of the money it requires. Further releases of money may be authorised by Consolidated Fund Acts. The process of Parliament providing the Government with money is known as "supply".

4.15.1 *Commons' Privileges*

The House of Commons is pre-eminent in matters of taxation and expenditure. The Crown addresses its demands for supply primarily to the House (although in so doing it also requests the concurrence of the House of Lords) and it is an established convention that the Lords will not interfere in the passage of Consolidated Fund and Finance Bills.

4.15.2 *Grants of Expenditure*

The formal procedure for Parliamentary scrutiny and authorisation of Government expenditure is based on the consideration of estimates and the enactment of Consolidated Fund Bills. The Consolidated Fund is the Government's 'bank account' at the Bank of England and consists of the proceeds of taxation and other Government revenues. The Bank of England may only make payments out of the Consolidated Fund where it has statutory authority to do so. This is generally provided by way of Consolidated Fund and Appropriation Acts, although the Bank also has standing statutory authority to make payments out of the Fund for certain specified purposes (such as payments to the European Union). An annual programme of votes, Consolidated Fund Bills and an Appropriation Bill provide the House of Commons with an opportunity to consider Government expenditure, authorise payments out of the Consolidated Fund and appropriate those payments to specified purposes.

Specific proposals for new expenditure may also require a vote in Parliament as any legislative proposals involving significant additional expenditure or other charges on public funds must be supported by a money resolution. Money resolutions are generally taken immediately after the second reading of a bill although it is possible to move further money resolutions at a later stage if amendments to the bill make this necessary. As is the case with ways and means resolutions (see paragraph 4.15.3), money resolutions may only be moved by a Minister. This restricts the scope of Private Members' Bills as, unless they attract support from the Government, they may not make provision for significant public expenditure. If narrowly drawn, money resolutions once agreed to, restrict the scope of amendments that may be made to bills as amendments are generally out of order if they would increase expenditure beyond the level authorised by the resolution.

4.15.3 *Taxation*

In the spring of each year the Chancellor of the Exchequer makes his budget statement to the House in which he announces the Government's taxation plans for the coming year. Immediately after the statement a motion is moved to allow specified alterations in taxation to come into effect immediately. The statutory authority required for taxation is provided for these alterations by section 5 of the Provisional Collection of Taxes Act 1968. A debate begun by the leader of the opposition then follows. This lasts about a week and, at the conclusion of the debate, the House votes on a series of ways and means resolutions which embody the taxation proposals of the budget. These resolutions will then form the taxation elements of the Finance Bill.

Where taxation is the main purpose of a bill, as is the case with the Finance Bill, that bill will be founded on ways and means resolutions. Ways and means resolutions are also required to authorise the levying of taxes or charges in legislation where the taxes or charges imposed are subordinate to the main purpose of the legislation. They are thus regularly needed in connection with items of the Government's legislative programme other than the Finance Bill. In such cases the resolutions are generally moved immediately after the second reading of the bill in question. Ways and means resolutions may only be moved by Ministers and (as with money resolutions) this constitutes a significant restriction on the power of the House to take the initiative in taxation.

4.15.4 *The Annual Programme*

The Government's financial year runs from 1st April to 31st March. Before the financial year begins there is a vote on account. This is generally presented in November and voted on in December. It is followed by a Consolidated Fund Bill, generally enacted in December, which authorises the Bank of England to pay out of the Consolidated Fund a sum of money sufficient to meet the needs of the Government until the main estimates are considered. This Consolidated Fund Act (generally the second of the calendar year and accordingly numbered as the Consolidated Fund (No. 2) Act of the year) also makes provision for a further payment out of the Consolidated Fund for the purposes of the financial year current at the time at which it is passed.

The main estimates are generally laid in March and voted on in June. The main estimates set out the specific grants which the Government anticipates as being necessary during the forthcoming year for the purposes of civil and defence services, House of Commons administration and works and the National Audit Office. Following a vote on the estimates the Commons consider the Consolidated Fund (Appropriation) Bill. This, when enacted, becomes the Appropriation Act. The Appropriation Act authorises the release of a further sum from the Consolidated Fund and authorises the Government to appropriate the sums released from the Consolidated Fund over the course of the year to the purposes set out in the Act.

There is also a need for supplementary estimates. These are generally considered in the summer (July), the winter (November/December) and in the spring (February/March). These cover further grants required for existing services and grants required for objects of expenditure that have arisen since the main estimates. The summer estimates, once voted upon, are generally rolled into that year's Consolidated Fund

(Appropriation) Bill and the winter estimates are authorised by the Consolidated Fund Bill presented in the autumn in order to authorise the issue of sums on account for the following financial year.

The spring (February/March) estimates lead to a further Consolidated Fund Bill covering the end of the financial year. This (which is the first Consolidated Fund Act of the calendar year but the second of the financial year) authorises the supply of a further sum from the Consolidated Fund for the remainder of the financial year and may also contain provision for the supply of a further sum for the previous financial year in respect of the excess votes for that year.

Where a department has exceeded its authorised limit of expenditure excess votes may be required after the end of the financial year. These are generally presented in February and voted on in March and they are reflected in the Consolidated Fund Act which authorises the following year's spring estimates.

Three days are provided specifically for the consideration of estimates recommended for debate by a committee consisting of chairmen of select committees (the Liaison Committee). The value of debates on estimates is, however, limited by the rule that, although Parliament can reduce the estimates, it may not increase them. Even amendments seeking to reduce the estimates are, in practice, comparatively rare.

4.15.5 *Scrutiny of Public Accounts*

Under the National Audit Act 1983, the National Audit Office (NAO) headed by the Comptroller and Auditor General (C&AG) carries out certification audits of the appropriation accounts of Government departments. It also carries out "value for money" audits which examine the economy, efficiency and effectiveness with which the body being audited has used its resources. Its reports are then presented to Parliament and may be considered by the Committee of Public Accounts. The C&AG also answers for the management of the NAO to the Public Accounts Commission which is made up of certain members of the House.

The Public Accounts Committee examines the appropriation accounts and other reports from the NAO and regularly takes evidence from the accounting officers of departments and from other civil servants. The C&AG's reports are responded to by the Government in the form of Treasury Minutes and are subject to annual debate.

Chapter 5

The House of Lords

5.8   Public Access & Information

5.8.1	Access to Sittings
5.8.2	Access to Committees
5.8.3	Tours
5.8.4	Information
5.8.5	Documentation
5.8.6	Broadcasting

5.9   Conduct and Ethics

5.9.1	Oaths of Allegiance
5.9.2	Language
5.9.3	Forms of Address
5.9.4	Dress Code
5.9.5	Calling of Speakers
5.9.6	Order in the Chamber
5.9.7	Sub judice
5.9.8	Members' Interests
5.9.9	Investigation of Conduct
5.9.10	Exclusion
5.9.11	Disqualification and Resignation
5.9.12	Public Disturbance

5.10   Powers and Privileges of Members

5.10.1	Defamation
5.10.2	Witnesses and Documents
5.10.3	Sanctions

5.11   Committees

5.11.1	Committees of the whole House
5.11.2	Select Committees

5.12   Parliamentary Bills

5.12.1	Types of Bill and Format
5.12.2	Accompanying documentation for Public Bills
5.12.3	Stages of Public Bills
5.12.4	Special Forms of Public Bill
5.12.5	Scrutiny of Public Bills
5.12.6	Approval of Commons Amendments
5.12.7	The Parliament Acts 1911 and 1949
5.12.8	Private Bills

5.13   Subordinate legislation

5.13.1	Overview
5.13.2	Hybrid Instruments

5.14   European Legislation

5.14.1	Documentation
5.14.2	European Communities Committee

5.15   Finance and Taxation

5.15.1	Commons' Privileges
5.15.2	Grants of Expenditure
5.15.3	Taxation
5.15.4	The Annual Programme
5.15.5	Scrutiny of Public Accounts

5.1   Form and Functions

5.1.1   Overview

The House of Lords, together with the House of Commons and the Sovereign, form the UK Parliament:

+ The Lords is a part hereditary and part appointed assembly comprising the Lords Spiritual and Lords Temporal.

+ It provides an additional pool of persons outside of the Commons from whom the Prime Minister can choose in making (normally junior) ministerial appointments. Life peerages can be conferred for that purpose.

+ It has the power (similar to the House of Commons) to initiate primary legislation not involving supply or taxation and formally agrees Commons' legislation in these areas: by convention, whilst Government bills may commence in the House, it limits its legislative role to that of a revising chamber.

+ It provides (together with the House of Commons and in certain respects the Scottish Parliament and the National Assembly of Wales) a degree of supervision of subordinate legislation.

+ It operates, alongside the House of Commons, as a national debating forum and investigative body.

+ Operating through its Appellate Committee it is the final UK domestic court of appeal other than in relation to Scottish criminal matters and devolution issues.

5.1.2   Abolition of Rights of Hereditary Peers

It is expected that the automatic right of hereditary peers to sit in the House will be abolished upon the enactment of the bill for this purposes during the 1998-99 Session. At the time of going to press, the bill includes provision for 91 hereditary peers specially chosen under standing orders to retain the right to sit.

5.1.3   Jurisdiction

See 4.1.2.

5.1.4   Legislative Competence

See 4.1.3.

5.2   Membership

5.2.1   *Composition*

The House of Lords comprises the Lords Spiritual and Lords Temporal, the former comprising the Archbishops of Canterbury and York and 24 other bishops of the Church of England and the latter comprising hereditary members (about 750), those created for life under the Life Peerages Act 1958 (a little less than 500) and the Lords of Appeal in Ordinary ("the Law Lords") created for life under the Appellate Jurisdiction Act 1876.

The peerage is divided into nine ranks which, in order of precedence, are princes, royal dukes, archbishops, dukes, marquesses, earls and countesses, viscounts, bishops and, finally, barons and baronesses.

5.2.2   *Elevation to Peerage and Disclaimer*

Most hereditary peerages only pass through the male line. Minors succeeding to a title do not receive a writ and are unable to sit in Parliament until they reach the age of 21. A person succeeding to an hereditary peerage is entitled within one year of succession to surrender it for life under the terms of the Peerage Act 1963.

New peerages, including life peerages, are bestowed by the Sovereign on the advice of the Prime Minister.

5.3   Opening and Dissolution

5.3.1   *Duration*

See 4.3.1 for the duration of Parliaments. The Lords' sessions are similar to those of the Commons and recesses are normally in the same weeks but may vary by a few days. The Lords often return from the summer recess a week earlier than the Commons.

5.3.2   *Opening*

See 4.3.2.

5.3.3   *Dissolution*

See 4.3.3.

5.4   The Role of the UK Government

5.4.1   *Representation*

In addition to those ministerial posts which are reserved for peers - the Lord Chancellor, the Leader of the House of Lords and the Lords' Chief Whip - the Government will ensure that each department of state is represented in the House of Lords. It is the usual practice for each department to have at least one Minister in the Lords and, in addition, peers will be appointed as spokesmen in the Lords to support or stand in for Ministers. Normally spokesmen will cover more than one department.

5.4.2   *Power in the House*

The Conservative Party currently has an inbuilt majority in the Lords - Conservative Peers outnumbering Labour Peers by approximately 3:1. Consequently party strength in the Lords is unaffected by the outcome of general elections, except to the extent that the new Government may create further life peers. In the main, however, the tendency of the House is to respect the democratic authority of the Government of the day.

5.5   Officials

5.5.1   *The Lord Chancellor*

The Lord Chancellor is appointed by the Sovereign on the recommendation of the Prime Minister. The Lord Chancellor is head of the judiciary and is also *ex officio* Speaker of the House of Lords. He presides over all deliberations of the House except when it is in Committee. He is not however empowered to keep order in the House, nor does he act as its representative unless the House confers this authority upon him. In his absence, one of the Deputy Speakers, also appointed by the Sovereign, will preside over the House, or the House may choose its own Speaker.

5.5.2   *The Leader of the House*

The Leader of the Lords is a member of the Government, appointed by the Prime Minister. Currently, she carries the title of Lord Privy Seal. Together with the Leader of the Opposition, she is responsible for the timetabling of business. In addition, she is responsible for advising the House of matters of procedure. She also represents the House on certain formal occasions.

5.5.3   *The Lord Chairman of Committees*

Peers are appointed by the House to the roles of Lord Chairman of Committees and Lord Principal Deputy Chairman of Committees and to a panel of Deputy Chairmen. The Lord Chairman chairs all committees of the whole House and is *ex officio* chairman of all other committees unless the House decides otherwise. He also exercises a general supervisory duty over private legislation and is the first Deputy Speaker. The Lord Principal Deputy Chairman is the chairman of the European Communities Committee.

5.5.4   *Permanent Officers of the House*

The Clerk of the Parliaments is the head of the administration of the House and is its main adviser on procedural matters. He is appointed and may only be removed by the Sovereign. He signs all official communications on behalf of the House and is responsible for the accuracy of the text of Acts.

The Gentleman Usher of Black Rod is also appointed by the Sovereign and is present whenever the Sovereign attends Parliament. He is present at the introduction of new peers and supervises the admission of strangers to the House; deals with disorder and disturbance; and is responsible for office accommodation, services and security in the House.

5.6 Sittings

5.6.1 Annual Programme

Similar to Commons (see 4.6.1) but the House tends to have slightly shorter recesses.

5.6.2 Sitting Times

The normal sitting time for the House is 2.30pm on Mondays, Tuesdays and Wednesdays, 3.00pm on Thursdays, and occasionally on Fridays at 11.00am (only in the latter part of the session will the House tend to sit on a Friday). The House usually rises between 9.00pm and 11.00pm. When judicial business is taken, the House meets early, typically at 2.00pm on a Thursday.

5.6.3 Adjournments and Prorogations

The Lords adjourns independently of the Commons. The Lords adjourns each day to a named day and hour. There is no fixed time for the adjournment of the House. The procedure for prorogation is as described for the Commons: see 4.6.3.

5.7 Business

5.7.1 Arrangement of Business

The rules of procedure in the Lords, unlike those in the Commons, do not give the Government any special rights. In practice, however, business is arranged by the Government Whips' Office in consultation with the usual channels and, where necessary, individual members of the House. Except towards the end of a session, Wednesdays are usually reserved for debates on motions. A programme of forthcoming business is issued by the Government Whips' Office every Thursday when the House is sitting.

5.7.2 Daily Programme

The usual daily programme on Mondays to Thursdays includes the following elements:-

Prayers

Said by one of the Lords Spiritual at the beginning of each day with no strangers admitted.

Business after Prayers

Judicial business, comprising the giving of judgments, takes place two or three times a month, usually at 2.00pm on Thursdays after which the House is briefly adjourned. Thereafter, or as first business when there is no judicial business, introductions, oaths of allegiance, messages from the Crown, notification of Royal Assent, tributes and personal statements are taken.

Question Time

Oral "starred" questions and, occasionally, private notice questions are then taken and are ordinarily completed within 45 minutes of the House sitting.

Business after Questions

A presentation of public petitions, ministerial statements, formal proceedings on private bills, business motions, introduction of bills and messages from the Commons are usually taken after questions. A peer presenting a public petition may only read out the prayer and specify the number of signatures to the petition.

Main Public Business

The ordinary public business for the day is then taken and may comprise stages of a bill, motions to approve affirmative instruments and motions to take note of or agree reports.

Unstarred Question

A short debate either during the dinner hour or at the close of business.

Adjournment

A motion to adjourn the House is put at the completion of the day's business and taken without debate.

Wednesdays

Up to the Whitsun recess, on one Wednesday per month, two short debates of up to 2 hours each take place, following a ballot of backbenchers and crossbenchers about one month in advance. Peers may not initiate more than one such debate a session and the subject matter for debate is limited to matters which are neither so weighty or controversial as to preclude proper debate in the time available. On other Wednesdays, one or two debates take place as agreed between the usual channels, on motions moved by opposition parties or back benchers.

Fridays

Occasionally, the House meets at 11.00am on Fridays. Starred questions, however, are not taken on a Friday.

5.7.3 Questions and Answers

Questions for Oral Answer

Up to four "starred" questions addressed to the Government (rather than a specific Minister) are taken each day together with supplementary questions which should be confined to two short and relevant points. Questions may be tabled between 24 hours and one month in advance with the final question on a Thursday being a topical question selected by ballot at 2.00pm the previous Tuesday. Each peer may have up to two starred questions on the Order Paper at any time (with no more than one for a particular day) and may ask two topical questions a session.

In addition to starred questions, a private notice question on a matter of urgency may be submitted in writing to the Leader of the House by 12.00am (or 10.00am on a day when the House sits before 1.00pm) and, when accepted, will be treated as if it were an additional starred question.

As indicated above, unstarred questions provide a formula for a short debate during the dinner hour or at the close of business.

Written Answers

Questions may be tabled for written answer in due course and are placed on the Order Paper. The reply is printed in the Official Report.

5.7.4 Motions

A notice of motion is tabled on the order paper in the name of the mover of the motion only and without the names of supporting peers being attached. The question on the motion is put by the Lord Chancellor or Chairman before it takes place and, with the exception of a motion for an Address in answer to the Queen's Speech, motions are not seconded. At the conclusion of the debate, the mover has the right of reply. The Lord Chancellor or Chairman then puts the question and, if decided against, the question cannot be put again in the same session.

Motions may be subject to amendment, the proponent of the amending motion also having a right of reply and typically speaking second. Motions may also be withdrawn but, once they have been moved, only with the leave of the House.

Business of the House motions, tabled in the name of the Leader of the House, either to vary or suspend standing orders or to apply time limits to debates, are taken before other notices relating to public business.

Motions for papers

The addition to a notice of a motion "and to move for papers" secures that the peer instigating the debate has a right of reply.

Motions for Resolutions

These are motions requiring a definite decision to be reached but, if the words "and to move a resolution" are adopted, notice can be given at a later stage before the motion is debated of the actual words of the resolution.

Motions "to take note"

This formula enables the House to debate a matter without coming to any positive decision and is regularly used in relation to select committee reports.

"Next Business" Motion

A motion "that the House do proceed to the next business" is a mechanism used to preclude the House recording an opinion on a motion that has been moved. It takes the place of the original motion and, if agreed to, the debate ends without the question on the original motion being put.

5.7.5 *Rules of Debate*

The Lord Chancellor has no general powers to control debate which in the Lords is a matter for the House. However, the Leader of the House, his deputy or, in their absence, a government whip will draw attention to breaches of order and procedure which are usually described as "undesirable".

Peers are ordinarily called to speak in the order of the list of speakers which is issued for most debates, but by way of guidance only, by the Government Whips Office. Those not listed may speak before the winding up speeches where time allows. The list of speakers is the responsibility of the Leader of the House and peers may place their names on it by 12.00 noon (or 6.00pm the night before if the House is sitting in the morning).

Where no list of speakers is issued, the order of speakers depends on the will of the House but, ordinarily, speakers from the Government benches will alternate with others.

Peers address their speeches to the House in general and may speak only once to any motion, except when the House is in committee or when replying, as the mover of a motion, to a debate. However, with the leave of the House, chairmen of committees, ministers to the crown and peers requiring to explain some element of their speech may speak again.

Speeches are meant to be kept short (i.e. less than 20 minutes in opening and closing and 15 minutes in other cases). In time limited debates, the time allocation for each speaker is noted on the list of speakers.

Peers speaking in a debate are expected to attend the greater part of the debate including the opening and winding up of speeches.

Interruptions (except in the case of maiden speeches) are permitted for the purpose of brief questions of clarification.

Reading of speeches is contrary to convention as is quotation (as opposed to summary) of a speech made in the Commons other than a speech by a Minister in relation to Government policy.

5.7.6 *Voting and Decisions*

Questions for decision are put by the Lord Chancellor or Chairman. A division is liable to be held if peers persist in calling out "Content" and "Not Content" when, within three minutes of the order then being giving to clear the bar, two tellers for each side are appointed. The question is then put again and, if both sides persist, peers have three minutes in which to enter one of the division lobbies to vote. The tellers return with their count following the vote and, once the Clerk has added the votes of the Lord Chancellor or Chairman and any infirm peer voting in his place, a teller for the winning side presents the vote to the Lord Chancellor or Chairman who reads the result. A quorum of 30 is required on a division upon a bill or for the approval, disapproval of subordinate legislation (the normal quorum of the House being three).

In the case of an equality of votes, bills, motions relating to the stages of bills and subordinate legislation are allowed to proceed but other motions are resolved in the negative. Where no more than one teller is appointed for each side, the question is decided against that side without a division and, where neither side manages to appoint two tellers, the question is resolved as if there had been an equality of votes.

5.8   Public Information & Access

5.8.1   *Access To Sittings*

The Strangers' Gallery is open whilst the House of Lords sits. Members of the public should join the queue (separate from the queue for the House of Commons) at St. Stephen's Entrance to the Houses of Parliament. Tickets can also be obtained through Black Rod's Office through a sponsoring peer.

5.8.2   *Access To Committees*

There is no system of tickets or advance booking for committees in the Lords.

5.8.3   *Tours*

Permits for tour along the "line of route" can be obtained from Black Rod's Office through the sponsorship of a peer.

5.8.4   *Information*

General enquiries about the role and work of the House of Lords are dealt with by the Journal and Information Office:

Telephone :	0171 219 3107
Fax :	0171 219 0620
Email :	hlinfo@parliament.uk

Enquiries about the judicial business of the House of Lords are dealt with by the Judicial Office:

Telephone :	0171 219 3111/3112/3113
Fax :	0171 219 2476

Enquiries about the work of select committees should be addressed to the Committee Office:

Telephone :	0171 219 3346
Fax :	0171 219 6715

Information about the House of Lords can also be found on the Parliament website (see 4.8.4).

5.8.5   Documentation

The working papers of the Lords is the *Minute* which is printed daily when the House is sitting. It begins with a formal record of the business conducted in the chamber the previous day, including the judicial decisions of the House, followed by motions and orders of the day for the coming month in so far as the business has been set down, then listed motions awaiting debate, questions for written answer, bills and orders, and forthcoming meetings of committees. A separate weekly list of the meetings of select committees is also printed. A Sessional Journal is compiled from the Minutes of Proceedings. The Journals also include a daily record of the peers present, the texts of reports from certain committees (such as the House of Lords' Offices and Procedure Committees) and an index.

A verbatim record of the proceedings of the House of Lords is published in *Hansard*. Debates in committees on public bills off the floor of the House are reported in an appendix to the daily *Hansard*.

5.8.6   Broadcasting

Recorded highlights of the proceedings of the Lords are shown on the Parliamentary Channel which is provided by the BBC and is available via cable (see 4.8.6).

5.9   Conduct and Ethics

5.9.1   Oaths of Allegiance

Peers can only sit and vote if they have taken the oath of allegiance which must be sworn by every peer on succession or introduction and in every new Parliament thereafter. Peers may also affirm. The House has ruled that peers may take the oath (or affirm) in Welsh but only in addition to and not instead of the English version.

5.9.2   Language

It is regarded as "undersirable" (i.e. out of order) for foreign language to be used in debate and therefore debates in the Lords are always conducted in English.

5.9.3 *Forms of Address*

As peers address their speeches to "the rest of the Lords in general" most speakers tend to use the phrases "my Lords" and "your Lordships" or "your Lordships' House" at appropriate points during their speeches. References to other peers in speeches can be prefaced by the words "the noble Lord (or Baroness etc.)", "the noble or learned Lord", in the case of Law Lords and Law Officers, "the most reverend Primate, the Archbishop ..." or "the most reverend Prelate, the Bishop ....." in the case of Lords Spiritual; and the "noble and gallant Lord" in the case of Admirals of the Fleet, a Field Marshal or Marshal of the RAF or a peer who holds the Victoria or George Cross. Peers from the same party are alternatively referred to as "my noble friend".

5.9.4 *Dress Code*

The Lords have no formal dress code but by tradition peers wear Parliamentary robes when they are first introduced into the House and for the State Opening of Parliament.

5.9.5 *Calling of Speakers*

As the House is self-regulating, the order in which peers speak depends "upon the will of the House". For most debates a speaking list is produced by the Government Whips' Office in consultation with the chief whips of the other parties and whilst this is for guidance only it is generally adhered to by peers.

5.9.6 *Order in the Chamber*

In line with its self-regulatory procedures, maintenance of order and the rules of debate is the responsibility of all peers who are present, who have a duty to call attention to breaches of order or procedure. If debate becomes heated it is open to any peer to move that the Clerk read the standing order which directs that "all personal, sharp, or taxing speeches be forborn"; and as an ultimate sanction, it is open to peers to move a motion "that the noble Lord be no longer heard". This rarely occurs and only in the most exceptional of circumstances.

5.9.7 *Sub judice*

The House regards as sub judice:

+ any matter awaiting or under adjudication by any criminal court (including a court-martial);

+ any matter awaiting or under adjudication by a civil court from the time the case has been set down for trial or otherwise brought before the court or before that time where there is a real and substantial danger of prejudice to the trial.

+ So far as possible the House seeks to ensure that practice in relation to sub judice matters is similar in both Houses of Parliament.

5.9.8 *Members' Interests*

Peers are required to register pecuniary and other interests which may have a bearing on the proceedings of the House and to declare such interests if they participate in a debate or other proceedings. The House regards it as undesirable for peers to advocate, promote or oppose matters in the House in which they have a pecuniary or other interest in the matter.

5.9.9 *Investigation of Conduct*

As the House of Lords is self-regulatory in its own proceedings there is limited provision in the standing orders relating to the conduct of peers. However, matters relating to conduct and, in particular, concerning the financial and other intervention of peers come within the jurisdiction of the Committee on Privileges.

5.9.10 *Exclusion*

There are no arrangements for excluding a peer from debate on grounds of conduct other than moving a motion that the peer be not heard further (see 5.9.6).

5.9.11 *Disqualification and Resignation*

A person is disqualified from membership of the House of Lords if they are:

+ an alien (which by virtue of the British Nationality Act 1981 means a person who is not a British citizen, Commonwealth citizen or citizen of the Republic of Ireland);
+ under 21 years of age;
+ bankrupt;
+ imprisoned for treason.

There is no mechanism by which peers may resign as such other than the Lords Spiritual (the Archbishops and Bishops of the Church of England) who, if they resign their See, also resign their seat in the Lords at the same time (by the Bishops (Retirement) Measure 1951). However, hereditary and life peers are under no obligation to attend the House and a person may disclaim a hereditary peerage within 12 months of succession (one month in the case of a member of, or candidate for, the House of Commons) under the Peerage Act 1963.

5.9.12 *Public Disturbance*

Disturbing the proceedings of the Lords is a contempt of the House and may be controlled and punished in a similar manner as contempts in the Commons (see 4.9.12).

5.10 Powers and Privileges of Members

5.10.1 *Defamation*

The House of Lords enjoys privilege in its role as the descendant body of the *Curia Regis* which advises the Sovereign and, in addition, article IX of the Bill of Rights 1689 applies to the Lords in the same manner as it does to the Commons (see 4.10.1). Therefore any matter raised in Lords' proceedings is absolutely privileged from action for defamation and the printing or publishing of anything relating to the proceedings of the Lords is also subject to the privilege of the House.

As with the Commons, reports of debates or proceedings published outside the House are privileged to the extent that they are a fair and accurate account of what took place and thus the extent of the privilege is a matter of law rather than parliamentary.

5.10.2 *Witnesses and Documents*

The power to summon witnesses and require the production of documents may be exercised by committees of the House of Lords without specific authority from the House itself (unlike the Commons where such powers have to be conferred on a committee) but the House will not compel members or officers of the Commons, foreign diplomats or witnesses from overseas to give evidence. The evidence of witnesses under examination is normally taken down verbatim and is printed and published in pursuance of an order of the House.

Witnesses are subject to the same privileges and protections of those applying to witnesses before the House of Commons.

5.10.3 *Sanctions*

The Lords has similar powers as those of the Commons to deal with contemnors but any warrants etc., which would normally be issued by the Speaker in the Commons are issued by the Clerk of the Parliaments rather than the Lord Chancellor in the House of Lords.

5.11 Committees

5.11.1 *Committees of the Whole House*

The committee stage on public bills is usually taken in the chamber as a Committee of the Whole House which every peer is entitled to attend. In such proceedings, peers are allowed to speak more than once on each question. Occasionally, other matters are referred to a Committee of the Whole House, to take advantage of this greater freedom of debate.

The committee stage may also be taken by a Grand Committee (Committee of the Whole House off the floor), usually in the Moses Room. Proceedings are the same as in a Committee of the whole House except that no divisions are taken.

5.11.2 Select Committees

The House appoints a number of Select Committees, both on a sessional and an *ad hoc* basis, the latter being appointed to investigate particular legislative proposals or other matters as they arise. The current sessional committees are:-

European Communities
To consider European legislation: see 5.14.

Science and Technology
To report on subjects of its choosing within the fields of science and technology.

Public Services
To consider the present condition and future development of public services in Great Britain.

✦ Legislative Committees

There are several legislative committees

Public Bill
Nominated to consider a particular non-controversial bill and comprising 12-16 peers together with the Chairman of Committees but all other peers may speak and may move amendments but cannot vote.

Special Public bill
Like a public bill committee but with power first to take written and oral evidence within a 28 day period.

Joint or select committee
To consider a particular bill in lieu of the ordinary committee stage.

Consolidation &c. bills
Joint committee with Commons - see 5.12.4.

Delegated powers and de-regulation
To scrutinise the delegated powers proposed to be taken in bills and to consider de-regulation orders - see 4.13.6.

Statutory instruments
A joint committee to consider the propriety of statutory instruments - see 4.13.1.

Local
There are various select committees in relation to local legislation, including the personal bills committee and hybrid bill, hybrid instrument and private bill committees selected for individual measures.

✦ Procedure

The House maintains four committees in relation to its own procedures:

Privileges
To consider questions of privilege and claims of peerage and of precedents. There is also now a joint committee on Parliamentary Privilege.

Procedure
To consider changes in the procedure of the House.

Liaison
To consider the work of select committees, requests for *ad hoc* committees and relationships between the two Houses.

Selection
To propose peers for membership of select committees.

✦ Administrative

There are currently two administrative committees in the House of Lords:

Offices Committee
To consider administrative affairs.

Broadcasting Committee
To consider the broadcasting of procedures.

5.12 Parliamentary Bills

5.12.1 Types of Bill and Format

Same as House of Commons : see 3.2 and 4.12.1. The equivalent of a Commons Private Members' Bill in the Lords is a Peers' Bill which can be presented by any member at any time. Such bills follow the same procedure in the Lords as Government bills and are not allocated a particular or limited slot in the sessional programme.

5.12.2 Accompanying Documentation for Public Bills

Same as House of Commons : see 4.12.3.

5.12.3 Stages of Public Bills

Public Bills in the House pass through the same stages as bills in the House of Commons but *subject to the following exceptions*.

Bills are introduced at the beginning of public business on any day by the peer who is presenting the bill reading out its long title and moving the first reading without debate.

After first reading, in the case of money bills and bills for aids and supplies, all stages are normally taken formally.

The committee stage is ordinarily taken on the floor of the House with all members entitled to participate. Amendments may be tabled by any member and there is no use of guillotine procedures but the conventions are such that only rarely will the House seek to defeat a key item of a Government bill. There is also a reluctance to put matters to a vote and, if the Government indicates that it will resist an amendment, the amendment is very frequently withdrawn.

Apart from Report, which can be taken immediately after the committee stage where there have been no amendments, each stage must be taken on a separate day.

Following the committee stage, there is no equivalent limitation to that in the Commons upon amendments being taken at report and third reading (these stages always being taken separately in the Lords). In practice, the committee stage nevertheless remains, as in the Commons, the principal opportunity for the proposal of amendments.

A "privilege amendment", when needed, is taken as the last amendment at third reading on a bill originating in the Lords to preserve the Commons' privileges respecting money and taxation by disclaiming any imposition in these areas. It is printed in bold in the Commons and subsequently struck out in that House.

ORDINARY STEPS	SPECIAL STEPS	COMMENTS
	Queen's Speech	Normally November
	Publication of draft and referral to joint committee	e.g. Financial Services and Markets Bill
	National Assembly for Wales consultation	Required under the Government of Wales Act 1998
	Bill brought from the Commons and printed	All H.C. Bills
FIRST READING		Purely formal
	All stages taken	Particularly Money Bills and Supply Bills
Printing		Includes Explanatory Memorandum
Consideration by Delegated Powers and Deregulation Committee		Report on delegated powers, usually before the committee stage
	Reference to Examiners	If bill is hybrid
SECOND READING		Decision in principle
	Instructions	Motion to instruct a committee to act in a particular way
Amendments tabled	- Hybrid Bill Select Committee	To consider petitions prior to ordinary committee stage.
	- Joint Committee on Consolidations	Consideration prior to ordinary Committee Stage
COMMITTEE OF WHOLE HOUSE		Detailed consideration
	Grand/Moses Room Committee	In lieu of committee stage in chamber but with no division.
	Public Bill Committee	In lieu of ordinary committee stage for technical and non-controversial bills.
	Special Public Bill (Jellicoe) Committee	In lieu of ordinary committee stage. Includes the taking of oral and written evidence.
	Recommitment to committee of Whole House	On motion, in cases where further consideration required.
Reprint		
Amendments tabled		
REPORT		Separate day from committee stage if bill has been amended.
Reprint		
Amendments tabled		
	Sovereign or Prince of Wales Consent	Immediately before third reading where prerogative etc. affected.
THIRD READING		Amendments to improve text and HC privilege amendment taken.
HC : ALL STAGES/APPROVAL HLAMENDMENTS		
ROYAL ASSENT		

5.12.4 Special Forms of Public Bill

Consolidation Bills

Such bills are invariably introduced into the House of Lords and, following second reading, are referred to the Joint Committee on Consolidation &c. Bills. Subsequently, such bills are re-committed to a committee of the whole House. Opportunities for amendment are restricted, the precise nature of the limitation being dependent upon the form of the bill as disclosed in its long title.

Hybrid bills

See House of Commons 4.12.5.

Provisional Order Confirmation Bills

See House of Commons 4.12.5.

Supply bills and bills of aids and supplies

Such bills cannot be amended in the House and are taken formally : see 4.15.

Money bills

A money bill passed by the Commons and sent to the House at least one month before the end of a session must be passed by the House within one month or the Commons may present the bill for Royal Assent without the consent of the House : see 4.15.

5.12.5 Scrutiny of Public Bills

Such bills may be amended in committee, on report and on third reading.

Tabling and printing of amendments

Amendments may be tabled by any peer at any time and are printed the day after they are tabled. The practice is to avoid tabling late amendments.

A marshalled list of amendments is published shortly before the committee stage and before report.

Admissibility

Any amendment may be tabled, but in general amendments are not tabled which-

- are beyond the scope of the bill and relevant to the clause or schedule to which they relate;
- are inconsistent with a previous decision taken at the same stage (other than by way of alternative amendments);

- impinge on the Commons' financial privilege by imposing a charge not covered by the terms of the relevant money or ways and means resolution;
- alter the title of a bill other than by way of correction.

Selection

There is no selection of amendments in the House. All amendments are called other than those which have been withdrawn but an amendment which has been called need not be moved.

Amendments may be grouped on an informal basis by agreement between the peers tabling the amendments and the Government Whips' Office.

Order of consideration

Clauses, schedules and amendments to them are taken in their natural order with amendments to amendments being considered immediately after the original amendment and priority being given in the case of alternative amendments to the amendment tabled first or that tabled by the peer in charge of the bill. Amendments to the preamble and title are taken last.

5.12.6 *Approval of Commons' Amendments*

See 4.12.7.

5.12.7 *The Parliament Acts 1911 and 1949*

See 4.12.8.

5.12.8 *Private Bills*

See 4.12.9.

5.13   Subordinate Legislation

5.13.1 *Overview*

As previously noted, the House shares with the Commons, a Joint Committee on Delegated Legislation. The requirements for laying instruments and the option of the affirmative resolution and negative resolution procedures are similar in both Houses but it would be unusual for an instrument to be subject to a motion to annul in the Lords (notwithstanding that the Government does not have the same control over the business programme) and, equally, affirmative resolutions would not ordinarily be taken to a division.

5.13.2 *Hybrid Instruments*

A special procedure exists for the consideration in the House of hybrid instruments which has no parallel in the Commons. Hybrid instruments are affirmative instruments which, in the opinion of the Chairman of Committees, would require to be enacted by a private or hybrid bill as opposed to a normal public bill but for the enabling Act. The procedure has a number of similarities with private bill procedure including the ability for those affected to petition and, in certain circumstances, to appear before a select committee.

5.14 *European Legislation*

5.14.1 *Documentation*

As for House of Commons, see 2.3 and 4.14.1.

5.14.2 *European Communities Committee*

This committee considers Community and European Union proposals and makes reports on both those which, in its opinion, raise important questions of policy or principle; and on other questions to which it considers the special attention of the House should be drawn. The chairman divides documents into those requiring no scrutiny (list A) and those requiring scrutiny (list B), the latter being referred to one of the committee's sub-committees of which there are currently five -

A: - Economic and Financial Affairs, Trade and External Relations
B: - Energy, Industry and Transport
C: - Environment, Public Health and Consumer Protection
D: - Agriculture, Fisheries and Food
E: - Law and Institutions

Reports of the sub-committees are subject to approval of the select committee. Reports are then subject to a reply from the Government within two months of publication with any debate recommended by the select committee taking place before adoption of the proposal by the Council.

Together with representatives from the Commons' European Legislation Committee, three members of the select committee are delegates to the Conference of European Affairs Committees (COSAC).

5.15   Finance and Taxation

5.15.1 *Commons' Privileges*

The role of the House of Lords in matters of finance and taxation is limited to a substantial extent by the pre-eminence of the House of Commons (see paragraph 4.15.1 above). The role of the House of Lords in expenditure and taxation is restricted to assenting to those financial provisions of the House of Commons which require statutory authority. The traditional pre-eminence of the House of Commons in financial matters has been further strengthened by the Parliament Acts of 1911 and 1949.

5.15.2 *Grants of Expenditure*

By convention the House does not amend bills of aids and supplies. As a result of this the committee stage of Consolidated Fund Bills is almost always negatived and proceedings on such bills are purely formal. Amendments by the Lords to provisions of bills other than Consolidated Fund Bills which involve expenditure are technically a breach of Commons privilege but the Commons may on occasion be prepared to waive such breaches of privilege.

5.15.3 *Taxation*

The convention preventing the House from amending bills of aids or supplies prevents amendments to the Finance Bills. In addition, the Parliament Acts of 1911 and 1949 prevent the Lords from rejecting bills that have been certified by the Speaker to be money bills, a category into which many (but not all) Finance Bills fall.

5.15.4 *The Annual Programme*

In considering Consolidated Fund Bills and Finance Bills the House of necessity follows the annual programme set by the Government and the House of Commons.

5.15.5 *Scrutiny of public accounts*

The House does not carry out any functions of scrutinising public accounts.

Chapter 6

The Scottish Parliament

6.6 *Sittings*

6.7 *Business*

6.8 *Public Access and Information*

6.9 *Conduct and Ethics*

6.10 *Powers and Privileges of Members*

6.1 Form and Functions

6.1.1 Overview

The Scottish Parliament was established by the Scotland Act 1998:

+ It is an elected assembly (129 members) from whose members the Queen appoints one member to form and preside as First Minister over the Scottish Executive and from whose members the First Minister, with its approval, appoints other Ministers.

+ It provides democratic legitimacy to the Scottish Executive of the day, notably by the requirement that the First Minister must resign if the Scottish Executive loses a vote of confidence in the Parliament.

+ It has the power, within its designated legislative competence, to make laws known as Acts of the Scottish Parliament.

+ It has the power to vary the basic rate of income tax for Scottish taxpayers by up to 3% and to sanction expenditure by the Scottish Executive within the assigned budget.

+ It provides a degree of supervision over subordinate legislation in Scotland.

+ It operates as a national debating forum and investigative body, both through its plenary sessions and by its committee system, in relation to matters of general public interest in Scotland. More specifically, it holds the Scottish Executive and others to account, scrutinises legislation and, pursuant to particular enactments, reviews the activities of certain public bodies.

+ It makes various public appointments pursuant to particular enactments.

6.1.2 Scotland and Cross-Border Bodies

Scotland includes the internal waters and territorial sea of the UK which are adjacent to Scotland. For this purpose, Orders in Council may determine which parts of internal waters or territorial sea are "adjacent to Scotland".

Special powers are conferred to enable Orders in Council to make provision for the conservation, management and exploitation of salmon, trout, eels and freshwater fish in the rivers Tweed and Esk which span the border between Scotland and England.

Special provision has been made for government departments, offices and office holders which are designated as cross-border public bodies by Orders in Council. Such bodies are excluded from the general ambit of the transfer of functions effected by the Scotland Act. Furthermore, UK Ministers are required to consult Scottish Ministers before exercising certain functions in relation to such bodies and, where such a body was required prior to devolution to lay any report before the UK Parliament, it is now required also to lay the report before the Scottish Parliament.

6.1.3 *Devolved and Legislative Competence*

Functions exercisable by the Scottish Parliament or the Scottish Executive (other than additional functions transferred to the Executive by Order in Council or on an agency basis) are only exercisable within "devolved competence" which means in effect that, were they to be the subject of an Act of the Scottish Parliament, they must be within its "legislative competence". This means that they must not -

- be applicable outside Scotland;
- concern "reserved matters";
- modify "protected provisions";
- be incompatible with Convention rights or Community law; or
- remove the Lord Advocate as head of criminal prosecution and investigation of deaths in Scotland.

Reserved Matters

Reserved matters are set out in detail in schedule 5 to the Scotland Act and comprise items under the following headings:

✦ Part I

General Reservations

- The Constitution
- Political Parties
- Foreign Affairs etc.
- Public Service
- Defence
- Treason

+ ## Part II

Head A

Financial and Economic Matters

- A1 Fiscal, economic and monetary policy
- A2 The currency
- A3 Financial services
- A4 Financial markets
- A5 Money laundering

Head B

Home Affairs

- B1 Misuse of drugs
- B2 Data protection
- B3 Elections
- B4 Firearms
- B5 Entertainment
- B6 Immigration and nationality
- B7 Scientific procedures on live animals
- B8 National security, interception of communications, official secrets and terrorism
- B9 Betting, gaming and lotteries
- B10 Emergency powers
- B11 Extradition
- B12 Lieutenancies

Head C

Trade and Industry

- C1 Business associations
- C2 Insolvency
- C3 Competition
- C4 Intellectual property
- C5 Import and export control
- C6 Sea fishing
- C7 Consumer protection
- C8 Product standards, safety and liability
- C9 Weights and measures
- C10 Telecommunications and wireless telegraphy
- C11 Post Office, posts and postal services
- C12 Research Councils
- C13 Designation of assisted areas
- C14 Industry Development Advisory Board
- C15 Protection of trading and economic interests

Head D

Energy

- D1 Electricity
- D2 Oil and Gas
- D3 Coal
- D4 Nuclear energy
- D5 Energy conservation

Head E

Transport

- E1 Road transport
- E2 Rail transport
- E3 Marine transport
- E4 Air transport
- E5 Other matters

Head F

Social Security

- F1 Social security schemes
- F2 Child support
- F3 Occupational and personal pensions
- F4 War pensions

Head G

Regulation of the Professions

- G1 Architects
- G2 Health professions
- G3 Auditors

Head H

Employment

- H1 Employment and industrial relations
- H2 Health and safety
- H3 Job search and support

Head J

Health and Medicines

- J1 Abortion
- J2 Xenotransplantation
- J3 Embryology, surrogacy and genetics
- J4 Medicines, medical supplies and poisons
- J5 Welfare foods

Head K

Media and Culture

- K1 Broadcasting
- K2 Public lending rights
- K3 Government Indemnity Scheme
- K4 Property accepted in satisfaction of tax

Head L

Miscellaneous

- L1 Judicial remuneration
- L2 Equal opportunities
- L3 Control of weapons
- L4 Ordnance survey
- L5 Time
- L6 Outer space

Protected Provisions

The protected provisions are:

- Union of Scotland Act 1706 and Union with England Act 1707 articles 4 and 6.
- Private Legislation Procedure (Scotland) Act 1936.
- European Communities Act 1972, ss 1, 2 (in part), 3(1) and (2) and 11(2) and Schedule 1.
- Local Government, Planning and Land Act 1980 Schedule 32, paragraphs 5(3)(b) and 15(4)(b) - designation of Enterprise zones.
- Social Security Administration Act 1992, ss 140A to 140G - rent rebate and rent allowance subsidy and council tax benefit.
- Human Rights Act 1998.

The Advocate General, the Lord Advocate and the Attorney General are entitled to refer the question of whether a bill or any provision in it is within legislative competence to the Judicial Committee of the Privy Council : see 3.3.

6.1.4 *Devolution Issues*

See generally 2.7. Any question concerning legislative competence, whether a function is a function of Scottish Ministers, the First Minister or the Lord Advocate, whether the exercise of functions by a member of the Scottish Executive is or would be within devolved competence and whether the exercise or failure to exercise such a function is incompatible with Convention rights or Community law is categorised as a "devolution issue".

6.2. Electoral Arrangements

6.2.1 *Composition and Electoral System*

The Scottish Parliament comprises 129 members (MSPs) 73 of whom are constituency members and 56 of whom are regional members. The constituencies are the same as the UK parliamentary constituencies except that Orkney and Shetland are separate constituencies for elections to the Scottish Parliament. The regional members are elected to represent eight regions each of which has seven regional members. Election is by means of the Additional Member System of proportional representation under which each elector has two votes, the first of which is cast for a constituency member on a simple majority ("first past the post") basis and the second is a regional vote cast either for a registered political party's regional list or for an individual candidate. Each list may have up to twelve candidates.

The Additional Member System allows regional seats to be allocated on the basis of the number of regional votes obtained taking into account the number of seats already won by a party in the region to arrive at what is called the party's electoral region figure. By this means, where the number of constituency seats won by a party is insufficient to reflect its share of the regional vote, it will gain one or more additional seats. However, no further seats are allocated to a party once that party has sufficient seats to reflect its share of the regional ballot.

6.2.2 *Franchise*

The electoral franchise is the same as for local government elections in Scotland. All British, other Commonwealth, and Irish citizens (including peers) and other EU citizens are entitled to be registered and may vote in one constituency if they are aged 18 or over and are resident there except convicted prisoners in detention or unlawfully at large, detained mental patients and those convicted of corrupt or illegal practices at elections.

6.2.3 *Candidacy and Election Rules*

Those eligible for election include all British, other Commonwealth, Irish, and EU citizens aged 21 or over and resident in the UK, including peers. No person can be a candidate, however, for more than one constituency or one regional list. The rules on election campaigns are set out in the Scottish Parliament (Elections etc.) Order 1997.

6.2.4 *Vacancies*

A by-election will be held following the death, resignation or disqualification of a constituency member if the vacancy occurs more than six months before the next ordinary general election. The by-election will be held within three months of the vacancy arising, on a date fixed by the Presiding Officer.

If a regional member's seat becomes vacant, it will be filled only if the member was returned from a regional list and then by the highest non-elected candidate on that list who is willing to serve, as notified to the Presiding Officer by the regional returning officer.

6.3 Opening and Dissolution

6.3.1 *Duration*

The Parliamentary session is the period from the date of the first meeting following a general election until the Parliament is dissolved.

A full session of the Parliament normally lasts for four years. The first full session of the Parliament began on 12th May 1999 which was the date of its first meeting after the general election.

Each session is divided into Parliamentary years for the purpose of arranging a calendar of meetings and business. These last for twelve months each new Parliamentary year in a session running from the anniversary of the first meeting of the Parliament following a general election.

6.3.2 *Opening*

The Scotland Act provides that the Parliament must meet within seven days of a general election or an extraordinary general election.

6.3.3   Dissolution

If a general election is to be held on the first Thursday in May, the Parliament is automatically dissolved at the beginning of the "minimum period" which ends with that day, the minimum period being determined by order for the conduct of elections made by the Secretary of State.

If the first Thursday in May would be inappropriate for the holding of an election, the Presiding Officer may propose an alternative date to the Sovereign. Provided the proposed date is neither more nor less than one month from the first Thursday in May the Sovereign may, by proclamation, dissolve Parliament and require the poll to be held on the proposed date.

An extraordinary general election may also be held on a proposal from the Presiding Officer if:

+ the Parliament resolves that it should be dissolved. Such a resolution, if passed on a division, requires a two-thirds majority;

+ the Parliament fails to nominate one of its members for appointment as First Minister within the time allowed under the Scotland Act.

On such a proposal the Sovereign may by proclamation dissolve the Parliament, require an extraordinary general election to be held on the day proposed and specify the date for the first meeting of the Parliament following the poll.

6.4   The Role of the Scottish Executive

The Scottish Executive comprises the First Minister, other ministers appointed by him and the Scottish Law Officers (i.e. the Lord Advocate and the Solicitor General for Scotland). They are collectively known as the Scottish Ministers.

6.4.1   The First Minister

While in theory the Sovereign has the power to appoint any member to be the First Minister, it is expected that this person will always have been chosen by the Parliament. Within 14 days of a Scottish general election and thereafter if the post of First Minister becomes vacant, the Parliament must vote to nominate a member for appointment as First Minister. The Presiding Officer then recommends that person for appointment. The date of the vote may be changed on a motion of the Parliamentary Bureau, but a member must be nominated within 28 days of the Scottish general election or of the post becoming vacant for any reason.

6.4.2 The Scottish Law Officers and Ministers

The Lord Advocate and Solicitor General for Scotland are appointed on the recommendation of the First Minister. The First Minister may also recommend members to be ministers or junior ministers. If the Parliament agrees to a motion that such persons should be appointed, the First Minister makes the recommendations to the Sovereign, who approves the appointments. If there is a division on a motion to recommend an appointment, the vote is only valid if at least 33 members vote (including those who vote to abstain). Ministers may resign or be removed from office by the First Minister.

6.4.3 The Crown - Sovereign and Executive

The exercise of the executive functions of government so far as of relevance to the Scottish Parliament are exercisable in part by the Sovereign directly, in part by Scottish Ministers and in part by the UK Government.

In addition to the Sovereign's powers of appointment and approval in relation to Scottish Ministers already mentioned, the Sovereign has a number of residual powers. In particular, she is able by Royal Proclamation to dissolve the Parliament and to require a general election to be held; and Royal Assent, by Letters Patent under the Scottish Seal signed by the Sovereign, is required before a bill passed by the Parliament becomes an Act.

Powers devolved to Scottish Ministers are typically powers formerly exercisable by a Minister of the Crown and will still be found expressed as such in pre-devolution legislation. The Scottish Executive thus exercises executive powers on behalf of the Crown (i.e. the Sovereign).

The UK Government also retains a number of powers directly in relation to the Parliament, for example the power of the Secretary of State by order to make provision in relation to elections, by order to prevent or require action bearing on international obligations, to make payments into the Scottish Consolidated Fund and to lend money to Scottish Ministers and the power of the Advocate General and Attorney General to initiate and participate in devolution proceedings.

In addition, through powers exercisable by Her Majesty in Council (that is, the Sovereign acting with and by the advice of the Privy Council), the UK Government is also able to exercise a number of powers over the Parliament, including—

- Disqualifying persons from standing for election to it;
- Altering its legislative competence;
- Transferring additional ministerial functions and property to the Scottish Ministers;
- Providing for the status and functions of public bodies whose remits cross the Anglo-Scottish border.

6.4.4 *Power of Scottish Executive in the Parliament*

The Scottish Executive will normally command majority support in the House (or face a vote of confidence) and should therefore be able to implement its policy relying upon that majority. Both the voting arrangements of the Parliamentary Bureau (which sets the business programme) and appointments to committees are required to reflect the balance of political parties in the House thereby further securing majority control. Only a limited amount of time is also specifically reserved for business that is not Scottish Executive business. Financial business which is necessarily the Scottish Executive's preserve is also given general priority and it has the sole right to propose tax varying motions and financial resolutions thereby limiting what other members may do.

6.4.5 *Votes of Confidence*

If the Parliament resolves that it has no confidence in the Scottish Executive, the Scottish Executive and junior Scottish Ministers are to resign and cease to hold office immediately. Notice of a motion of no confidence will be included in the Parliament's business if it is supported by 25 members. Usually, two days' notice is required although the

Parliamentary Bureau can approve a shorter period of notice in exceptional circumstances. A motion of no confidence may be passed by a simple majority.

6.5   Officials

6.5.1   *The Presiding Officer*

The Presiding Officer is to preside over all meetings of the Parliament; to exercise casting votes in those meetings; to convene and chair meetings of the Parliamentary Bureau; to rule on questions about the interpretation and application of the Standing Orders; and to represent the Parliament in discussions with other bodies - both within the United Kingdom and abroad. Should the Presiding Officer be unable to act, a deputy may exercise these roles.

The Presiding Officer is elected at the first meeting of the Parliament following a Scottish general election or as soon as possible after a vacancy arises. Once a Presiding Officer has been elected, he takes the chair immediately. The Parliament then elects two deputies if there are vacancies for those posts. A member may not be nominated, however, to be Presiding Officer or a deputy if two members of that member's party already hold such posts.

The Presiding Officer and deputies may resign at any time and may be removed from office by an absolute majority of the Parliament (65 votes).

6.5.2   *The Scottish Parliamentary Corporate Body*

The Scottish Parliamentary Corporate Body ("the Parliamentary Corporation") oversees the administration of the Parliament and represents it in legal matters. The Parliamentary Corporation consists of the Presiding Officer and four other members elected by the Parliament or appointed by the Presiding Officer. It appoints the Clerk of the Parliament and employs the Clerk and other staff of the Parliament. Most of the Parliamentary Corporation's day to day responsibilities are delegated to the Clerk. Members of the Parliamentary Corporation may resign or be removed by motion of the Parliament.

6.5.3 The Parliamentary Bureau

This Committee consists of the Presiding Officer, together with one member nominated by the leader of each of the parties that has at least five members. Parties with fewer than five members may group together to nominate a member of the committee, provided that their combined number is at least five.

The Bureau is to propose the Parliament's business programme and alterations to its daily business; to propose the establishment, remit, membership and duration of other committees; and to determine questions related to a committee's competence to deal with a matter. It is to meet in private and each member of the committee carries a number of votes equal to the number of members they represent. The Presiding Officer has only a casting vote.

6.5.4 The Clerk of the Parliament

The Clerk is appointed by the Parliamentary Corporation. The Clerk is to be responsible for keeping Acts of the Parliament and to exercise such functions in relation to the administration of the Parliament, the employment of its staff and the management of its property as the Parliamentary Corporation may delegate to him. If the office is vacant, or he is unable to act, the Clerk's functions may be carried out by an Assistant Clerk.

6.5.5 The Auditor General for Scotland

See generally 6.15.4. The Auditor General is appointed by the Sovereign after nomination by the Parliament and may only be removed by the Sovereign on a recommendation of the Parliament approved by two-thirds of its total membership.

6.5.6 Maladministration

The Parliament is required to make provision for the investigation of complaints made to its members about actions of the Scottish Administration. It may also make provision for investigation of complaints about the actions of the Parliamentary Corporation or of Scottish public bodies, except for actions relating solely to reserved matters. It is anticipated that these provisions will entail the establishment of a "Scottish Ombudsman" with a similar remit to the Parliamentary Commissioner for Administration (see 4.5.9).

6.6   Sittings

6.6.1   *Location*

The Parliament currently meets at the Church of Scotland Assembly Hall, the Mound, Edinburgh. This is also known as 'the Debating Chamber' or just 'the Chamber'. Committees generally meet in the Committee Chambers building on George IV Bridge, or in the Chamber itself. The Parliament may provide, on a motion of the Parliamentary Bureau, that a meeting can be held in any other place in Scotland. These accommodation arrangements are temporary, until the new Parliamentary buildings at Holyrood are completed, which is expected to be in the autumn of 2001.

6.6.2   *Annual Programme*

The Parliament follows an annual programme which enables the Scottish Executive to implement its legislative objectives and to vote the money required by the administration.

The pattern of the year's sittings will include the following:-

12th May	Beginning of Parliamentary Year.
June	Annual Statement by the First Minister setting out the proposed policy objectives and legislative programme of the Scottish Executive.
	Completion of consideration of financial proposals.
July-August	Summer recess.
October-November	Consideration of draft budgets.
Mid October	Autumn recess.
Late December/ Early January	Christmas recess.
January-February	Passage of Budget Bill.
Spring	Beginning of financial year (1st April) and Easter recess.

6.6.3   *Sitting Times*

Normally, sittings are between 2.30pm and 5.30pm on Mondays, 9.30am and 5.30pm on Tuesdays, Wednesdays and Thursdays and 9.30am and 12.30pm on Fridays.

A meeting of the Parliament may continue beyond 5.30pm on Mondays to Thursdays or 12.30pm on Fridays if:

+ it is necessary in order to complete any voting which is not adjourned to a later meeting;

+ it is necessary in order to complete the election of the Presiding Officer or a deputy Presiding Officer or the election of a members or members of the Parliamentary corporation or selection of a nominee for appointment as First Minister;

+ the Parliament so decides, on a motion of the Parliamentary Bureau, in order to consider Members' Business;

+ the Parliament so decides on a motion (which may be moved without notice) of a member of the Scottish Executive or of a member moving any business under consideration at that time. The motion may be debated for up to 10 minutes (each speaker being limited to a three minute speech).

A meeting of the Parliament normally begins and ends on the same day and normally not more than one meeting of the Parliament may take place on the same day. The full Parliament does not meet when its committees are sitting.

6.6.4 *Adjournments and Closure*

The Parliament decides, on a motion of the Parliamentary Bureau, the date and time for any meeting of the Parliament (after the first meeting), and, until the Parliament has so determined, the Presiding Officer appoints such dates and times (but see 6.6.3). The Presiding Officer may, if he considers it appropriate, at any time close a meeting of the Parliament.

6.7 Business

6.7.1 *Arrangement of Business*

The Parliament decides, on a business motion of the Parliamentary Bureau, a business programme for such a period as may be specified in the motion and this is notified to members in the Business Bulletin. The business motion is usually taken on a Wednesday to cover a two week period. The programme includes an agenda for meetings of the Parliament during the period in question and may include a timetable for the consideration by the Parliament, any committee or sub-committee of bills, EC legislation and subordinate legislation.

In proposing the business programme the Bureau must ensure that:

✦ on 12 half sitting days (i.e. 9.30am to 12.30pm and 2.30pm to 5.00pm or 09.30am to 12.00 noon on Fridays) in each Parliamentary year, the business of committees is given priority over the business of the Scottish Executive - the Parliamentary Bureau has proposed that committee convenors should provide a steer in setting the appropriate priorities;

✦ on 15 half sitting days in each Parliamentary year, the Parliament considers business chosen by political parties which are not represented in the Scottish Executive or by any group formed from political parties with fewer than five representatives or from members who do not represent a political party;

✦ at each meeting of the Parliament there is a period of up to 30 minutes for any Members' Business at the end of the meeting following Decision Time (i.e. the last half hour). The Parliamentary Bureau has ruled that such business should not normally lead to a decision having to be taken;

✦ between the beginning of May and the end of June each year there is time for the consideration of financial proposals;

✦ between the beginning of October and the end of November each year there is time for consideration of draft budgets;

✦ between the beginning of January and the end of February each year there is time for the stages of the Budget Bill.

The Bureau must also ensure that sufficient time is set aside in the business programme for the First Minister to make a statement to Parliament setting out the proposed policy objectives and legislative programme of the Scottish Executive for any Parliamentary year.

6.7.2 Daily Programme

The daily programme, as determined by the business programme (see 6.7.1), is set out in the daily business list drawn up by the Clerk and may include the following elements:-

+ Ministerial Statements

    A member of the Scottish Executive or junior Scottish Minister may make a ministerial statement on giving notice to the Presiding Officer who notifies the Parliamentary Bureau and then includes it in the business programme. Ministerial statements can be debated. Where a statement is of an urgent nature, a request can be made to make it that day and, if the Presiding Officer considers it sufficiently urgent, he will alter the daily business list accordingly.

+ Personal Statements

    Any member may make a personal statement at the discretion of the Presiding Officer who notifies the Parliamentary Bureau and it is then included in the business programme. Personal statements are not debated.

+ Question Time

    See 6.7.3.

+ Consideration of Motions and Legislation

    See 6.7.4 and 6.12 and 13.

+ Decision Time

    Provision is made for decisions and votes to be taken half an hour before the end of the ordinary sitting day.

+ Members' Business

    A period of up to 30 minutes is allowed at the end of each sitting day for debates instigated by individual members, normally on matters which do not require a division.

6.7.3 Questions and Answers

+ Question Time

Question Time is a period of up to 30 minutes each week (normally on Thursdays) when questions which have been selected by the Clerk on a random basis may be put to and answered by members of the Scottish Executive or junior Scottish Ministers. Open Question Time is a period of up to 15 minutes each week immediately following Question Time. Up to three Open Questions are selected by the Presiding Officer at the end of the eighth day before Question Time from all admissible oral questions prior to the Clerk selecting from the remaining questions those to be answered in Question Time.

Oral questions to the Scottish Executive may be answered at Question Time or Open Question Time. Members may lodge an oral question only on the eighth day (up to 2.00pm) or ninth day at any time before the Question Time at which he or she wishes the question to be answered. A member may lodge only one question for answer at any Question Time. Notices of questions will appear in the Business Bulletin.

An oral question concerning the matter for which the First Minister is alone responsible will normally be answered by the First Minister but may exceptionally be answered by any other member of the Scottish Executive. Questions about the operation of the systems of criminal prosecution and investigation of deaths in Scotland will normally be answered by the Lord Advocate or the Solicitor General for Scotland but may exceptionally be answered by another member of the Scottish Executive. Other oral questions may be answered by any members of the Scottish Executive or a junior Scottish Minister.

Questions are taken in the order in which they are printed in the Business Bulletin and may only be asked by the member who lodged it. After a question is answered, the member who asked it may ask one supplementary question. Further supplementary questions may be asked at the discretion of the Presiding Officer. At Open Question Time any members may at the discretion of the Presiding Officer ask a supplementary question. A question selected for answer at Question Time or Open Question Time but which is not taken is treated as a question for written answer.

Exceptionally, an oral question to the Presiding Officer on a matter concerning the Parliamentary Corporation or the staff of the Parliament may be lodged. Normally such questions are for written answer.

✦ Emergency Questions

Where an oral question is of an urgent nature the member lodging it may, if it is lodged by 10.00am on a day on which there is a meeting of the Parliament, request that it is answered as an emergency question that day, whether or not there is a period set aside for Question Time that day. If an emergency question is, in the opinion of the Presiding Officer, sufficiently urgent, he will allow the question to be put and answered at an appropriate point during the meeting of the Parliament. After an emergency question is answered the member who asked it may ask one supplementary question and may, at the discretion of the Presiding Officer, ask further supplementary questions.

✦ Written Answers

Questions to the Scottish Executive (or to the Presiding Officer on a matter concerning the Parliamentary Corporation or the staff of the Parliament) may be lodged by any member for a written answer which should normally be made within 14 days. The questions are first published in the Business Bulletin and then, with the answers, in the Official Report.

Oral Questions selected for Question Time or Open Question Time but not taken are treated as questions for written answer.

6.7.4 *Motions*

Except where standing orders provide otherwise, any member may give notice of a motion or move a motion about any matter. Notice of a motion must normally be given at least the day before it is moved unless the Parliament decides with the agreement of the Presiding Officer that it may be moved without notice.

Notices containing the text and the name of the member giving notice of it are submitted to the Clerk. Any member may indicate his or her support for a motion by notifying the Clerk. Motions are printed in the Business Bulletin. Where time has been allocated for a debate on a particular subject, the Presiding Officer considers all motions on that subject of which notice has been given and decides which of those motions are to be taken by the Parliament. In all other cases, the Parliamentary Bureau considers motions of which notice has been given and by motion proposes which of those motions are to be taken by the Parliament. A business motion is always taken by the Parliament.

Immediately after the motion is moved, the Presiding Officer may call on any other members to speak. After a motion is moved, it may be withdrawn by the member who moved it at any time before the question is put unless any member objects to it being withdrawn.

A motion may be amended. The text of an amendment and the name of the member who gave notice of it and of any members supporting it are printed in the Business Bulletin. The Presiding Officer decides which amendments are to be taken by the Parliament. If an amendment to a motion is to be taken by the Parliament, it is taken immediately after the motion is moved. When an amendment is taken, it may be moved by the member who gave notice of it or by any member who has indicated his or her support for it. Before the member moves the amendment, he or she may speak in support of it. An amendment may be debated only if the motion may be debated. The question on an amendment is put at Decision Time.

✛ Motions by First Minister

The following motions may be moved only by the First Minister:

- a motion seeking the agreement of the Parliament that a recommendation be made to the Sovereign for the appointment or removal of a person as Lord Advocate or Solicitor General for Scotland;
- a motion seeking the agreement of the Parliament that a member be appointed a Minister or a junior Scottish Minister respectively;
- a motion that a recommendation be made to the Sovereign for the removal of a judge.

✛ Motion for a tax varying resolution

A motion for a tax-varying resolution may be moved only by a member of the Scottish Executive - see 6.15.2. Such a motion may not be amended. A motion for a tax-varying resolution may be moved no earlier than 12 months before the beginning of the year of assessment to which it relates, save that a motion may be moved after the beginning of the year of assessment to which it relates only at Stage 3 of a Budget Bill, or a Bill to amend a Budget Act, relating to that year.

✦ Business Motions

A motion seeking the approval of the Parliament to the Parliamentary Bureau's proposals on the business programme is known as a business motion, and can only be moved by a member of the Parliamentary Bureau. Any debate on a business motion is restricted to 30 minutes. No more than one speaker for and one speaker against the motion and any amendment to it is permitted and each speaker may speak for no more than five minutes. Members may propose amendments to a business motion. If, when notice of an amendment is given, it is supported by at least 10 members, that amendment is taken by the Parliament.

✦ Motions of no confidence

Any member may give notice of a motion that the Scottish Executive or a member of the Scottish Executive or a junior Scottish Minister no longer enjoys the confidence of the Parliament ('a motion of no confidence') : see 6.4.5.

✦ Motions for Closure of Debate

A member may, by motion without notice, propose that a debate be closed earlier than the end of the period of time allocated for that debate, or extended for up to 30 minutes. Such motions may be taken only with the agreement of the Presiding Officer. If the motion is agreed to, the debate is closed or extended accordingly. If the motion is not agreed to, the same or similar motion may not be moved again during the debate.

✦ Motions for Adjournment of Debate

At any time during a debate a member may propose that the debate be adjourned. Such a motion may be taken only with the agreement of the Presiding Officer. If the motion is agreed to, the Parliament proceeds to the next business. If the motion is not agreed to, the same or a similar motion may not be moved again during that debate.

✦ Motions for Adjournment or Closure of Meeting

Any member may without notice propose that a meeting of the Parliament be adjourned or closed. Such a motion may be taken only with the agreement of the Presiding Officer. A meeting may be adjourned only to a time later in the same day.

6.7.5 *Rules of Debate*

Meetings of the Parliament are chaired by the Presiding Officer or the deputy Presiding Officer or, where neither is available, the oldest qualified member. No member except the Presiding Officer may speak unless called upon to do so by the Presiding Officer. Normally, members speak standing at their places and address the Presiding Officer.

The Presiding Officer may allocate speaking time, whether for proceedings in relation to a particular item of business or for a particular speaker in any proceedings, and may do so whether or not the proceedings have started or the speaker has started to speak. In doing so, however, he must not disrupt any timetable of business set out in the daily business list.

The Presiding Officer may order a member to stop speaking if that member continues to speak beyond any time allocated to him or her or to that item of business or if, in the opinion of the Presiding Officer, the member departs from the subject or indulges in repetition. A speaker may not be interrupted except by the Presiding Officer but a speaker may give way to allow another member to intervene. Members must not speak or stand when the Presiding Officer is speaking.

6.7.6 *Voting and Decisions*

All decisions of the Parliament are taken by resolution and, if any member disagrees with the question put by the Presiding Officer who asks "whether we are all agreed", a division follows. All members may vote, the vote normally being taken using the Parliament's electronic voting system or, when that cannot be used, by an alphabetical roll call with members calling out "Yes", "No" or "Abstain". In the event of a tie, the Presiding Officer has a casting vote.

Many decisions are left to be taken at the "Decision Time" programmed for the last half hour of the ordinary sitting.

Decisions which must be taken at times other than Decision Time include:-

+ a motion seeking the agreement of the Parliament to the First Minister's recommendation for the appointment or removal of a person as Lord Advocate or Solicitor General for Scotland;

+ a motion seeking the agreement of the Parliament that a person be appointed a Minister or a junior Scottish Minister;

+ a business motion;

+ a motion for the closure of a debate;

+ a motion for the adjournment of a debate;

+ a motion to refer a bill back to the lead committee for a further report on the general principles of the bill at Stage 1;

+ a motion to adjourn Stage 3 proceedings of a bill or refer back to committee for further Stage 2 consideration;

+ a motion in relation to an Emergency Bill;

+ a motion for the exclusion of a member;

+ a motion for the adjournment or closure of a meeting of the Parliament;

+ a motion on Members' Business; and

+ the question on an amendment to a bill.

Unless the Presiding Officer otherwise determines, all other decisions of the Parliament are ordinarily taken on the same day as the question for decision arises, at the time known as "Decision Time" which is usually the last half hour of the sitting (i.e. from 5.00pm or, on Fridays, 12.00 noon). The Parliament may, however, on a motion of the Parliamentary Bureau, decide that Decision Time should begin at another time. Normally, Decision Time ends not later than 30 minutes after it begins but it may continue in order to complete any voting which is not adjourned to a later meeting as a result of a motion from any member.

Decisions in committees are taken by a show of hands unless a member requests a roll call vote and the convenor agrees. Only members of the committee may vote and, in the event of a tie, the convenor has a casting vote. Questions on an amendment to a bill are taken immediately after the amendment is moved (with or without debate) but, in other cases, the convenor determines the time for decisions.

6.7.7 Petitions

Petitions from persons or bodies may be submitted by being lodged with the Clerk or sent by e-mail. A petition must state the name and address of the petitioner and the names and addresses of any supporters. As long as the petition is determined by the Public Petitions Committee to be admissible (i.e. it complies with the requirements mentioned above, contains no offensive language and does not require Parliament to do anything which it clearly has no power to do), that committee must consider the petition and refer it to the Scottish Ministers, a Parliamentary committee or some other person or body, report to the Parliamentary Bureau or to the Parliament or take any other action which the committee considers appropriate.

6.8 Public Access and Information

6.8.1 Access to the Sittings

Access for visitors is via Mylne's Court which is reached from the Lawnmarket on the junction of North Bank Street and Mound Place. Over 300 seats are available, 140 of which require no pre-booking. Tickets for seats in the West Gallery are allocated on a 'first come, first served basis' available in advance from the Public Information Service. Tickets must be collected from the Visitor Centre.

6.8.2 Access to Committees

Committees of the Parliament will normally meet in the Committee Chambers building on George IV Bridge. Seats must be reserved in advance through the Public Information Service and tickets collected from the Visitor Centre. It is not normally possible to admit groups to committee rooms due to the small number of seats available.

6.8.3 Tours

No arrangements for organised tours are yet in place.

6.8.4 Information

The Scottish Parliament Visitor Centre, situated in the Committee Chambers building on George IV Bridge, provides information about the Parliament and its work to the general public.

The Public Information Service provides information about the Parliament's history, structure and procedures, MSPs, and current and future business. The PIS does not deal with matters relating to Executive policy, the implementation or interpretation of legislation, or the policies of political parties.

Telephone:	0131 348 5000
Switchboard/	0845 278 1999
public information :	
Fax:	0131 348 5601
Email:	sp.info@scottish.parliament.uk

Information can also be found at the Parliament's website at http://www.scottish.parliament.uk

The Parliament also maintains close contacts with a designated public library in each of the 73 Scottish constituencies. These 'Partner Libraries' act as a focal point for information about the Parliament. They will answer public enquiries about the Parliament and its documentation, and will provide, where available, online access to the Parliament's website.

6.8.5   *Documentation*

The Scottish Parliament Official Report is the record of the proceedings of the Parliament and its committees. The Official Report is published daily when the Parliament is sitting. The text is also posted on the Parliament's web site by 8.00am on the following working day. Every month, the daily editions of the Official Report will be published in a bound volume. This will be the definitive edition and will contain an index.

What's Happening in The Scottish Parliament is published weekly.

The Parliamentary Corporation will publish a Journal of the Scottish Parliament containing minutes of proceedings, notices of the titles of subordinate legislation and the date such legislation was laid, and titles of reports and the dates when they were lodged with the Clerk.

6.8.6 *Broadcasting*

Live coverage of the proceedings of the Scottish Parliament, both in the chamber and the main committee room, is provided by BBC Resources Scotland.

6.9 Conduct and Ethics

6.9.1 *Oaths of Allegiance*

Members may not take part in any proceedings of the Parliament until they have sworn the oath of allegiance or affirmed. A member must take the oath (or affirm) in English but may repeat that oath (or affirmation) in another language immediately afterwards.

6.9.2 *Language*

The Parliament's business is normally conducted in English but members may speak in Scots Gaelic. Members or any person invited to address the Parliament may also speak in any other language with the agreement of the Presiding Officer.

6.9.3 *Forms of Address*

Members are referred to in proceedings by name but the Presiding Officer and Deputy Presiding Officer may be referred to by their titles, as may members of the Scottish Executive.

6.9.4 *Dress Code*

The Parliament has no formal dress code.

6.9.5 *Calling of Speakers*

Speakers are called by the Presiding Officer who in deciding which members are to be called will have regard to the nature of the business under consideration. Subject to any timetable set out in the daily business list, the Presiding Officer may also allocate speaking time for a particular item of business or a particular speech.

6.9.6 *Order in the Chamber*

The Presiding Officer is responsible for maintaining order in the chamber and members must not speak or stand when the Presiding Officer is speaking. The Presiding Officer may order a member to stop speaking if the member continues to speak beyond any allocated time or departs from the subject or becomes repetitive. Members are required to conduct themselves in an orderly manner and in particular not act in a way which would constitute a criminal offence or contempt of court. A member who acts in breach of that requirement may be excluded from the chamber by the Presiding Officer for as long as he thinks fit up to the end of the next sitting day (or for any further period which the Parliament may decide on a motion moved by the Parliamentary Bureau). A suspension motion cannot be amended and if it is a subject of debate only the member concerned and one member for and one member against the motion may speak before the matter is put to a vote.

6.9.7 *Sub judice*

Except to the extent permitted by the Presiding Officer, a member may not refer to any matter which is the subject of active legal proceedings as defined in section 2 of the Contempt of Court Act 1981.

6.9.8 *Members' Interests*

Members are required to register with the Clerk the following registerable interests:

+ any remunerated employment, trade, profession etc.;

+ membership of a "related undertaking", that is an undertaking which is a parent or subsidiary of one of which the member is a director and from which he or she receives remuneration as such;

+ any campaign contribution which exceeded 25% of the member's election expenses;

+ any sponsorship;

+ gifts for the value exceeding £250;

+ overseas visits which have not been paid for by the member, the member's immediate family by or with the approval of the Parliament or from public funds;

+ any heritable property in which the member has an interest; and

+ shareholdings of more than 1% of the issued share capital of a company or with the value of more than £25,000.

A member is required to make a declaration of any registerable interest before participating in any proceedings of the Parliament if that interest would prejudice or give the appearance of prejudicing the member's ability to participate in a disinterested manner. Failure to comply with the registration and declaration requirements is a criminal offence.

6.9.9 *Investigation of Conduct*

The Parliament's Standards Committee is responsible for considering and reporting on whether a member's conduct accords with the Parliament's rules or code of conduct for members, any matter relating to members' interests or complaints relating to the conduct of members in performing their parliamentary duties. The Committee may by motion make a recommendation that a member's rights and privileges be withdrawn to the extent and for such period as the Committee may specify in the motion.

6.9.10 *Exclusion*

A member may be excluded on a motion proposed by the Standards Committee (see 6.9.9) or, in relation to misconduct in the chamber, on the order of the Presiding Officer or in accordance with a motion moved by the Parliamentary Bureau (see 6.9.6).

6.9.11 *Disqualification and Resignation*

A person is disqualified from being a member of the Parliament if he or she:

+ holds judicial office;
+ is a civil servant, member of the armed forces or police force or a member of a foreign legislature;
+ is disqualified (otherwise than under the House of Commons Disqualification Act 1975) from being a member of that House or from sitting and voting in it;
+ is a Lord of Appeal in Ordinary;
+ is bankrupt;
+ is detained as a mental patient; or
+ holds any public office specified in an Order in Council made under section 15 of the Scotland Act 1998.
+ A person is not disqualified from being a member by virtue of being a peer (other than a Lord of Appeal in Ordinary) or minister of religion.

6.9.12 Public Disturbance

The Presiding Officer may determine "reasonable conditions" under which the public is to be admitted and may order any person who fails to comply with those conditions to leave and may exclude them for such period as he considers appropriate.

6.10 Powers and Privileges of Members

6.10.1 Defamation and Contempt

The Scotland Act 1998 provides that any statement which is made in proceedings of the Parliament or published under the authority of a Parliament is absolutely privileged.

The strict liability rule in relation to publication of court proceedings being a contempt of court does not apply to publication made in proceedings in Parliament in relation to a bill or subordinate legislation or to the extent that it consists of a fair and accurate report of such proceedings made in good faith.

6.10.2 Witnesses and Documents

The Parliament may require any person to attend its proceedings and give evidence or produce documents in their custody or control where their evidence or those documents concern a matter which is within the responsibility of the Scottish Executive. A witness is not obliged to answer any question or produce any document which he would be entitled to refuse to answer or produce in proceedings before a court in Scotland.   The power may not be exercised against judges or the members of a quasi-judicial tribunal (in their capacity as such) or a Procurator Fiscal where to answer would prejudice criminal proceedings or otherwise be contrary to the public interest. There are also limitations on the exercise of the power in relation to ministers and other crown employees and in respect of any witness outside of Scotland.

A person who, without reasonable excuse, refuses or fails to attend proceedings when required to do so, refuses or fails to answer questions or refuses or fails to produce a document commits an offence, as does a person who deliberately alters, suppresses, conceals or destroys any document which is required to be produced. The Parliament may require witnesses to give evidence on oath and it is an offence to refuse to take an oath when required to do so.

6.10.3 Sanctions

Unlike the UK Parliament, the Scottish Parliament has no inherent jurisdiction to punish contempts but any action which constitutes a contempt may be punished as a criminal offence before the courts.

6.11 Committees

6.11.1 Establishment, Powers and Procedures

There are eight mandatory committees and, in addition, the Parliament may establish committees as it sees fit, on motions from the Parliamentary Bureau. The motions should also cover the membership, remits and duration of the committees.

All the committees have the power to conduct inquiries into matters within their remits and may consider relevant policies of the Scottish Administration, proposals for legislation, EC legislation and international conventions, possible law reforms and the financial proposals of the Scottish Administration. They can also initiate bills on subjects within their remits.

Each committee has a convenor and deputy convenor chosen by the committee but the Parliamentary Bureau may decide from which political party they shall be chosen. Other members may attend public meetings but not vote and, in relation to UK, Scottish and EC legislation, international conventions and law reform, the relevant members of the Scottish Executive, junior Scottish Minister or other member in charge of the bill in question may participate but not vote. The committees can determine when they meet as long as they do not meet during a parliamentary sitting and may meet in private. The committees can also appoint members as reporters and, with the approval of the Parliamentary Bureau, special advisers. With the approval of the Parliament on a motion from the Parliamentary Bureau, committees can also appoint sub-committees. In addition to other reports, each committee is required to make an annual report.

6.11.2 Mandatory Committees

The eight mandatory committees together with an indication of their remit and maximum membership are as follows:-

Procedures	Practice and Procedures of the Parliament (7).
Standards	Conduct of members (7).
Finance	Scottish Executive proposals for budgets, public expenditure and taxation and related matters (11) - see 6.15.4.
Audit	Accounts laid before the Parliament, reports by the Auditor General for Scotland and related matters (11) - see 6.15.4.
European	EC legislation, its implementation and EC and EU issues (13) - see 6.14.
Equal opportunities	
	Equal opportunities within and outside Parliament (13).
Public petitions	
	Admissibility and action upon such petitions (7).
Subordinate legislation	
	Instruments laid before Parliament, powers to make such legislation and related matters (7).

6.11.3 Subject Committees

The Parliament has established committees, each with a maximum membership of 11 members, to shadow the portfolios of the Scottish Ministers. The committees are: Justice and Home Affairs; Education, Culture and Sport; Social Inclusion, Housing and the Voluntary Sector; Enterprise and Life Long Learning; Health and Community Care; Transport and the Environment; Rural Affairs and Local Government.

6.12 Bills of the Scottish Parliament

6.12.1 Types of Bill

There are two types of domestic legislation with which the Parliament is concerned: bills which become Acts of the Scottish Parliament and subordinate (secondary or delegated) legislation made by ministers or the Sovereign under an Act of the UK Parliament or of the Scottish Parliament.

Parliamentary bills can be further categorised by the manner of their treatment in Parliament as follows:-

Public Bills	Executive Bills
	Committee Bills
	Members Bills
Private Bills	Local Bills
	Personal Bills

6.12.2 Format of Legislation

Similar to UK : see 4.12.2.

6.12.3 Accompanying Documentation

Every bill must, unless otherwise agreed by the Parliament, be accompanied on its introduction by:-

+ A written statement by the Presiding Officer as to its legislative competence.
+ A financial memorandum giving estimates of administrative, compliance and other costs and distinguishing between costs falling on the Scottish Administration, local authorities and others.

And, in the case of executive bills :

+ a written statement by the member in charge that in his or her view it is within the legislative competence of the Parliament.
+ explanatory notes, containing an objective summary of the provisions.
+ a policy memorandum, setting out the policy objectives, why alternatives were discounted, consultation undertaken and an assessment of effects on equal opportunities, human rights, island communities, local government, sustainable development and other matters of relevance.

And, in the case of a Bill charging expenditure on the Scottish consolidated fund, an Auditor General's Report giving an opinion on whether the charge is appropriate.

6.12.4 *Stages of a Bill*

Each Bill must pass through three stages -

+ Stage 1 - consideration of general principles
+ Stage 2 - consideration of detail
+ Stage 3 - final consideration.

Royal Assent is given by Letters Patent under the Scottish Seal signed by the Sovereign.

The arrangements of the usual stages, together with an indication of the main variations, is shown on the accompanying table.

Two weeks must ordinarily elapse between the conclusion of stage 1 and the commencement of stage 2 and between the conclusion of stage 2 (if a bill is amended) and the commencement of stage 3. These programming requirements do not apply, however, to Budget Bills and Emergency Bills.

A bill cannot be submitted by the Presiding Officer for Royal Assent if it is the subject of on-going devolution proceedings, a determination by the Judicial Committee that it is outside legislative competence (see : 3.3 and 6.1.3) or a prohibition order. The Secretary of State is empowered to make an order prohibiting the Presiding Officer from submitting a bill for Royal Assent if it contains provision which either he has reasonable grounds for believing are incompatible with international obligations or the interests of defence and national security or which modify the law in relation to reserved matters and which he has reasonable grounds for believing would have an adverse effect on the operation of the law applicable to reserved matters. Such a prohibition order can be made within four weeks of the bill passing (whether on a first occasion or following reconsideration) or within four weeks of a referral to the Judicial Committee on the question of legislative competence.

A bill is lost if it is not passed by the end of the session or if it is voted down at stage 1 or stage 3 or, at stage 3, if there is a division with less than 25% of members voting. A bill in the same or similar terms to a bill so lost at stages 2 or 3 may not then be introduced within a period of six months.

Ordinary Steps	Special Steps	Comments
	First Minister's Legislative Programme	
	Agreement to Committee Bill proposal	In plenary session : see 6.12.5
INTRODUCTION		Purely formal - notification in Business Bulletin and accompanying documents and Presiding Officer's certificate
Printing		Together with the accompanying documents
STAGE 1		Consideration of principle
	Financial Resolutions	Necessary prior to any stage for money or taxation proposals
Parliamentary Bureau ("PB") refers to subject ("lead") committee		PB reference to additional committee where falls within remit of more than one committee
(Lead) committee consideration		
	Reference to consolidation/statute law repeals committee	In lieu of lead committee for consolidation/statute law repeals bills.
Report by Lead Committee		In case of Executive Bill, also on policy memorandum
	No committee referral or report	Budget Bills and, on motion by members of S.E., Emergency Bills
	All stages taken in plenary session	Emergency Bills
	Recommittal	On motion of any member
Stage 1 consideration in principle		Decision in principle in plenary session
STAGE 2		Consideration in detail
PB motion referring bill to Lead Committee		
	PB motion referring bill to Whole Parliament or non-Lead Committee	In lieu of Lead Committee consideration.
Amendments tabled		
Stage 2 consideration in detail		By Lead Committee
	Committee of whole Parliament	Emergency bills and others on motion of PB
	Consideration by consolidation/statute law repeals committee	For such bills in lieu of other consideration
Reprint		
	Reference back to Subordinate Legislation Committee	Where bill amended re powers for subordinate legislation
STAGE 3		Final Consideration
Amendments tabled		

	Crown consent	Where royal prerogative affected
	Recommitment	Up to half the bill or motion by member in charge as first business before stage 3 consideration
Stage 3 final consideration		In plenary session
	Reconsideration	In plenary session in relation to devolution issues or motion by member in charge
	Reconsideration by Parliament	On motion by member in charge
	Prohibition Order	By Secretary of State precluding Royal Assent
ROYAL ASSENT		On submission by Presiding Officer

6.12.5 *Special forms of Public Bill*

+ Member's Bill

a bill introduced by a member who is not a member of the Executive. Such a bill may be introduced, following notice by a member to the Clerk of the proposed short title together with a brief explanation of the bill, if within one month the proposal obtains the support of at least 11 other members. The Parliamentary Bureau is then obliged to propose time for stage 1 consideration. Each member may introduce no more than two bills a session (inclusive of any committee bill resulting from a proposal by that member).

+ Committee Bill

a bill resulting from a proposal by a committee agreed to by the Parliament but not taken up by the Executive. Such a proposal may be on the committee's own initiative or on a referral by the Parliamentary Bureau of a draft from a member.

+ Budget Bills

these are Executive bills to authorise sums to be paid out of the Scottish Consolidated Fund, to authorise sums received to be applied without being paid into the Fund or to amend a Budget Act. Such bills do not require a financial memorandum, explanatory notes or a policy memorandum and are not referred to a committee prior to stage 1 consideration. Stage 3 of such a bill must be commenced within 20 days of the bill's introduction. For more details, see 6.15.

+ Consolidation Bills

Bills giving effect to recommendations of the Scottish Law Commission on its own or jointly with the Law Commission. Such bills are referred to a consolidation committee prior to decision by the Parliament without debate on stage 1, are referred back to that committee for stage 2 and are decided by the Parliament at stage 3, again without debate.

+ Statute Law Revision or Repeal Bills

Bills to repeal spent enactments in accordance with recommendations of the Scottish Law Commission or to partly repeal and revise laws now out of date. Similar procedures to consolidation bills apply.

+ Emergency Bills

Executive bills proceeding on an emergency motion without a committee report before stage 1 consideration of general principles and, usually, with all stages being taken in one day in the Parliament.

6.12.6 *Private Bills*

Private bills are bills of a local or personal nature introduced by outside interests ("promoters").

Private bills may be introduced only on 27th March or 27th November or, if not a sitting day, the next available sitting day. At stage 1 of such a Bill, the Lead Committee may require the promoters to comply with additional procedural requirements (e.g. as to notices) and provide an opportunity for objections to be deposited. At stage 2, the relevant committee can appoint a members as a reporter or an outside adviser to hold an inquiry into the bill and objections to it.

Scottish Provisional Orders Procedure, (see the Private Legislation Procedure (Scotland) Act 1936) which was the principal legislative approach required for local legislation in Scotland prior to devolution, continues in existence in relation to applications prior to 1st July 1999 and for non-devolved matters (i.e. where a Scottish Private Bill cannot be promoted).

6.12.7 *Scrutiny and Amendment of Bills*

Consideration of the principles of a bill takes place before the lead committee and in debate for stage 1.

Bills can be amended at the stage 2 committee, the stage 3 debate and, for the purposes of resolving any problem giving rise to such additional proceedings, on reconsideration.

✦ Tabling and printing of amendments

Notice of an amendment may be given by any member after the completion of stage 1 or stage 2 by lodging it with the Clerk not later than two sitting days in advance or, for stage 2, with less notice if the convenor agrees (a "manuscript amendment"). The notice must set out the text of the amendment together with the name of the proposer. The member in charge plus up to four other members may indicate their support by notifying the Clerk. Admissible amendments are printed in the Business Bulletin.

A marshalled list of amendments is prepared by the Clerk for each day of proceedings on a bill.

✦ Admissibility

An amendment is admissible unless:

(a) it is not in proper form;

(b) it is not relevant to the bill or to the provision in question;

(c) it is inconsistent with the general principles of the bill as agreed by Parliament;

(d) it is inconsistent with the decision already taken at that stage; or

(e) it goes beyond the terms of any financial resolution in relation to the bill.

The convenor or, as the case may be, the Presiding Officer determines admissibility prior to printing.

✦ Selection

At stage 3, the Presiding Officer may select as he sees fit the amendments to be taken.

✦ Order of Consideration

The marshalled list sets out the amendments proposed to a bill and the order in which they are to be disposed of as determined by the Clerk. The convenor or, as the case may be, the Presiding Officer may group amendments.

Unless the Parliament otherwise determines on a motion of the Parliamentary Bureau, the committee decides the order in which provisions are taken at stage 2. Each section and schedule and the long title are considered separately, a schedule normally being taken with the section introducing it. The question that a section or schedule is agreed is put by the convenor without the need for a motion and is treated as decided if a motion to leave out is not agreed to. A member who is not a member of the committee may participate in the committee proceedings (but not vote) in relation to an amendment in his or her name or generally, if he or she is the member in charge of the bill or, for a non-Executive Bill, is the relevant member of the Scottish Executive.

Unless the Parliament otherwise decides on a motion of the Parliamentary Bureau, amendments are taken at stage 3 in the order of the provisions to which they relate before the Parliament debates the question whether the bill is passed.

The member moving an amendment, the member in charge of the bill, any members of the Scottish Executive or a junior Scottish Minister may speak on an amendment. Other members may do so at the discretion of the convenor or, as the case may be, the Presiding Officer.

6.13 Subordinate Legislation

6.13.1 *Procedural Scrutiny*

All instruments laid before the Parliament are referred to the Subordinate Legislation Committee to consider the impact on public finances and certain procedural aspects not touching on the substance or the policy behind the instrument. The Committee has 20 days from laying of the instrument to report to Parliament and the Lead Committee.

6.13.2 *Laying before Parliament*

Laying is achieved by lodging a copy or, where required, the draft with the Clerk who then refers the instrument to the Lead Committee and the Subordinate Legislation Committee.

6.13.3 *Lead Committee*

The lead committee is the committee within whose remit the subject matter of the instrument falls or where it falls within the remit of more than one committee that designated by the Parliament on a motion of the Parliamentary Bureau.

6.13.4 Negative Procedure

Any member may by motion within 40 days of the instrument being laid propose to the Lead Committee that it recommends that no further action be taken on it.

That member and the relevant minister may participate in the debate on the motion (maximum length 90 minutes) but may not vote.

The Lead Committee must report its recommendations (taking into account recommendations made by any other committee) within 40 days of the instrument being laid and, if it recommends annulment, the Parliamentary Bureau must within the same period by motion proposed that nothing further is done on the instrument. Only the members moving the motion and the relevant minister may speak, each for a maximum of three minutes.

6.13.5 Affirmative Procedure

Any minister may, by motion, propose that the Lead Committee recommend that the instrument be approved and may participate in the debate on the motion (maximum length 90 minutes) but may not vote.

The Lead Committee must report its recommendation (taking into account recommendations made by any other committee) within 40 days of the instrument being laid or, if different, in the case of an order already in force, the period beyond which it cannot remain in force without approval. If the Lead Committee recommends approval, the Parliamentary Bureau must, by motion, propose that Parliament approve the instrument. Only the relevant minister and one member opposing the motion may speak, each for a maximum of three minutes.

6.14   European Legislation

6.14.1 Documentation etc.

See 2.3 and 4.14.1. It is likely that similar arrangements respecting the deposit of draft documentation in the Parliament will be adopted as apply in the case of the House of Commons.

6.14.2 *European Committee*

The European Committee will normally comprise members of other committees having a relevant remit but its convenor cannot be a convenor of such a committee. He considers and reports on proposals for and the implementation of EC legislation and any EC or EU issue.

6.15   Finance and Taxation

6.15.1 *Grants of Expenditure*

The Barnett formula (named after former Chief Secretary to the Treasury Joel [now Lord] Barnett) has been used since the late 1970s to determine the budgets of the Northern Ireland Office, the Scottish Office and the Welsh Office. Under the formula changes to programmes in England (or, in the case of Northern Ireland, programmes in Great Britain) result in equivalent changes in the budgets of the Welsh Office, the Scottish Office and the Northern Ireland Office. The budgets are calculated as a block based on population shares and each Secretary of State has had the freedom to distribute as they see fit the resources they have received between the programmes run by their department. There is no obligation for the block grant to be spent according to the same pattern as the expenditure in England upon which it is based. Although not directly a factor in the procedure of determining any individual year's block grant, built into the system is a higher level of spending per capita in Wales, Scotland and Northern Ireland than in England. Spending on agriculture does not form part of the block grant determined under the Barnett formula as this is determined primarily by UK and European Union policies.

Following devolution, the Barnett formula will continue to be used as part of the mechanism for determining the level of Scottish expenditure, most of which will become the responsibility of the Parliament. As the formula is an administrative measure and is not given statutory force by the devolution legislation, it will be possible for future UK Governments to change or replace it.

The Scotland Act 1998 establishes a Scottish Consolidated Fund which will be separate from the United Kingdom Consolidated Fund (as to which see 4.15.2). The Secretary of State for Scotland makes payments into the Fund out of money provided by the UK Parliament and, in addition, sums received by an office holder of the Scottish Administration are paid into it. It is likely that the block grant received by the Secretary of State according to the Barnett formula will be paid into the Fund.

The Scotland Act 1998 and the Standing Orders of the Scottish Parliament apply to the management of the Scottish Consolidated Fund many of the principles that apply to the United Kingdom Consolidated Fund. For payments to be made out of the Scottish Consolidated Fund, legislative authority will be required. In addition, various specific provisions have been made in the rules of the Scottish Parliament for financial matters.

Bills and amendments to bills which introduce new, or increase existing, expenditure require a financial resolution which may only be moved by a member of the Scottish Executive or a junior Scottish Minister. In addition, all bills introduced into the Parliament will be required to be accompanied by a Financial Memorandum, setting out the administrative, compliance and other costs to which the bill will give rise. Standing Orders also require any bill containing any provision for charging expenditure to the Scottish Consolidated Fund to be accompanied by a report signed by the Auditor General for Scotland setting out his or her views as to whether the charge is appropriate.

6.15.2 *Taxation*

The Scotland Act 1998 confers a limited tax-raising power on the Parliament. This power allows the Parliament to vary the basic rate of income tax for those resident in Scotland by up to 3% from that applying in the remainder of the UK. If the Parliament exercises its power to increase the basic rate of income tax in Scotland, the Inland Revenue will be required to pay into the Scottish Consolidated Fund an amount equal to the estimated yield of the increased rate of tax being paid. If the Parliament reduces tax rates, a payment will be made out of the Fund to the Inland Revenue to account for the shortfall in the tax yield.

Motions varying the rate of Scottish income tax may only be moved by a member of the Scottish Executive. As with new expenditure, any bill or amendment to a bill which would impose or increase any tax or charge also requires a financial resolution which may only be moved by a member of the Scottish Executive or a junior Scottish Minister.

6.15.3 *The Annual Programme*

Standing Orders require that the business programme proposed by the Parliamentary Bureau must include adequate time between May and June for the consideration of financial proposals, between the beginning of October and the end of November for the consideration of draft budgets and between the beginning of January and the end of February for the stages of the main Budget bill.

6.15.4 *Scrutiny of Public Accounts*

The Auditor General for Scotland takes over the responsibilities of the Comptroller and Auditor General where those responsibilities are in respect of functions transferred to the Parliament and Executive under the Scotland Act. Scottish legislation is to require the preparation of accounts by Scottish Ministers, the Lord Advocate and other persons to whom sums are paid out of the Scottish Consolidated Fund and for the examination of such accounts by the Auditor General for Scotland. The Auditor General will also be able to carry out investigations into the economy, efficiency and effectiveness with which Scottish Ministers, the Lord Advocate and other persons receiving sums from the Scottish Consolidated Fund have discharged their functions. The Scotland Act 1998 envisages that Scottish legislation will make provision for the publication of accounts and reports on accounts and for their laying before the Parliament.

In addition to scrutiny of financial matters by the Parliament as a whole, the Parliament has an Audit Committee and a Finance Committee. The Audit Committee has a convenor from a party not forming part of the Executive and no Minister is a member. It considers and reports on any accounts laid before the Parliament, any report laid before the Parliament by the Auditor General for Scotland and other documents laid before the Parliament concerning financial control, accounting and auditing in relation to public expenditure.

The remit of the Finance Committee is to consider and report on Budget Bills, on any proposals laid before the Parliament by members of the Scottish Executive containing proposals or budgets for public expenditure and on any proposals by Committees of the Parliament for public expenditure. The Audit Committee is also able to consider and report on the timetable for stages of the Budget Bill and on the handling of financial business.

Chapter 7

The National Assembly for Wales

7.1   Form and Functions

7.1.1   *Overview*

The National Assembly for Wales (Cynulliad Cenedlaethol Cymru) was established by the Government of Wales Act 1998:

+ It is an elected Assembly exercising statutory functions in relation to Wales and English border areas and may consider and make representations about any matter affecting Wales.

+ It is a body corporate with general powers to act within the scope of the functions conferred upon it.

+ It exercises functions conferred on it by legislation including most of the executive/administrative functions formerly exercisable by the Secretary of State and the Welsh Office which were transferred to it by the National Assembly for Wales (Transfer of Functions) Order 1999.

+ It can make regulations under section 2(2) of the European Communities Act 1972 to the extent permitted by Order in Council.

+ It has a right of consultation in relation to appointments to the extent specified in Order in Council.

+ It has a right of consultation at the beginning of each session of the UK Parliament in relation to the Government's legislative programme for the session.

+ It has wide general powers in relation to culture, sporting and recreational activities in Wales.

+ It operates as a national debating forum and investigative body in Wales, both through its plenary sessions and by its committee system and, in addition, through its powers to conduct public inquiries and polls.

+ It maintains the Partnership Council for Wales (Cyngor Partneriaeth Cymru) and operates, together with Welsh local authorities, a statutory scheme in relation to voluntary organisations.

+ It may by order transfer to itself functions of a Welsh Health Authority.

+ It may by order make provision for the transfer of functions of certain other public bodies.

7.1.2 *Transferred Functions*

Functions exercisable by a Minister of the Crown in relation to Wales can be transferred to the Assembly or made exercisable only with the agreement of, or after consultation with the Assembly, in each case by Order in Council made by the Crown at the behest of the UK Government. The first such order, the National Assembly for Wales (Transfer of Functions) Order 1999, was made to come into force on 1st July 1999 transferring certain functions in the following fields:-

1   Agriculture, forestry, fisheries and food

2   Ancient monuments and historic buildings

3   Culture (including museums, galleries and libraries)

4   Economic development

5   Education and training

6   The environment

7   Health and health services

8   Highways

9   Housing

10 Industry

11 Local government

12 Social services

13 Sport and recreation

14 Tourism

15 Town and country planning

16 Transport

17 Water and flood defence

18 The Welsh language

Functions which are transferred to the Assembly may be transferred so as to be exercisable exclusively by the Assembly or jointly or concurrently with the relevant Minister(s).

7.1.3   Conferred Functions

The specific functions conferred on the Assembly by the Government of Wales Act include-

+ Order-making powers for the transfer to the Assembly of functions of a Welsh Health Authority and certain other bodies.

+ Power to make regulations under s. 2(2) of the European Communities Act 1972 implementing community obligations to the extent permitted by Order in Council.

+ Power to support Welsh culture, specifically museums, art galleries, libraries and places of historic interest in Wales, the Welsh language and arts, crafts, sport or other cultural or recreational activities in Wales.

The following rights are also conferred on the Assembly:-

+ The right to be consulted in relation to certain appointments to the extent specified by Order in Council.

+ The right to be consulted about the UK Government's legislative programme.

+ The right to consider, and make representations about, any matter affecting Wales.

+ The right to cause inquiries to be held in relation to any matter relevant to the exercise of its functions and to hold polls for ascertaining views as to whether or how its functions should be exercised.

+ The right to promote and oppose Private Bills in the UK Parliament.

+ The right to take and defend legal proceedings.

+ The right to do anything which is calculated to facilitate, or is conducive or incidental to, the exercise of any of its functions.

7.1.4 Devolved and Legislative Competence

Functions exercisable by the Assembly or members of the Assembly Cabinet are only exercisable within the scope of the powers transferred to or conferred upon them. The Assembly in particular has no power to make, confirm or approve any subordinate legislation or to do any other act which is incompatible with either Community law, obligations imposed on it by a Minister of the Crown in relation to Community law or Convention rights.

7.1.5 Devolution Issues

See generally 2.7 and 2.8. Any question concerning whether a function is exercisable by the Assembly or is within its powers, whether the Assembly has failed to comply with a duty imposed on it and whether a failure to act by the Assembly is incompatible with any Convention rights is categorised as a devolution issue.

7.1.6 Wales and Cross Border Arrangements

Wales includes the territorial sea adjacent to Wales. The Secretary of State can by order determine what part of the sea is "adjacent to Wales" and determine the boundary of "Welsh controlled waters" in relation to deposits at sea and abandonment of offshore installations. The Transfer Order provides which parts of the Severn and Dee estuaries are to be treated as adjacent to Wales.

The following functions may also be transferred to the Assembly:

(a) functions in relation to a "cross-border body" i.e. any body exercising functions, or carrying out activities, in or with respect to Wales (or any part of Wales) and anywhere else,

(b) functions in relation to an "English border area" i.e. a part of England adjoining Wales (but not the whole of England) if:

(i) the function in question relates to water resources management, water supply, rivers or other watercourses, control of pollution of water resources, sewerage or land drainage; and

(ii) corresponding provision is made in relation to Wales or the part adjoining England.

All functions in relation to Welsh language or culture are regarded as exercisable in relation to Wales and may be transferred to the Assembly.

7.1.7 *Local Government Scheme and The Partnership Council*

The Assembly is required to make a "Local Government Scheme" setting out how it proposes, in the exercise of its functions, to sustain and promote local government in Wales.

The Partnership Council for Wales ("Cyngor Partneriaeth Cymru) is a body to be established and maintained by the Assembly consisting of members of the Assembly and of local authorities in Wales. It is empowered to:

(a) give advice to the Assembly about matters affecting the exercise of any of the Assembly's functions;

(b) make representations to the Assembly about any matters affecting, or of concern to, those involved in local government in Wales;

(c) give advice to those involved in local government in Wales.

It is expected that the Council will consist of 10 Assembly members and 15 local government representatives and be chaired by the First Secretary. Its first meeting is likely to be in October 1999.

7.1.8 *Scheme for Voluntary Organisations*

The Assembly is required to make a scheme setting out how it proposes, in the exercise of its functions, to promote the interests of relevant voluntary organisations, being bodies (other than local or public authorities) whose activities-

(a) are carried on otherwise than for profit;

(b) directly or indirectly benefit the whole or any part of Wales (whether or not they also benefit any other area).

The scheme, which must be published, has to be kept under review by the Assembly.

7.1.9 *Consultation with Business*

The Assembly is required to consult with organisations representative of business and any other organisations it considers appropriate on the Assembly's impact on the interests of business.

7.1.10 Equality of Opportunity

The Assembly is required to secure that its functions are exercised with due regard to the principle that there should be equality of opportunity for all people. This includes publishing a report after each financial year detailing the arrangements made and assessing their effectiveness.

7.1.11 Sustainable Development

The Assembly is required to make a scheme setting out how it proposes to promote sustainable development in the exercise of its functions. The scheme is required to be kept under review and, in the year following each ordinary election, the Assembly must publish an assessment of the effectiveness of its proposals to date and give consideration to remaking or revising the scheme.

7.2 Electoral Arrangements

7.2.1 Composition and electoral system

The Assembly comprises 60 members, 40 of whom are constituency members and 20 of whom are additional members, four from each of five electoral regions. The constituencies are the same as the UK parliamentary constituencies and the regions are each made up of between seven and nine constituencies.

Election is by means of the Additional Member System of proportional representation under which each elector has two votes, the first of which is cast for a constituency member on a simple majority ("first past the post") basis and the second is a regional vote cast either for a registered political party's regional list or for an individual candidate. Each list may have up to twelve candidates.

The Additional Member System allows regional seats to be allocated on the basis of the number of regional votes obtained taking into account the number of seats already won by a party in the region to arrive at what is called the party's electoral region figure. By this means, where the number of constituency seats won by a party is insufficient to reflect its share of the regional vote, it will gain one or more additional seats. However, no further seats are allocated to a party once that party has sufficient seats to reflect its share of the regional ballot.

7.2.2 Franchise

The electoral franchise is the same as for local government elections in Wales. All British, Commonwealth, and Irish citizens (including peers) and other EU citizens, where resident in Wales, are entitled to be registered and may vote in one constituency if they are aged 18 or over except those of unsound mind, convicted prisoners in detention or unlawfully at large and those convicted of corrupt or illegal practices at elections.

7.2.3 Candidacy and Election Rules

Those eligible for election will include all British, other Commonwealth, Irish, and EU citizens aged 21 or over resident in the UK, including peers. No person can be a candidate, however, for more than one constituency or one regional list. The rules on election campaigns are set out in the National Assembly for Wales (Representation of the People) Order 1999.

7.2.4 Vacancies

A by-election will be held following the death, resignation or disqualification of a constituency member if the vacancy occurs more than six months before the next ordinary general election. The by-election will be held within three months of the vacancy arising, on a date fixed by the Presiding Officer.

7.3 The First Secretary & Assembly Cabinet

7.3.1 Election of First Secretary

Once the Presiding Officer (Llywydd) and Deputy Presiding Officer (Is-Lywydd) have been elected, the Assembly elects a First Secretary (Prif Ysgrifennydd). If there is only one nomination, that member is elected, otherwise the Assembly is balloted until one member receives a majority of the votes cast.

7.3.2 Assembly Cabinet

The First Secretary then appoints Assembly Secretaries (Ysgrifennyddion y Cynulliad) to the Assembly Cabinet and allocates responsibilities among them. No more than eight Assembly Secretaries may be appointed and all but two of them have to be members of a subject committee. The First Secretary must then notify the Assembly of the Assembly Cabinet's membership. An Assembly Secretary may resign at any time or be dismissed by the First Secretary. The current portfolios are: Economic Development; Post-16 Education and Training; Health and Social Services; Environment (incorporating Local Government and Planning); Pre-16 Education, Schools and Early Learning; and Agriculture and Rural Development. There are also Assembly Secretaries responsible for the Assembly's finances and for its business.

7.3.3 *The Crown - Sovereign and Executive*

Executive functions of government in Wales are exercisable in part by the Assembly and, through it, by members of the Assembly Cabinet and in part by the UK Government.

Most of the powers devolved to the Assembly were formerly exercisable by Ministers of the Crown and will still be found expressed as such in pre-devolution legislation. The Assembly thus exercises executive powers on behalf of the Crown (i.e. the Sovereign).

The UK Government retains a number of powers directly in relation to the Assembly, for example the power of the Secretary of State to make provision in relation to elections and to make payments of money and loans to the Assembly, the power of Ministers to require action by the Assembly bearing on international obligations and the power of the Attorney General to initiate and participate in devolution proceedings. The Secretary of State for Wales also has two specific functions in relation to the Assembly. Firstly, he must consult the Assembly on the UK Government's legislative proposals. This consultation is to involve attending and participating in the Assembly's proceedings at least once each Parliamentary session. Secondly, he is entitled to attend and participate in any other proceedings of the Assembly and to have the same access to documents relating to such proceedings as ordinary Assembly Members have. He does not, however, have the right to vote or to participate in the proceedings of an Assembly committee or sub-committee.

In addition, through powers exercisable by Order in Council, the UK Government may exercise a number of powers in relation to the Assembly, most notably the power to transfer functions to and from the Assembly.

7.3.4 *Power in the Assembly and Votes of Confidence*

As the First Secretary is elected by the Assembly and in turn appoints the Assembly Secretaries including the Assembly Business Secretary he ought to be able to command the support of a majority of members. Presently, no single party or coalition commands a majority in the Assembly but the First Secretary is leader of the largest party.

In general, Assembly Committees are required to reflect the balance of the political groups in the Assembly thereby bolstering the power of the First Secretary if he heads a majority group.

Should the Assembly resolve - by a simple majority - that it has no confidence in the First Secretary, he must resign. A motion of no confidence is only valid if supported by at least six members. The Assembly must then elect a new First Secretary. The other Assembly Secretaries remain in office and elect one of their number to discharge the First Secretary's responsibilities (including chairing the Assembly Cabinet) until a new First Secretary is elected.

7.4   Officials

7.4.1 *The Presiding Officer*

The Presiding Officer or, in his absence, the Deputy presides at plenary meetings of the Assembly and has the duties given to him by the Assembly and may only vote in the exercise of a casting vote. This vote is to be cast in favour of a matter if further debate is possible and against the matter if it is not or if the vote is on an amendment.

The Presiding Officer and Deputy are elected at the first meeting after an ordinary election. Nominations to the post of Presiding Officer are only valid in the first instance if those nominating and seconding a candidate represent different political groups from each other. If it appears to the chair that no such nominations will be received, the meeting is to be adjourned for a short period, after which nominations of a single political group may be accepted. If two or more candidates are nominated, elections take place until one candidate has received at least half the votes cast. Once elected, the Presiding Officer immediately takes the chair.

A person may not be nominated to be Deputy Presiding Officer if they are from the same political group as the Presiding Officer.

The Presiding Officer or Deputy may resign at any time and is required to do so immediately if the Assembly resolves that it has no confidence in him or her. Should a vacancy arise, the election of a new Presiding Officer or Deputy takes priority over any other business of the Assembly.

7.4.2 *The Permanent Secretary and Clerk to the Assembly*

The Assembly has the power to appoint its own staff who are members of the Home Civil Service. Should the Assembly or any of its committees delegate any of their functions to its staff, the Permanent Secretary to the Assembly is responsible for allocating functions among the staff. The Permanent Secretary is also responsible both for ensuring that complaints procedures about the Assembly's actions exist and are published and for liaising with the Welsh Administration Ombudsman in the course of his investigations.

The Clerk to the Assembly is appointed by the Assembly. He or she will take the chair for the election of the Presiding Officer following future ordinary elections. He or she is also empowered to take the chair when both the Presiding Officer and Deputy are absent or unable to act - but only to arrange the election of a temporary chair. Should the Presiding Officer or Deputy resign, this is done by giving notice in writing to the Clerk.

7.4.3 *The Auditor General for Wales*

The Auditor General is appointed by the Sovereign and may only be removed by her on a recommendation of the Secretary of State, after consultation with the Assembly. The Auditor General has the right of access to documents, information and the accounts of the Assembly and its subsidiaries (including trusts and charities established by it). The Auditor General is also to examine the economy, efficiency and effectiveness of the Assembly's use of resources. He may exchange information with the Comptroller and Auditor General. Reports by the Auditor General are to be considered by the Assembly's Audit Committee and he is to be consulted by that committee before it determines its work programme.

7.4.4 *The Independent Adviser on Standards*

The Assembly is to appoint an Independent Adviser to provide advice and assistance to the Presiding Officer on matters relating to the conduct of members. The Adviser may also carry out investigations on behalf of the Assembly's Committee on Standards of Conduct.

7.4.5 *The Welsh Administration Ombudsman*

The Ombudsman is appointed by the Sovereign and may be removed from office by her only on the advice of the Secretary of State after consultation with the Assembly. The Ombudsman is able to conduct investigations into actions of the Assembly and specified public authorities in Wales. Where the Ombudsman makes a report into the activities of the Assembly, the Assembly must make a response within three months. A proposed response must be considered by the relevant Subject Committee before being submitted to the Ombudsman.

7.5 Opening and Dissolution

7.5.1 *Duration of Sessions*

A full session of the Assembly lasts for four years from the date of an ordinary election. This is held on the first Thursday in May. At the end of a session, the Assembly is dissolved and a further ordinary election is held. The first full session of the Assembly began on 12th May 1999 which was the date of its first meeting after the first election.

Each session is divided into 12 month periods for the purpose of arranging a calendar of meetings and business. There will be recesses within these periods.

7.5.2   Opening

Provision is made for the first meeting of the Assembly to be held on a day, and at a time and a place, appointed by order by the Secretary of State. The National Assembly for Wales (First Meeting) Order 1999 (S.I. 1999 No. 944) provided for the first meeting to be held on 12th May 1999 at 11.00am in the chamber which has been provided for the Assembly in Crickhowell House, Cardiff Bay.

7.5.3   Dissolution

The Assembly can continue to sit until the end of the day before the day of the poll at the next ordinary election.

7.6   Sittings

7.6.1   Location

The Assembly is currently located in Crickhowell House in Cardiff Bay. The new Assembly chamber, to be constructed next to Crickhowell House, is due to be completed in the second quarter of 2001.

7.6.2   Annual Programme

In each 12 month period time must be provided to debate the following business:

+ the annual report of the First Secretary;

+ the allocation of the Budget of the Assembly;

+ motions proposed on behalf of opposition groups;

+ reports submitted by subject committees;

+ reports by the Audit Committee;

+ the annual report of the Committee on Standards;

+ the Government's legislative programme;

+ the annual report on the equal opportunity arrangements;

+ the annual report on the local government scheme;

+ the annual report on the sustainable development scheme;

+ the annual report on the voluntary sector scheme;

+ the Assembly's arrangements for co-operation with business;

+ European Union matters;

+ the annual reports of the Welsh Administration Ombudsman and the Health Service Commissioner for Wales.

At least eight plenary meetings in the 12 month period must include time for motions proposed by opposition groups. These meetings must be distributed so far as possible in accordance with each group's representation in the Assembly. At least six plenary meetings must include time for debates on reports submitted by subject committees.

The Assembly must ensure that time is made available for consideration, either in plenary meeting or in committee, of the reports of the Equal Opportunities Commission, the Commission for Racial Equality and the Disability Rights Commission. Consideration may also be given to reports from voluntary bodies in Wales concerned with these matters.

7.6.3 *Sitting Times*

Assembly business normally takes place on Tuesdays, Wednesdays and Thursdays, with plenary sessions typically from 2.00pm to 5.30pm on Tuesdays and Wednesdays and committee meetings usually from 9.00am to 12.30pm.

Timetable motions, which outline proposed meetings and recesses over three month periods (see 7.7.1), are required to be framed, wherever possible, having regard to the family and constituency or electoral region responsibilities of members, and their likely travel arrangements. The motions must also seek to avoid programming business before 9.00am or after 5.30pm on any working day.

7.6.4 *Adjournment and closure*

A plenary session is closed in accordance with the agreed timetable for Assembly business unless a member proposes otherwise. If a member proposes earlier or later closure and is supported by at least 10 other members, the Presiding Officer must put the proposition to the vote.

7.7 Business

7.7.1 *Arrangement of Business*

+ Periodic Timetable Statements

The Assembly Business Secretary is required to table motions proposing outline timetables of plenary meetings, times available for committee meetings, meetings of political groups, and recesses. These motions must contain proposed timetables for periods of not less than three months and include dates for questions for oral answer by specific Assembly Secretaries.

The motions must specify which Assembly Secretaries should answer questions on which dates and should avoid programming business before 9.00am or after 5.30pm on any working day: see 7.6.3.

+ Weekly Business Statements

Each week that the Assembly meets, the Assembly Business Secretary must propose a statement about the organisation of its business for the next two weeks, and, so far as possible, the following week. The statement must inform the Assembly of business to be considered in each plenary meeting and the timetable for that business (including the period allocated to any individual item of business). The timetable for the third week is regarded as provisional, but the Assembly Business Secretary must avoid changes to the business proposed for the second week unless there is compelling reason for a change.

The Assembly Business Secretary's statement constitutes the agreed timetable for Assembly business unless at least 10 members object. If there is an objection, the Presiding Officer may allow the Assembly Business Secretary to propose that the statement should be adopted. Then, one member from each political group speaks briefly in response. The Assembly Business Secretary is entitled to reply and the Presiding Officer then puts the proposition to the vote. If the business statement is rejected, the Assembly Business Secretary must bring forward a revised statement.

+ Variations on the Day

At any plenary session, a member may propose, with the prior permission of the Presiding Officer, that the Assembly should immediately consider a particular matter of public importance. If anyone other than an Assembly Secretary proposes the matter, an Assembly Secretary is given an opportunity to comment before the proposition is put to the vote. If the Assembly agrees to the proposition, the matter is taken during that day's meeting or, if the Presiding Officer so decides, at the next meeting and the timetable is adjusted accordingly.

Subject to such a variation, business is called by the Presiding Officer and taken in the order in which it appears in the notice of business. However, when an item of business is called, a motion to postpone it until a later time that day or a subsequent day may be proposed either by the member in charge of it or, in the case of Assembly Cabinet business, by an Assembly Secretary. The proposition to postpone is immediately put to the vote, but such postponement cannot be agreed if at least 10 members object.

7.7.2 *Daily Programme*

Business in plenary sessions is ordinarily taken in the following order:-

+ Statements by the Presiding Officer;

+ Introduction of new Assembly members;

+ Obituary Tributes;

+ Election of Officers and members of committees;

+ Personal Statements;

+ Questions for Oral Answer

+ Statements by Assembly Secretaries;

+ Main plenary business;

+ Short debates prior to the conclusion of plenary meetings.

Personal Statements

The Presiding Officer may, on receiving written notice from a member, allow that member to make a brief, factual personal statement which is not subject to debate.

Statements by Assembly Secretaries

Statements by Assembly Secretaries are subject to debate.

Questions

See 7.7.3.

Motions and main business

See 7.7.4.

Adjournment Debates

Every week that the Assembly meets in plenary, the Presiding Officer holds a ballot to determine the name of a backbencher member to propose a topic or motion for debate in the next week. That member must notify the Presiding Officer of the topic or table the motion at least four working days before the debate. No amendment to the motion may be tabled. In the debate, the successful member speaks and an Assembly Secretary may respond. No other member may speak unless he or she has the permission of the member who succeeded in the ballot or is permitted to intervene by the Assembly Secretary responding.

7.7.3 *Questions and Answers*

✦ Question Time

The First Secretary answers oral questions once for at least 15 minutes each week that the Assembly meets in plenary. Assembly Secretaries other than the First Secretary and the Assembly Business Secretary must answer oral questions at least once, for at least 15 minutes, in every four weeks that the Assembly meets in plenary.

Members may table oral questions about any matters relating to an Assembly Secretary's responsibilities. Questions must be provided to the Table Office between five and 10 working days before they are due to be answered. Questions are accepted at the discretion of the Presiding Officer, who has regard to any guidance which the Assembly adopts. A member may table no more than two questions for oral answer by a particular Assembly Secretary at any plenary meeting.

Questions received between 9.00am and 5.00pm on the first allowed day are ordered by means of random selection. Questions received after that time are called in the order in which they are received.

The member asking an oral question is permitted to ask a related supplementary question. The Presiding Officer may then invite other members to ask supplementary questions subject to balancing the need to explore the issue under discussion with the need to secure that as many tabled questions are answered as possible.

At the end of question time, or at another time if the Presiding Officer so determines, the Presiding Officer may call a member to ask a question for which the usual notice has not been given if he and the Assembly Secretary have been given at least two hours prior notice and he is satisfied that the question is of an urgent character and relates to a matter of public importance.

Oral questions which are not reached receive a written answer which is recorded in the report of plenary proceedings for that day.

✦ Written Answers

Members may table questions for written answer by any Assembly Secretary by providing the text to the Table Office at least five days in advance. Questions are accepted at the discretion of the Presiding Officer having regard to any Assembly guidance on the subject. They are published in the notice of business on the day on which they are answered and the answers are recorded in the report of plenary proceedings for that day.

7.7.4 Motions

Except for oral questions, statements, introduction of new members, obituary tributes, or where a member proposes a topic (rather than a motion) for a short debate, business in plenary meetings proceeds on the basis of motions proposed. Except where standing orders provide otherwise, any motion must be tabled at least three working days before it is to be debated. A motion so tabled may be proposed by any member. Except where standing orders provide otherwise, amendments may be proposed to any motion, and must be tabled at least two working days before the motion is to be debated, subject to the discretion of the Presiding Officer. At the end of the period allocated to any motion and unless any procedural motion relating to that motion has been agreed to, the Presiding Officer invites the Assembly to decide on any amendments proposed and on the motion.

Procedural motions take precedence over other business. The Presiding Officer may permit a member to speak briefly in favour of any such motion, and another member to speak briefly against, and then puts the proposition to the vote.

The following matters may be proposed in procedural motions:-

✦ postponement of an item of business;

✦ referral of a matter to a committee;

✦ the closure of a debate;

✦ the continuation, or the adjournment, of debate after the period of time allocated to any individual item of business has expired;

✦ such other matters as the Presiding Officer considers appropriate.

At any time after a motion or an amendment has been proposed, a member may propose that it should be voted on immediately or allowed to continue for a specified period on that day or adjourned to another day. The Presiding Officer puts that proposition (which is not subject to debate) to the vote only if at least 10 members express support and if he is satisfied that to do so would not be an abuse of the Assembly's procedures, an infringement of the rights of minorities in the Assembly, or cause excessive delay.

7.7.5 *Rules of Debate*

The Presiding Officer and, in his absence, his deputy are reponsible for order in the Assembly (see 7.9.6).

Members called to speak address the chair. Members may speak in English or Welsh and simultaneous translation facilities are provided for speeches made in Welsh. The Presiding Officer may call the Secretary of State for Wales to speak in any debate. Speeches must be relevant to the business before the Assembly, and avoid tedious repetition.

The Presiding Officer may, at the beginning of any debate, announce a time limit on members' speeches. He may also direct a member who has spoken for too long to stop speaking. A member, other than the proposer of a motion or an amendment who is exercising a right of reply, may not speak more than once on any matter except, with leave of the Presiding Officer, for the purpose of briefly explaining some material point of his or her original speech.

A member who is speaking may allow other members to intervene for the purposes of clarification before resuming a speech. A member may not speak after the proposer of a motion has exercised a right of reply. A member may not speak after a proposition has been voted on except on a point of order relating to it.

7.7.6 *Voting and Decisions*

Decisions are ordinarily taken at the moment when they are reached during proceedings rather than being postponed to a later time.

Members must cast their votes individually and in person, but are not obliged to vote. The Presiding Officer may put a motion or an amendment to the vote by a show of hands and then announce the results. If the Presiding Officer considers that the result is doubtful, or if the announcement is challenged, the Presiding Officer calls for a confirmatory vote. Confirmatory votes can be taken by electronic means, or failing that, by roll call, in alphabetical order, of the membership. When one or more confirmatory votes has been called for, bells are rung. After an interval of five minutes, the vote or votes are taken. The Presiding Officer declares the vote closed and announces the result. The names of members voting, including those recording an abstention, are included in the reports of the Assembly's plenary proceedings.

A confirmatory vote is not valid unless at least 10 members participate. If fewer than 10 members participate, the business is held over to the next plenary meeting and the Assembly proceeds to the next item of business. In determining the number of members participating in a confirmatory vote, the chair and those recording an abstention are regarded as participants.

7.7.7   *Written Statements and Petitions*

Written statements of opinion not exceeding 100 words on matters affecting Wales may be tabled by any member (other than an Assembly Secretary) and may be supported, opposed or otherwise commented upon in writing by any member. If deemed by the Presiding Officer to be in order, written statements are published, together with any expressions of support or opposition tabled by other members.

Petitions may be addressed to the Assembly by members of the public. The Presiding Officer is responsible for informing the Assembly of the content and signatures of any petition received. The Assembly, or one of its committees, may then resolve to debate it.

7.8   Public Access and Information

7.8.1   *Access to Sittings*

Seats are allocated on a first come first served basis. 50 seats are available in the public gallery (30 of which are available through members).

7.8.2   *Access to Committees*

Approximately 25 seats are available for each committee by booking in advance.

7.8.3   *Tours*

No formal arrangements for tours of the Assembly have yet been made.

7.8.4   *Information*

The Assembly has an information office which can be contacted on:

Telephone:	01222 898 200
Fax:	01222 898 229
EMail:	assemblyinfo@wales.gov.uk

The Assembly also has its own website at http://www.wales.gov.uk.

7.8.5   *Documentation*

The Assembly is producing in electronic form an agenda for each day's sitting, a record of votes and proceedings for the previous day's sitting, and a forward look at forthcoming business. The Record of Proceedings is a verbatim report of the previous day's plenary meeting. It is available in the language spoken (with Welsh translated into English) the following day and in a fully bilingual version after five days.

7.8.6   *Broadcasting*

All plenary sessions of the Assembly are recorded for both visual and audio transmission. Five of the Assembly's six Committee rooms are wired for sound recording; and three for video recording.

7.9   Conduct and Ethics

7.9.1   *Oaths of Allegiance*

An Assembly member may not take part in any Assembly proceedings until he or she has taken the oath of allegiance or made the corresponding affirmation.

7.9.2 Language

The Assembly is required to conduct its business so, that so far as reasonably practicable, the English and Welsh languages are treated on a basis of equality. The Standing Orders are in both English and Welsh and the Assembly is required to have regard to the spirit of any guidelines made under section 9 of the Welsh Language Act 1993. Members may speak in English or Welsh and simultaneous interpretation is provided for speeches made in Welsh.

7.9.3 Forms of Address

Members address each other by name.

7.9.4 Dress Code

The Assembly has no formal dress code.

7.9.5 Calling of Speakers

Members are called to speak by the Presiding Officer and are required to address the Chair. The Presiding Officer may, at the beginning of a debate, announce a time limit on members' speeches and may direct a member who has spoken for too long to cease speaking.

7.9.6 Order in the Chamber

The Presiding Officer is responsible for maintaining order in the Assembly and may call to order any member who engages in conduct which is a criminal offence, obstructs the business of the Assembly, seeks to raise matters outside the scope of the debate, is discourteous, uses offensive language, refuses to conform to the Standing Orders or disregards the authority of the Chair.

Members are required to comply with any directions given by the Presiding Officer about their conduct and a member may be asked to withdraw for the remainder of the day if the Presiding Officer regards their conduct as warranting such withdrawal. If a member refuses to withdraw when required to do so by the Presiding Officer, a motion to exclude the member from the Assembly may be proposed and voted on immediately. On the first occasion exclusion is for one working day, on the second occasion in the same calendar year for five working days and on the third or any subsequent occasion for twenty working days. The Presiding Officer may adjourn the meeting or suspend the sitting for a specified time in the event of grave disorder.

7.9.7   Sub judice

Members are not prevented from raising matters of general public importance in respect of which court proceedings have been initiated provided the Presiding Officer is satisfied that the matter is clearly related to public policy, it does not relate to a case which is to be heard or is being heard before a jury, the matter is raised by means of a motion or question and the comments of the member concerned do not encroach on the functions of the courts or a judicial tribunal.

7.9.8   Members' Interests

Members are required to register interests of the following kind:-

+ directorships in public and private companies;

+ employment, office, trade, profession or vocation for which the member is remunerated or has pecuniary interest;

+ Any remunerated activity in the areas of public relations, political advice or consultancy relating to the functions of the Assembly and, where there is such a registerable interest, the member is required to register names of the clients concerned;

+ gifts, hospitality, material benefits or advantages, remuneration or other benefits received from a company or other body which is a contractor to the Assembly or has tendered or is tendering for a contract with the Assembly;

+ any financial sponsorship as a member of the Assembly or as a candidate for election where the sponsorship exceeds 25% of the candidate's election expenses;

+ overseas visits relating to or arising out of membership of the Assembly where the costs have not been borne by the member or from public funds;

+ any land or property other than the member's home;

+ any shareholdings above 1% of the issued share capital of the company concerned;

+ membership of any body which is funded wholly or partly by the Assembly; and

+ membership of the freemasons.

A member must also make a declaration of any pertinent registered interest before participating in proceedings. Any member who has or proposes to enter into an employment agreement involving the provision of services by him or her in his or her capacity as an Assembly member is required to provide the Presiding Officer with a copy of the agreement which shall be open to public inspection.

7.9.9 *Investigation of Conduct*

The investigation of complaints relating to the conduct of members is a matter for the Committee on Standards of Conduct. The Committee is empowered to investigate, report on and, if appropriate, recommend action in respect of any complaint referred to it by the Presiding Officer relating to a member's financial or other interests or the member's conduct.

7.9.10 *Exclusion*

In addition to the power of the Presiding Officer to order the withdrawal of a member for misconduct and for a vote to be taken to exclude a member (see 7.9.6), the Assembly may, on a motion proposed by a member of the Committee on Standards of Conduct, resolve to exclude a member from the Assembly for a period specified in the motion. Such a motion must arise from the consideration by the Committee of a complaint relating to a member's registerable interest.

7.9.11 *Disqualification and Resignation*

A person is disqualified from being an Assembly member if he or she:-

+ holds judicial office;

+ is a member of the civil service, armed forces, police force or a foreign legislature;

+ holds the office of Auditor General for Wales or the Welsh Administration Ombudsman;

+ holds an office designated by Order in Council;

+ are disqualified from being a member of a local authority under the Audit Commission Act 1998;

✦ is disqualified, otherwise than under the House of Commons Disqualification Act 1975, from being a member of the House of Commons;

✦ is the Lord Lieutenant, Lieutenant or High Sheriff of any area in Wales (but the disqualification only relates to that Assembly constituency or electoral region);

✦ is imprisoned or unlawfully at large;

✦ is bankrupt; or

✦ is a detained mental patient.

A person is not disqualified from being a member of the Assembly by being a peer or minister of religion. A member may resign his or her seat in the Assembly by giving notice in writing to the Presiding Officer of the Assembly.

7.9.12 *Public Disturbance*

The Presiding Officer may require members of the public who are observing the proceedings of the Assembly to withdraw if they act in a disruptive or disorderly manner or otherwise interfere with the Assembly's proper discharge of its business.

7.10   Powers and Privileges of Members

7.10.1 *Defamation and Contempt*

For the purposes of the law of defamation, any statement made in, for the purposes of or incidental to, proceedings of the Assembly (including any of its committees or sub committees), and the publication of a report of such proceedings by or under the authority of the Assembly, is absolutely privileged.

The Assembly is a legislature for the purposes of Schedule 1 to the Defamation Act 1996 and therefore qualified privilege extends to the fair and accurate reporting of its proceedings. The Assembly is also treated under that Act as if it were a Minister of the Crown, so that privilege extends to the reporting of an inquiry appointed by the Assembly as it does to the reporting of inquiries appointed by a Minister.

The strict liability rule in relation to publication of court proceedings does not apply to any publication made in, for the purposes of or purposes incidental to, Assembly proceedings (including committee proceedings) or to the extent that it consists of a fair and accurate report of such proceedings made in good faith.

7.10.2 *Witnesses and Documents*

The Assembly has the power to require witnesses to attend before it and to give evidence or produce any document which is in their possession or control. The power to require attendance and production of documents may be exercised by any of the Assembly's subject committees. Witnesses are not obliged to answer any question or produce a document which they would be entitled to refuse to answer or produce for the purpose of proceedings in a court in England and Wales but, subject to that qualification, a person who refuses to comply without reasonable excuse or who intentionally alters, supresses, conceals or destroys any document commits a criminal offence.

7.10.3 *Sanctions*

Unlike the UK Parliament, the Assembly has no inherent jurisdiction to deal with contemnors but persons causing a disturbance or refusing to comply with an order to give evidence or produce documents are subject to the criminal law.

7.11 Committees

7.11.1 *Establishment, Powers and Procedures*

In addition to the committees that it is required to establish under the Government of Wales Act, the Assembly may establish a committee on a motion tabled by an Assembly Secretary or at least three Assembly members. Such a motion must be accompanied by a cost-benefit analysis of the establishment of that committee. The motion must specify the committee's proposed terms of reference and the date on which it will cease to exist, which must be within 12 months of the committee's first meeting.

The members of a committee are elected by the Assembly, ordinarily for the term until the next election, on a motion of the Assembly Business Secretary following consultation with the other political parties. Each committee has a quorum of two members or one third of its total number of members, whichever is higher. A meeting will also be declared inquorate if the members present represent only one political group unless the committee is solely advisory.

Committees have the power to appoint expert advisers; to invite persons to attend their meetings and to submit evidence and produce documents to them; and to hold joint meetings with other committees or provide those committees with information or documents. Committees' procedures are determined by their chairs, following guidelines issued by the Presiding Officer. Committee proceedings may be in English or in Welsh, are ordinarily held in public, and simultaneous interpretation facilities are available for proceedings in Welsh. Committees also have a general power to appoint sub-committees to exist for a maximum of 12 months or until completion of the business referred to them.

The Assembly can delegate functions to committees and committees (other than the Audit Committee) can delegate their functions to sub-committees.

7.11.2 *Assembly Cabinet*

The Assembly Cabinet (referred to in the Act as "the executive committee") unlike other committees is appointed by the First Secretary, subject to the approval of the Assembly. Its members are the Assembly Secretaries (a maximum of nine) including the First Secretary. It may meet in private and determine its own procedure. Should the First Secretary resign, the Assembly Cabinet may elect one of its members to take over until a new Assembly First Secretary is elected by the Assembly. The Assembly Cabinet can delegate its functions to the First Secretary or an Assembly Secretary, as may one of its sub-committees.

7.11.3 *Business Committee*

This committee is chaired by the Deputy Presiding Officer and consists of the Assembly Business Secretary and the Chief Whips of the opposition parties. It is required to meet in private each week that the Assembly holds a plenary meeting. The Committee advises the

Assembly Business Secretary on the management of the Assembly's business, advises the Deputy Presiding Officer in relation to subordinate legislation procedure and makes recommendations to the Assembly as it thinks fit on the conduct of business. The Committee's advice should be taken into account by the Assembly Business Secretary when he tables business statements and by the Deputy Presiding Officer when she determines how subordinate legislation is to be dealt with by the Assembly. The Committee also makes recommendations on the procedures of the Assembly and is involved in determining the membership of the Assembly's other committees.

7.11.4 Subject Committees

Each Assembly Secretary's work is scrutinised by a subject committee of nine or ten members, of which the Secretary is one. Each committee is elected by the Assembly and reflects the party balance within the Assembly. The six subject committee Chairs are also elected by the Assembly to reflect party balance. All members may attend a subject committee's proceedings when they are held in public and, with advance permission from the Chair, make brief representations. An Assembly Secretary may also attend and, with the consent of the Chair, participate.

Subject committees can require persons to attend proceedings and to produce documents, non-compliance being the subject of a criminal offence.

Each committee contributes towards policy development in its subject area; reviews the expenditure connected with it; and reviews the performance of related public bodies. It may scrutinise proposed legislation and advise on the budget allocation. It may also hold inquiries and call witnesses.

7.11.5 Regional Committees

There are regional committees for the four "regional economic forums" of Wales, namely North Wales, Mid Wales, South West Wales and South East Wales. They are to meet in their regions at least twice a year and advise the Assembly on matters affecting their regions.

7.11.6 Other Committees

+ Legislation Committee

This committee scrutinises all subordinate legislation that comes before the Assembly to ensure that it is not defective and that all necessary requirements have been complied with by the Assembly. The committee is chaired by a member of an opposition party.

+ Audit Committee

This committee, which must also be chaired by a member of an opposition party, has responsibility for ensuring that Assembly resources are used properly and efficiently: see 7.14.4. The House of Commons' Public Accounts Committee may require this committee to take evidence on its behalf.

Like subject committees, the Audit Committee can require persons to give evidence and produce documents, non-compliance giving rise to a possible criminal offence.

+ Equal Opportunities and European Affairs Committees

These committees, which consist of members of each subject committee and are chaired by Assembly Secretaries, are to scrutinise the Assembly's arrangements in relation to equality of opportunity; and its relations with the institutions of the European Union and the impact of Community policies in Wales: see 7.14.

+ Committee on Standards of Conduct

This committee investigates complaints into Assembly members' behaviour and may recommend action by the Assembly. It also supervises the Register of Interests. The Committee has an independent adviser to assist it in its work.

7.12 Legislative Functions

The National Assembly has no power conferred upon it to initiate primary legislation.

7.12.1 Consultation on the Government's Legislative Programme

As soon as reasonably practicable after the beginning of each session of the UK Parliament, the Secretary of State for Wales is required to consult the Assembly upon the Government's legislative programme for the session as appears to him to be appropriate. This includes attending and participating in proceedings of the Assembly relating to the programme on at least one occasion each session. Further consultation is then required if a bill is introduced by the government at a later stage upon which no consultation has already taken place.

7.13   Subordinate Legislation

7.13.1   *Types of Procedure*

Standing Order 22 prescribes different procedures for seven categories of instrument:-

Part 1   General Subordinate Legislation:

i.e. "relevant Welsh subordinate legislation" (being instruments to be made, confirmed or approved by the Assembly) which are to be made by statutory instrument and do not involve UK Parliamentary Procedure.

Part 2   Subordinate   legislation   subject   to   Parliamentary
                           Procedure.

i.e. instruments with which the UK Parliament remains involved.

Part 3   Subordinate legislation otherwise subject to Special
                           Parliamentary Procedure.

i.e. instruments which but for the Government of Wales Act 1998 would be subject to such procedure before the UK Parliament.

Part 4   Local statutory instruments.

i.e. instruments made by the Assembly which are local in nature.

Part 5   Instruments not required to be made by statutory
                           instrument.

i.e. where neither the enabling Act nor the Statutory Instruments Act 1946 requires the instrument to be made as a statutory instrument.

Part 6   Confirmation and Approval Powers.

i.e. where the Assembly confirms or approves instruments made by others.

Part 7   Instruments proposed by Assembly members.

i.e. on a motion as a result of the ballot.

7.13.2   *General Subordinate Legislation: Normal Procedure*

Such instruments are subject to certain preliminary requirements and then go through initial consideration procedures involving subject committees before final approval procedures before the Assembly.

✦ Preliminary Requirements

- Preparation of draft by an Assembly Secretary in English and Welsh unless he or she considers it would be inappropriate or not reasonably practicable for the order to be in both languages.
- Notification of members including invitation to make representations as to possible referral to a subject committee.
- Conduct by the Assembly Secretary of regulatory appraisal (including appropriate consultation if the appraisal indicates that the costs will be significant) unless he or she considers an appraisal would be inappropriate or not reasonably practicable.
- Publication of regulatory appraisal (including responses to any consultation) if the Assembly Secretary decides to proceed.

✦ Initial Consideration

- Submission of draft Order, Explanatory Memorandum and any regulatory appraisal by the Assembly Secretary to the Business Committee with or without a recommendation that the Order should be considered by one or more subject committees.
- The Deputy Presiding Officer determines whether to refer a draft Order to subject committees (the Assembly can reverse a decision) and allows between two and eight weeks for the committee(s) to report.
- Where reference is made, the subject committee(s) considers the draft, taking evidence, if desired, including evidence from other committees and members and submits a report.
- The Assembly Secretary lays the draft order (possibly in amended form) together with the Explanatory Memorandum and regulatory appraisal (but not before receipt of any requisite committee report or the expiry of the allotted time for this) before the Assembly . He or she also submits the draft order to the Legislation Committee.
- In the case of an order giving rise to the payment of sums by the Assembly, a recommendation is required from the Assembly Cabinet that the order be made.

✦ Final Approval

- The Legislation Committee considers the propriety of the draft order and submits a report as soon as possible.
- Amendments (if any) must be tabled by at least three members at least two working days in advance and accompanied by a statement as to their purpose and cost implications.
- The Assembly considers the principle of the draft Order on a motion proposed by the Assembly Secretary who, where a debate ensues, has a right of reply before any vote is then taken.
- Following agreement to the principle of the Order, amendments are taken in the order in which they relate to the text subject to selection and any grouping order determinations by the Presiding Officer. Ordinarily, one member will be allowed to propose an amendment, one member to speak against it and the Assembly Secretary will be heard before the amendment is voted upon.
- The Assembly Secretary proposes the approval of the draft Order which is immediately voted upon.
- If the Order has been amended, the Assembly Secretary prepares a revised draft and a further regulatory appraisal if he or she considers that such an appraisal is required. The revised draft is then re-considered by the Assembly but upon the basis that approval in principle has been given and amendments, other than to a part of the text which has been revised, are out of order.
- The draft Order is made by being signed by the Presiding Officer or, in his absence, by the Deputy, the First Secretary or a member of the Assembly Cabinet.

7.13.3 *General Subordinate Legislation : Urgent Procedure*

The Assembly Cabinet is empowered to determine in cases of urgency that all or part of the ordinary procedures described in 7.13.2 (other than the preparation of a draft together with an Explanatory Memorandum and regulatory appraisal (but without consultation) shall not apply. In such cases, the Legislation Committee must still report to the Assembly on the Order and, where the Order has not been laid before and approved by resolution of the Assembly, any member may, within 40 working days, table a motion that the Order should be revoked.

7.13.4 *Instruments subject to Parliamentary Procedure*

The procedure depends upon whether the instrument can only be made after the UK Parliament or the House of Commons has approved it in draft or whether it is to be made together with the UK Minister.

✦ Prior Parliamentary Approval

The ordinary procedures for general subordinate legislation described above apply in advance of the separate parliamentary procedures but the draft Order need not be prepared initially in Welsh and, except in those cases where the instrument can be made forthwith by the Assembly, the Order cannot be made (i.e. signed by the Presiding Officer or others) until the Assembly has been notified that the parliamentary approval process has been completed.

✦ Instruments made together with a UK Minister

In these cases, the ordinary procedures for general subordinate legislation do not apply. After a draft of the Order together with a statement explaining its intended effect and financial implications has been laid by the relevant Assembly Secretary, a motion to approve the draft (which again need not be prepared also in Welsh at this stage) proposed by the Assembly Secretary is considered. No amendments can be moved. If the motion is approved, the Assembly Secretary notifies the UK Minister concerned and, except in those cases where the instrument can be made forthwith by the Assembly, the final step of making the Order is delayed until the Assembly has been notified that the parliamentary approval process has been completed. The Presiding Officer (or other authorised officer) then makes the Order by signing it.

7.13.5 *Instruments otherwise subject to Special Parliamentary Procedure*

A procedure equivalent to special parliamentary procedure is followed.

The relevant Assembly Secretary is required to lay a draft of the instrument before the Assembly and give notice of it by advertisement, inviting those affected to present petitions within 21 working days. The Presiding Officer determines whether petitions should be considered against the criteria of whether they disclose a substantial ground of objection. If he considers that they do not, he then affords an opportunity for representations. Petitioners whose property or interests are affected and amenity societies representing interests who are affected are treated as satisfying the "substantial ground" test. Where petitions are allowed, counter-petitions may then be invited following a further advertisement. Those petitions and counter-petitions that are allowed to be heard are then referred to a committee selected for the purpose who hear the parties, in person, by counsel or by agent, and report to the Assembly. If the committee reports against the instrument, no further proceedings on it take place. If the committee reports in favour of the instrument, it is then made or confirmed. If the committee proposes amendments, the instrument is made with those amendments. However, where amendments have been proposed, it is also open to the Assembly Secretary to withdraw the instrument or to move a motion that it be made or confirmed without the amendments.

7.13.6 *Local Statutory Instruments*

The Assembly Secretary proposing to make the instrument prepares a draft in both English and Welsh (unless considered unnecessary or not reasonably practicable) and gives at least 10 working days notice of it. The instrument can then be made unless, within five working days, at least 10 members table a motion against it and, thereafter, the Assembly resolves to apply the normal general subordinate legislation procedures to it. Where such a motion is passed, the initial consideration and final approval stages applicable to general subordinate legislation apply in the ordinary way.

7.13.7 *Non-statutory Instruments*

Such instruments follow the same procedure as for local statutory instruments unless the Assembly Secretary considers it appropriate to -

(i) lay a draft before a subject committee and allow it to report upon the draft within 2-8 weeks;

(ii) lay it before the Legislation Committee following any such subject committee consideration; or

(iii) lay it before the Assembly for debate in plenary session following consideration by a subject committee or the Legislation Committee.

7.13.8 *Confirmation and Approval Powers*

The relevant Assembly Secretary or authorised officer may confirm or approve the instrument in writing but must give at least 10 days notice. If, within five working days, at least 10 members table a motion against it, the Assembly Secretary is required to table a motion (which cannot be amended) proposing that the Assembly confirm or approve it.

Special provision is made for Forestry Commissioners' instruments enabling members to table a motion to annul these instruments.

7.13.9 *Instruments Proposed by Members*

A ballot is held by the Presiding Officer from time to time which members (other than Assembly Secretaries) can enter to win the right to table a motion instructing an Assembly Secretary to bring forward draft subordinate legislation. The member must name the subject of the motion in the ballot. The motion itself must identify the relevant legal powers, specify the object to be achieved and be accompanied by a cost-benefit and general assessment which must be tabled not less than two days before the motion is considered. If the motion is successful, the Assembly Secretary must bring forward a draft instrument in accordance with the motion as soon as possible.

7.14 European Legislation

7.14.1 *Documentation etc.*

See 2.3 and 4.14.1. It is likely that similar arrangements respecting the deposit of draft documentation in the Assembly will be adopted as apply to the House of Commons.

7.14.2 *The Committee on European Affairs*

This committee keeps under review all aspects of the European Union including liaison arrangements with UKREP and UK departments. It is required to avoid duplicating the work of subject committees and to report to the Assembly from time to time.

The committee is chaired by an Assembly Secretary elected by the Assembly, the other members of the committee being elected to reflect the political groups and to give representation on the committee to subject committees. MEPs for Wales and Welsh representatives on the Council of the Regions may attend and, with permission, speak at public meetings of the committee. Assembly members may also, with permission from the chair, make representations in advance and may submit observations to be tabled by the chair.

7.15   Finance and Taxation

7.15.1   *Grants of Expenditure*

As is the case with Scotland (see paragraph 6.15.1 above), the Barnett formula will continue to be used to assess the block grant paid by the UK Parliament to the Secretary of State. This arrangement is not contained in the devolution legislation and it will be open to future Governments of the United Kingdom to change the way in which Welsh spending is assessed and funded.

The block grant determined under the Barnett formula will be paid to the National Assembly for Wales by the Secretary of State for Wales following the deduction of an appropriate sum for the running of the Secretary of State's office and the exercise of his remaining functions. The Assembly will be able to set and manage its own spending priorities, although its ability to set priorities will inevitably be constrained by existing spending commitments and needs. In relation to the making of general subordinate legislation, the Assembly requires a recommendation from the Assembly Cabinet before making the instrument if it gives rise to the payment of any sums by the Assembly.

7.15.2   *Taxation*

The National Assembly for Wales has no tax raising powers.

7.15.3   *The Annual Programme*

Standing Orders require the Assembly Secretary for Finance to invite the subject committees of the Assembly to submit their views on priorities for the Assembly's expenditure priorities for the following three financial years no later than 30th September each year. She will then be obliged to table (not later than 10th December) a preliminary draft budget for the following three financial years and a motion that this draft budget should be adopted. The motion may not be amended by the Assembly. Following adoption of the budget, the subject committees of the Assembly will be consulted on the allocation of resources from the overall budget within their areas of responsibility and (not later than 15th February) the Secretary for Finance is required to lay a detailed budget before the Assembly setting out the proposed allocation of resources for the following year and the provisional financial allocations for the two following years. At this stage, the Secretary for Finance must also table a motion that the detailed budget should be ratified. Again, it will not be possible for the Assembly to amend this motion.

Except in cases of urgency, the transfer of resources between the main expenditure groups of the Assembly in the course of a financial year may only be made on a motion proposed by the Assembly Secretary for Finance.

7.15.4 *Scrutiny of Public Accounts*

An Auditor General for Wales has been appointed under the Government of Wales Act 1998. He is responsible for auditing the accounts of the Assembly and those of many of the bodies it sponsors. The Auditor General is able to call upon the resources of the National Audit Office to assist him.

There is an Audit Committee of the National Assembly for Wales chaired by a member of an opposition group. The Committee's role is to examine the reports on the accounts of the Assembly prepared by the Auditor General for Wales and to consider the Auditor General's reports on the efficiency and effectiveness with which the Assembly has used its resources. The House of Commons Committee of Public Accounts will continue to be able to investigate public expenditure in Wales and the Government of Wales Act 1998 provides that the Audit Committee of the Assembly may, if requested so to do by the Committee of Public Accounts, take evidence on behalf of the Committee of Public Accounts from the Assembly's principal accounting officer and report to the Committee.

The head of the Assembly's permanent staff will be designated by the Treasury as the Assembly's principal accounting officer and will be responsible for ensuring the propriety and regularity of the Assembly's finances. This replicates the position in Whitehall Departments, where the Permanent Secretary is generally the principal accounting officer, is responsible to the Treasury for the financial management of the Department and may be required to give evidence to the Committee of Public Accounts.

Chapter 8

The Northern Ireland Assembly

8.1 Form and Functions

8.1.1 Overview

The Northern Ireland Assembly will only become fully operational once the Secretary of State for Northern Ireland concludes that sufficient progress has been made in implementing the Belfast ("Good Friday") Agreement of 10th April 1998. The Assembly is the product of that agreement and the Northern Ireland Act 1998:

✦ It will be an elected Assembly (108 members) which will elect the First Minister and the deputy First Minister from amongst its members and from whose members the remaining Northern Ireland Ministers and Junior Ministers are chosen.

✦ It will have the power to exclude Northern Ireland Ministers or members of a political party from office for not respecting their pledge of office.

✦ It will have the power, within its designated legislative competence, to make laws known as Acts of the Northern Ireland Assembly.

✦ It will provide a degree of supervision over subordinate legislation in Northern Ireland.

✦ It will operate as a national debating forum and investigative body, both through its plenary sessions and by its committee system, in relation to matters of general public interest in Northern Ireland. More specifically, it will hold the Northern Ireland Executive to account, scrutinise legislation and, pursuant to particular enactments, review the activities of certain bodies.

8.1.2 Transitional Arrangements

Elections for an Assembly were held in Northern Ireland on 25th June 1998 under the Northern Ireland (Elections) Act 1998, and those elected form the "new Northern Ireland Assembly" which will become the Northern Ireland Assembly once an Order in Council is made implementing Parts I and III of the Northern Ireland Act 1998. However, that Order will not be laid until the Secretary of State considers sufficient progress has been made in implementing the Belfast Agreement. Until then Northern Ireland remains subject to direct rule with legislation for it being made by the UK Government by Order in Council.

The new Northern Ireland Assembly has elected a First Minister (designate) and deputy First Minister (designate) and has established a Shadow Assembly Committee in anticipation of the appointment of the Northern Ireland Executive, a number of other committees and a Shadow Assembly Commission. Its initial Presiding Officer was appointed by the Secretary of State

8.1.3 *Devolved and Legislative Competence*

The Northern Ireland Assembly and the Northern Ireland Executive will have functions in relation to "transferred matters", that is any matter which is not classified as an "excepted matter" or a "reserved matter". Even within the scope of a transferred matter, a Minister or Northern Ireland Department will not be able to do anything which -

(a) is incompatible with a Convention right;

(b) is incompatible with Community law;

(c) discriminates against a person or class of person on the ground of religious belief or political opinion;

(d) aids or incites another person to discriminate against a person or class of person on that ground; or

(e) in the case of legislation, modifies an "entrenched enactment".

Likewise, the Assembly will have no power to make laws outside its "legislative competence". This means that Acts must not -

(a) have extra-territorial application;

(b) deal with an "excepted matter" other than in an ancillary way;

(c) be incompatible with any of the Convention rights;

(d) be incompatible with Community law;

(e) discriminate against any person or class of person on the ground of religious belief or political opinion;

(f) modify an "entrenched enactment".

Excepted Matters

These are set out in detail in Schedule 2 to the Northern Ireland Act 1998 and comprise items in relation to:-

1. Crown matters.

2. Parliament.

3. International relations.

4. Defence.

5. Weapons of mass destruction.

6. Titles.

7. Treason.

8. Nationality and immigration.

9. National taxes and duty and stamp duty.

10. National Insurance.

11. Appointment of judges.

12. Elections.

13. Registration and political parties.

14. Coinage and bank notes.

15. National Savings Bank.

16. Protection of Trading Interests Act 1980.

17. National security.

18. Nuclear energy.

19. Sea fishing outside Northern Ireland Zone.

20. Outer space.

21. Northern Ireland Constitution.

22. Most of the Northern Ireland Act 1998 (see also reserved matter 42).

Reserved Matters

These are set out in detail in Schedule 3 to the Northern Ireland Act 1998 and comprise matters in the following areas:-

1. Conferral of functions on Ministers.

2. Crown property.

3. Navigation and shipping except harbours and inland waters.

4. Civil aviation except aerodromes.

5. Foreshore and sea bed.

6. Domicile.

7. Post Office and postal services.

8. Assembly powers and privileges.

9. Criminal law.

10. Public order.

11. RUC, police and traffic wardens.

12. Firearms and explosives.

13. Civil defence.

14. Emergency Powers Act (N.I.) 1926.

15. Courts.

16. Civil Service Commissioners (N.I.).

17. Social Security and Child Support Commissioners (N.I.).

18. Social Security and Industrial Injuries Advisory Councils.

19. Vaccine Damage Payment Scheme.

20. Import, export and trade.

21. The minimum wage.

22. Occupational and personal pension schemes and Pensions Ombudsman.

23. Financial services and markets.

24. Building societies and friendly societies.

25. Money laundering.

26. Competition.

27. Intellectual property.

28. Measurements.

29. Telecommunications.

30. National Lottery.

31. Xenotransplantation.

32. Surrogacy.

33. Human fertilisation and embryology.

34. Human genetics.

35. Research Councils.

36. Areas for assistance under Part III of the Industrial Development Act 1982.

37. Consumer safety.

38. EC technical standards (except food, feeding stuff, fertilisers and pesticides).

39. Emission limits and the environmental protection technology scheme.

40. Data protection.

41. Oaths and declarations.

42. Parts of the Northern Ireland Act 1998 (see also excepted matter 22).

Entrenched Enactments

The enactments which cannot be modified are -

(a) the European Communities Act 1972 (except s.3(3) or (4) or 11(1);

(b) the Human Rights Act 1998; and

(c) the following sections of the Northern Ireland Act 1998:-

s.43(1)-(6) and (8) (members' interests)

s.67 information to Treasury

s.84-86 (provisions by Order in Council)

s.95(3) and (4) (savings for existing laws)

s.98 (interpretation).

8.1.4 Devolution Issues

See generally 2.7. Any question concerning legislative competence, whether the exercise of a function by a Minister or Northern Ireland Department would be outside their general competence, any question whether a Minister or Northern Ireland Department has failed to comply with any Convention right, any obligation under Community law or an order under s.27 of the Northern Ireland Act 1998 (quotas for international obligations) and any question about excepted or reserved matters is categorised as a "devolution issue".

8.2 Electoral Arrangements

8.2.1 Composition and electoral system

The Assembly comprises 108 members, six members representing each of the 18 UK parliamentary constituencies in Northern Ireland. Election is by means of the Single Transferable Vote method of proportional representation whereby voters express an order of preference and votes are transferred to the voter's next choice when the prior choice is not needed to give a candidate the necessary quota of votes or because the candidate has been eliminated due to a deficiency of votes.

8.2.2 *Franchise*

The electoral franchise is the same as for local government elections in Northern Ireland. All British, other Commonwealth, Irish and other EU citizens (including peers), where resident in Northern Ireland, are entitled to be registered and may vote in one constituency if they are aged 18 or over except convicted prisoners in detention or unlawfully at large, detained mental patients and those convicted of corrupt or illegal practices at elections.

8.2.3 **Candidacy and Election Rules**

Those eligible for election will include all British, other Commonwealth, Irish, and EU citizens resident in the UK aged 21 or over, including peers. The ban on membership of foreign (i.e. non-commonwealth) legislatures which applies under the House of Commons Disqualification Act 1975 has been specifically removed for members of Seanad Eireann, the Senate of the Irish Republic. The rules on election campaigns are set out in the New Northern Ireland Assembly (Elections) Order 1998.

8.2.4 *Vacancies*

A system of substitutes has been provided for vacancies arising after the initial election but, thereafter or where a seat cannot be filled by this means, a by-election will be held.

8.3 The Role of Ministers etc.

8.3.1 *First Minister and Deputy First Minister*

The First Minister and deputy First Minister are elected by a cross-community vote of the Assembly. They must stand for election jointly and act jointly in exercising their functions, which include nominating Ministers to the North-South and British-Irish Councils, determining Ministerial portfolios and exercising certain prerogative powers of the Crown in Northern Ireland.

8.3.2 *Ministers and Votes of Confidence*

10 Ministers, who together with the First and deputy First Minister form the Executive Committee, are nominated from among the Assembly

members in proportion to the party strength in the Assembly. This is done using the same system of proportional representation as is used for elections to the European Parliament and in calculating the additional members in Scotland and in Wales.

The Ministerial portfolios are currently:
- Agriculture & Rural Development;
- Environment; Regional Development;
- Social Development; Education;
- Higher & Further Education, Training & Employment;
- Enterprise, Trade & Investment;
- Culture, Arts & Leisure;
- Health, Social Services & Public Safety; and
- Finance & Personnel.

The number of Ministers and their portfolios is determined by the First and deputy First Ministers, subject to approval by a cross-community vote in the Assembly.

Each Minister may only hold office while subscribing to the Pledge of Office. Should the Assembly resolve, by a cross-community vote, that it has no confidence in a Minister, either because the Minister is not committed to non-violence and exclusively peaceful and democratic means, or because he or she has failed to observe any of the other terms of the pledge of office, the Minister may be excluded from holding office for a 12 month period. The Assembly may similarly resolve that it has no confidence in a particular party. This prevents members of that party from holding office for the same period.

The First and deputy First Ministers may also, with the approval of the Assembly, make arrangements for the appointment of junior Ministers.

8.3.3   *The Crown*

Executive power in Northern Ireland will continue to be vested in the Sovereign but, as respects transferred matters, will be exercisable by Northern Ireland Ministers and Departments.

The Sovereign (and thus the UK Government) retains a number of powers under the Northern Ireland Act to legislate for the Assembly by

Order in Council. Such Orders may be used to appoint the date on which powers will be devolved to the Assembly and to amend the list of reserved and excepted matters, following a request from the Assembly. The Sovereign also has the role of giving Royal Assent to Acts of the Assembly. The Secretary of State's consent is required for the Assembly to pass a bill that deals with excepted or reserved matters and it is the Secretary of State who submits bills to the Sovereign for Royal Assent.

8.3.4 *Power in the Assembly*

Under the proportional system, a political party will have a Minister in the Assembly's Executive Committee if that party has slightly over 1/11th of the seats in the Assembly (10 members). The four parties that are likely to be represented on the Executive Committee if one should be formed have between them 90 of the 108 seats in the Assembly. The Assembly does not rely on a single party or a coalition having a majority of the seats. If, however, the Assembly cannot elect a First Minister and a Deputy First Minister within six weeks of its election or of the posts becoming vacant, a new election to the Assembly will be held. The Assembly may also resolve that an extraordinary election should be held. Such a resolution requires two thirds of the total membership of the Assembly to vote in favour.

8.3.5 *North/South Ministerial Council and Implementation Bodies*

The North/South Ministerial Council is to deal with matters of mutual interest within the competence of both the Assembly and the Irish Government. The First Minister and deputy First Minister may nominate Ministers and junior Ministers to serve on the Council.

Decisions and policies of the Council have to be agreed by both sides and are to be implemented on an all-Ireland and cross-border basis. The Council is due to be located in Armagh and staffed by a standing joint secretariat consisting of members of both the Northern Ireland Civil Service and the Irish Civil Service.

The implementation of the policies of the Council is to be carried out by a number of Implementation Bodies. The current Implementation

Bodies are:

- Waterways Ireland;
- the Food Safety Promotion Board;
- the Trade and Business Development Body;
- the Special EU Programmes Body;
- the North/South Language Body, (An Foras Teanga or Tha Boord o Leid);
- the Foyle, Carlingford and Irish Lights Commission.

If a Minister of the Assembly enters into an agreement to establish a new implementation body this agreement must be approved by the Assembly.

8.3.6 *The British-Irish Council*

The Assembly's representation on the Council is to be nominated by the First Minister and Deputy First Minister. There is required to be cross-community participation on the Council. Ministers who participate must report back to the Executive Committee and the Assembly. See generally 2.6.

8.3.7 *The British-Irish Intergovernmental Conference*

The Conference is to promote bi-lateral co-operation in matters of mutual interest between the United Kingdom and Irish Governments. It is required under the Belfast Agreement to meet frequently to discuss non-devolved Northern Ireland matters, including rights, justice, prisons and policing. The Conference is to be chaired by the Irish Minister of Foreign Affairs and the Secretary of State for Northern Ireland. When excepted and reserved matters relating to Northern Ireland are to be discussed, the First Minister and Deputy First Minister must ensure cross-community attendance by Ministers of the Assembly.

8.3.8 *The Civic Forum*

The Forum is to advise the First Minister and Deputy First Minister on social, economic and cultural matters. The Forum comprises 60 members and a chairman, nominated under the Nolan principles. Seven nominees represent business interests; three represent agriculture and fisheries; seven represent unions; 18 represent voluntary bodies and community bodies; five represent churches, four represent cultural organisations; four represents arts and sporting bodies; two represent victims; two represent community relations groups; two represent educational interests; and six are directly nominated by the First Minister and Deputy First Minister. The chairman is also appointed by the First Minister and Deputy First Minister. Members of the Forum are to serve for three years on a staggered basis.

8.3.9 *Northern Ireland Human Rights Commission*

The Commission is to be appointed by the Secretary of State to be representative of the community in Northern Ireland. It is to review the adequacy and effectiveness in Northern Ireland of law and practice in relation to the protection of Human Rights. The Commission is also to advise the Secretary of State and the Executive Committee of legislative and other measures that may be taken to protect Human Rights and the Assembly as to whether bills before it are compatible with Human Rights. It may also give assistance to proceedings relating to Human Rights brought by individuals and it may bring proceedings itself.

8.3.10 *The Equality Commission for Northern Ireland*

The Commission is to comprise 14 to 20 Commissioners appointed by the Secretary of State. It will take over functions in relation to fair employment, equal opportunities, racial equality and disability rights. Furthermore, public authorities carrying out functions relating to Northern Ireland will be under a duty to have regard to the need to promote equality of opportunity. This incorporates equality of opportunity:

(a) between persons of different religious belief, political opinion, racial group, age, marital status and sexual orientation;

(b) between men and women generally;

(c) between persons with a disability and persons without; and

(d) between persons with dependants and persons without.

It will also be unlawful for public authorities to discriminate on grounds of religious belief or political opinions.

8.4   Officials

8.4.1   The Speaker and Assembly Commission

As its first item of business after election, the Assembly is to elect a Presiding Officer ("the Speaker") and Deputies. They must be elected with cross-community support and have a number of functions, including ruling on conduct within the Assembly and chairing the Assembly's debates. The Speaker is also chairman of the Northern Ireland Assembly Commission, which employs the Assembly's staff, holds its property and represents it in legal proceedings.

8.4.2   The Comptroller and Auditor General

See generally 8.14.4. The Comptroller and Auditor General for Northern Ireland is appointed by the Sovereign on the nomination of the Assembly and may only be removed by the Sovereign on a recommendation of the Assembly approved by two-thirds of its total membership.

8.5   Opening and Dissolution

8.5.1   Duration

A full session of the Assembly is to last for four years from the date of a general election. After this the Assembly is dissolved and a general election is held. The first full session of the Assembly began on 1st July 1998 which was the date of the first meeting of the New Northern Ireland Assembly after the election of 25 June 1998. The next election is on 1st May 2003.

8.5.2   Opening

The Assembly is to meet within a period of eight days beginning with the day of the poll at which it is elected.

At the first meeting of an Assembly after a dissolution, the Clerk reads a notice convening the meeting and the outgoing Speaker, if re-elected to the Assembly, takes the Chair. Alternatively the eldest member takes the role of acting Speaker. Members then take their seats by signing the Assembly's Roll of Membership. When all members have had the opportunity to take their seats, the Assembly proceeds to elect a Speaker.

8.5.3 **Dissolution**

The Assembly is dissolved prior to an election by an order of the Secretary of State. The same order sets the date of the poll.

The Assembly may pass a resolution to dissolve itself if two-thirds of its members vote to do so. The Secretary of State then proposes a date for an election. If the period for electing a First Minister and deputy First Minister ends without these offices being filled, the Secretary of State must also propose a date for a fresh election. In either of these cases, the Sovereign by Order in Council will provide for the Assembly to be dissolved on a date specified in the Order.

8.6   Sittings

8.6.1   **Location**

The Assembly is to sit in the Parliament Buildings, Stormont, Belfast.

8.6.2   **Annual Programme**

This will be a matter for the Northern Ireland Executive to determine once it is established.

8.6.3   **Sitting Times**

The Assembly is to sit from 10.30am to 6.00pm on Monday and Tuesday. The following indicative timetable has been agreed:

Monday:	
Committee Business	11.00am - 12.30pm
Questions	2.30pm - 4.00pm
Government Business	4.00pm - 6.00pm
Tuesday:	
Government Business	10.30am - 12.30pm
Private Members Business	2.00pm - 3.00pm
Adjournment Debate	3.00pm - 6.00pm

If the business cannot be completed in that time, the sitting may be extended into Tuesday evening, Wednesday or both. Additional sittings may be arranged by the Business Committee according to the exigencies of the Assembly.

8.6.4 **Adjournments**

An adjournment of the Assembly is to the next sitting day unless the Assembly, on a motion made by a member of the Executive Committee after notice, has ordered an adjournment to some other definite date.

Whenever notice is given to the Speaker by the First Minister and Deputy First Minister or by not less than 30 members that the Assembly should meet at an earlier date than that to which it stands adjourned for the purpose of discussing a specific matter or matters of urgent public inportance, the Speaker then summons the Assembly to meet.

8.7 Business

8.7.1 **Arrangement of Business**

The Business Committee, chaired by the Speaker, arranges the Assembly's business. A Notice Paper is prepared by the Clerk. Motions relating to the business of the Assembly are taken at the commencement of public business after notice and are decided without amendment or debate.

8.7.2 **Daily Programme**

✦ Prayers

On taking the chair each day and before the commencement of business the Speaker announces a period of two minutes silent prayer or contemplation.

✦ Executive committee business

✦ Statutory committee business

✦ Statements

A member of the Executive Committee makes statements to the Assembly on matters for which the Executive Committee is responsible. Notice of such statements must be given to the Speaker not less than two and a half hours before they are due to be made. A period of questions on the statement is limited to one hour. Statements must ordinarily be made outside the time bands specified for questions and adjournment debates. However where a statement is of such urgency or impact that it impinges upon any of these times the Speaker must make provision to schedule appropriate additional time in the same week for questions and/or an adjournment debate unless this requirement is dispensed with by leave of the Assembly.

✦ Private Members' Business

Unless the Assembly otherwise directs Private Members' business is arranged on the order paper in such order as the Speaker thinks fit. In determining the order of Private Member's business the Business Committee must have regard to:

- the wishes expressed by the members in charge of the various items;
- the relative public importance in its opinion of the various items;
- the desirability of giving precedence to those bills which are furthest advanced in their passage through the Assembly.

✦ Private Business

Private Bills are to be subject to the same stages as those laid down for Public Bills. All private business which is set down for any sitting day and which is not disposed of in the time allotted for it is postponed until such time as the Business Committee determines. Where the time allocated for private business is insufficient for the transaction of all private business tabled the private business to be transacted must be chosen by ballot and the resulting unopposed private business is to have precedence over the resulting opposed private business.

✦ Adjournment debates

These are to take place on Tuesdays between 3.00pm and 6.00pm. Any member who wishes to raise a matter must give at least eight days' notice to the Speaker.

✦ Public Petitions

A member who presents a public petition to the Assembly may only state who the petition comes from, the number of signatories and the material allegations contained in it. The member may also read the "prayer" of the petition. Every petition presented must be notified to the clerk of the Business Committee, which decides whether and when it is to be taken in the Assembly.

8.7.3 Question Time

Questions may be asked of a member of the Executive Committee and a member representing the Assembly Commission in relation to any matter for which the Commission carries responsibility. Questions are taken between 2.30pm and 4.30pm on Mondays. If this allocation of time is insufficient the Speaker may allocate appropriate additional time following the completion of other scheduled business. The Speaker must consult the Business Committee on the need to provide additional time for questions. No questions are to be taken after 4.00pm except questions which have not been answered because of the absence of the Executive Committee member or Commission representative to whom they are addressed.

Questions which have not appeared on the Order Paper but which in the opinion of the Speaker are of an urgent nature and relate to matters of public importance may, if the Speaker is satisfied that adequate notice has been given to the members of the Executive Committee concerned (normally by 10.30am on a Monday), be asked immediately prior to the Adjournment debate on Tuesdays.

8.7.4 Motions

Any member may, except where Standing Orders provide otherwise, give notice of a motion or move a motion about any matter. No motion or amendment (other than the nomination of a candidate for the election of a Speaker, Deputy Speaker or First Minister and deputy First Minister) needs to be seconded before the question is put. Amendments to motions must be given in writing to the Speaker at least one hour before the commencement of business on the day in which the motion is to be taken. A member may not speak more than once in the same motion, but a right of reply shall be allowed to a member who has moved a motion or an amendment.

After the question of a motion has been proposed, any member who has not already spoken to it, or to any amendment to it which has been proposed, may move that the question be decided and the Speaker shall put this forthwith (unless it appears to the Speaker that any of the parties present has not had a reasonable opportunity to contribute to the debate or the motion is an abuse of standing orders).

Motions relating to the business of the Assembly are to be taken at the commencement of public business after notice and decided without amendment or debate.

8.7.5 *Rules of Debate*

A member must not address the Assembly unless called on to speak by the Speaker. A member may not speak more than once to the same motion, but a member who has moved a motion or an amendment has a right of reply. Any member may seek to intervene while another member is speaking but may not persist in so doing if the member refuses to give way. The Business Committee is to consult with the Speaker in order to establish the total time to be allocated to each debate and the general arrangements for the debate. The Speaker determines the order of speaking and the number of speakers in any debate having due regard to the balance of opinion of the matter, the party strengths in the Assembly and the number of members who have indicated a desire to speak. The Speaker must announce to the Assembly the established speaking times for any debate as a preliminary to the debate. The Speaker, after having called the attention of the Assembly to the conduct of a member who persists in irrelevance or tedious repetition, may direct the member to discontinue his speech.

8.7.6 *Voting and Decisions*

Decisions are taken by the Assembly by a simple majority of those voting, except:

+ a vote, resolution or Act which appropriates a sum out of the Consolidated Fund of Northern Ireland or increases a sum to be appropriated, or imposes or increases a tax, which shall not be passed without cross-community support;

+ where there is a motion to suspend standing orders;

+ where a provision of the Northern Ireland Act 1998 provides otherwise.

A decision which requires "cross community support" must achieve an overall majority plus a majority of both the Nationalists and Unionists voting or a 60 per cent majority plus the support of 40 per cent of both the Nationalists and the Unionists.

If the votes in a division are equal the amendment or motion is not carried.

A vote must not be taken on any matter if a quorum is not present (ten members including the Speaker). The Speaker or a Deputy Speaker when in the Chair is not entitled to a vote on any matter. The Speaker judges whether the motion is carried, or not, by collecting voices or by a show of hands as he considers appropriate. If the opinion of the Speaker is challenged the Division bells are sounded and after three minutes the Speaker puts the question again and, if it is challenged, may either:

- call for the nomination of tellers and divide the Assembly. When tellers have been nominated the Speaker directs the Assembly to divide, 'ayes' to the right and 'noes' to the left. The Division bells are rung and four minutes after putting the question again the Speaker directs that the doors to the division lobbies be locked. The tellers then bring the division lists to the Clerk who will announce the result; or
- if in the Speaker's opinion the division is unnecessarily claimed, take the vote of the Assembly by calling upon the members who support and who challenge the Speaker's decision successively to rise in their places. The Speaker then either declares the determination of the Assembly or divides the Assembly as described above.

Where a division is held on closure of a debate on an issue the resolution of which requires cross-community support, the question is not carried unless at least 30 members have voted in support of it.

8.8   Public Access and Information

8.8.1   *Access to Sittings*

44 seats are available in the public gallery which are allocated on a first come first served basis.

8.8.2   *Access to Committees*

Seats for the public are available on a first come first served basis.

8.8.3   *Tours*

These are available through a sponsoring member (up to a limit of 40 guests per member).

8.8.4 Information

The Assembly has an information office for general enquiries:

Telephone:	01232 521137
Fax:	01232 521961
Email:	info.office@ni-assembly.gov.uk

Information can also be obtained from the Assembly's website (http://www.ni-assembly.gov.uk). This contains details of Assembly publications, committees, the Commission, political representation and general background.

8.8.5 Documentation

A verbatim report of the proceedings of the Assembly is contained in the Official Report (Hansard). Information on Assembly business is contained in an Order Paper for each sitting and a list of forthcoming business. Committee work is listed in a Business Diary. A record of the previous day's proceedings is contained in the Minutes of Proceedings.

8.8.6 Broadcasting

Proceedings of the plenary sessions are recorded and made available to broadcasters.

8.9 Conduct and Ethics

8.9.1 Oaths of Allegiance

Members are not required to swear an oath of allegiance but become members on signing the roll. Ministers are required to make a pledge of office which commits them to democratic and non-violent government.

8.9.2 Language

Members may speak in English, Irish or Ulster Scots.

8.9.3 Forms of Address

The Presiding Officer may be called "Mr (or Madam) Speaker" and the Deputy Presiding Officer referred to as "Mr (or Madam) Deputy Speaker". There are no other formal modes of address and members may refer to one another by name.

8.9.4   Dress Code

The Assembly has no formal dress code.

8.9.5   Calling of Speakers

A member is not permitted to address the Assembly unless called on to speak by the Speaker. The Speaker determines the order and number of speakers having due regard to the balance of opinion, the party strengths and the number of members who have indicated the desire to speak. The Business Committee in consultation with the Speaker establishes the time to be allocated for each debate and the general arrangements for ensuring that the requirement to have regard to the balance of opinion and party strengths is adhered to. The Speaker announces the speaking times at the beginning of each debate.

8.9.6   Order in the Chamber

The Speaker is responsible for maintaining order in the Assembly and when the Speaker rises to speak members must cease speaking and resume their place. The Speaker may require a member to withdraw for the remainder of the day's sitting where the member wilfully assaults or obstructs or acts in a disorderly manner, obstructs the business of the Assembly, is guilty of disorderly conduct, uses unparliamentary language, refuses to conform to the Standing Orders, disregards the authority of the Speaker or assaults, obstructs or resists any constable or officer of the Assembly acting on the Speaker's authority . If the Speaker "names" a member the question is immediately put that the member be suspended from the service of the House for a period of up to five sitting days. The Speaker is required to take whatever steps are necessary to prevent conduct which would constitute a criminal offence or a contempt of court and where there is grave disorder may adjourn the Assembly or suspend the sitting for an hour.

8.9.7 **Sub judice**

Subject to the discretion of the Chair, matters should not be referred to in any debate or other proceedings:

+ Where they are awaiting or under adjudication in any court exercising criminal jurisdiction (including courts martial) from the moment the law is set in motion by a charge being made; and

+ In the case of a civil case from the time that the case is set down for trial or otherwise brought before the court and until a verdict or sentence has been announced.

Where a notice of appeal is given the matter is sub judice until the appeal is decided. Reference may be made to matters which relate to a ministerial decision which cannot be challenged in the courts except on grounds of misdirection or bad faith or concern issues of importance such as the economy, public order or essentials of life but in any event the Chair must exercise discretion so as not to allow references to matters where there is a real and substantial danger of prejudice to the proceedings.

8.9.8 **Members' Interests**

Members are required to inform the Registrar of Members' Interests of the particulars of any "registerable interest" which they have and they must declare any such interest before taking part in any debate or proceedings of the Assembly or its committees. No member is permitted in return for payment or any other benefit to advocate or initiate any cause on behalf of an outside body or urge another member to do so.

8.9.9 **Investigation of Conduct**

The Committee on Standards and Privileges is responsible for overseeing the work of the Assembly Clerk of Standards and considering any matter relating to the conduct of members including specific complaints in relation to breaches of the Code of Conduct which the Assembly agrees. Breach of the requirements in relation to members' interests is a criminal offence.

8.9.10 *Exclusion*

Members may be excluded in accordance with the "naming" procedure (see 8.9.6).

8.9.11 *Disqualification and Resignation*

A member is disqualified from membership of the Assembly if disqualified under the Northern Ireland Assembly Disqualification Act 1975 and for that purpose references in that Act to the Assembly established under the Northern Ireland Assembly Act 1973 are to be read as references to the Assembly established under the 1998 Act.

In addition, a person is disqualified from being a member for a constituency which comprises the whole or part of any county or county borough of which the person is the Lord Lieutenant or Lieutenant. A person is also disqualified if he or she is disqualified from membership of the House of Commons otherwise than under the House of Commons Disqualification Act 1975 but is specifically not disqualified from membership by reason only of being a member of Seanad Eireann (the Senate of the Irish Republic). Peers and ministers of religion are not disqualified from being a member.

A member may resign from the Assembly by giving notice in writing at any time to the Presiding Officer.

8.9.12 *Public Disturbance*

The Speaker has the power to order the withdrawal of visitors from all or any part of the Parliament buildings whenever he or she thinks fit. In addition, the Keeper of the House who is responsible for exercising the Speaker's orders in relation to the maintenance of order, is required to remove any visitor to the Assembly who misconducts himself or herself, occupies any part of the Assembly or gallery which is appropriated to members or refuses to withdraw when requested to do so whilst the Assembly or any of its committees is sitting.

8.10 Powers and Privileges of Members

8.10.1 *Defamation and Contempt*

Absolute privilege attaches to any statement made in proceedings of the Assembly and to the publication of a statement under the Assembly's authority. Qualified privilege attaches to publications which consist of a fair and accurate report of such proceedings made in good faith.

The strict liability rule in relation to publication of court proceedings does not apply to any publication made in, for the purposes of or purposes incidental to, Assembly proceedings (including committee proceedings) or to the extent that it consists of a fair and accurate report of such proceedings made in good faith.

8.10.2 *Witnesses and Documents*

The Assembly has the power to require any person to attend its proceedings for the purpose of giving evidence or to produce a document which is in his or her custody or control, provided the evidence or document relates to matters which are within the competence of the Assembly (i.e. transferred matters concerning Northern Ireland and other matters in relation to which statutory functions are exercisable by ministers or the Northern Ireland Departments). A person is not obliged to answer any question or produce any document which he or she would be entitled to refuse to answer or produce in proceedings in a court in Northern Ireland but subject to that qualification, refusing to comply with an Order of the Assembly or deliberately altering, suppressing, concealing or destroying a document is a criminal offence.

Witnesses may be required to give their evidence on oath and a person who refuses to take an oath when required to do so is guilty of an offence.

8.10.3 *Sanctions*

Unlike the UK Parliament, the Assembly has no inherent jurisdiction to deal with contemnors but disturbing proceedings, failing to comply with orders of the Assembly etc. are offences which are punishable under criminal law.

8.11 Committees

8.11.1 Establishment, Powers and Procedures

The Assembly is required to establish a number of committees by the Northern Ireland Act 1998. It is also required to establish a number of committees by its standing orders. In addition to these, the Assembly is free to establish further committees as it sees fit. Such committees are appointed by a motion of the Assembly, setting out the terms of reference, the quorum and the composition of the committee. All committees may, with the approval of the Business Committee and the Assembly, establish sub-committees. Committees may report on matters referred to them and those they see fit to draw to the attention of the Assembly.

8.11.2 Statutory Committees

The Assembly is required to establish a committee to scrutinise the work of each of the Northern Ireland Ministers. The chairs of these committees are distributed between the political parties using the same formula that is used to calculate their entitlement to ministerial posts. No statutory committee may be chaired by a Minister or a Junior Minister. A statutory committee consists of 11 members, including its chair and deputy chairman, who should be in proportion to the party strengths within the Assembly. Membership of the committees should be arranged so that all non-Ministers have a place on at least one statutory committee. The quorum for a statutory committee is five and each of these committees may call for witnesses and documents.

8.11.3 Standing Committees

The Assembly is required to establish the following standing committees: a Committee on Procedures, a Business Committee, a Special Committee on Conformity with Equality Requirements, a Public Accounts Committee, a Committee on Standards and Privileges, and an Audit Committee. Each of these committees is to have a membership of 11 and a quorum of five, except for the Audit Committee which is to have a membership of five and a quorum of two. Chairmen of the standing committees are to be elected in proportion to the parties' strengths within the Assembly.

8.11.4 Ad hoc *Committees*

In addition to the above-mentioned committees the Assembly is able to establish further committees on a motion. The procedures and powers of these committees are prescribed by the terms of the motion by which they are established. The motions should also determine the membership and operation of the committees together with the date by which they will cease to operate. To date, the new Northern Ireland Assembly has established two *ad hoc* committees: one on the Procedural Consequences of Devolution, which has reported and been wound up, and one on the Port of Belfast.

8.12 Assembly Bills

8.12.1 *Types of Legislation*

The Assembly will be empowered to initiate and pass Bills which will become Acts upon receipt of Royal Assent.

8.12.2 *Format of Legislation*

Similar to UK : see 3.2 and 4.12.1.

8.12.3 *Accompanying Documentation*

Public bills are required to be accompanied by an explanatory and financial memorandum detailing the nature of the issues addressed by the bill, the consultative process undertaken, the main options considered, the option selected and why and the cost implications of the proposals.

8.12.4 *Stages of a Public Bill*

Each bill must pass through nine or ten phases -

✦ Prior Clearance

This involves submission of the text in advance to the Speaker together with a statement asserting that the bill is within legislative competence. In the case of a bill which the Speaker considers deals with an excepted matter in an ancillary fashion or with a reserved matter (in either case other than in a manner ancillary to provisions dealing with transferred matters), the Secretary of State's consent is required for the bill to be progressed.

+ First Stage

The bill is introduced by its title being read by the Clerk. It is then ordered to be printed and set down in the list of pending future business.

+ Second Stage

This involves a debate on the principle of the bill, followed by referral to the appropriate statutory committee, unless the Assembly otherwise determines.

+ Committee Stage

The appropriate statutory committee is given 30 days (or such longer period as may be agreed by motion) in which to consider and take evidence and report its opinion on the bill.

Bills and draft bills may also be referred at any time to the Northern Ireland Human Rights Commission and to the Special Committee on Conformity with Equality Requirements.

+ Consideration Stage

The provisions of the bill and any amendments proposed to it are considered.

+ Reconsideration

A bill is subject to reconsideration if it is found by the Judicial Committee to be outside legislative competence, if the Assembly so resolves in the context of devolution issue proceedings, if the Secretary of State determines not to submit the bill for Royal Assent or if the UK Parliament resolves that it should not be submitted for Royal Assent.

+ Further Procedural Clearance

Following the Consideration Stage, a bill cannot proceed to the Final Stage until the Speaker has certified that it remains within legislative competence or, having referred it to the Secretary of State, the Secretary of State signifies his or her consent to any provision dealing with an excepted or reserved matter or signifies his or her opinion that no such reference was necessary.

+ Final Stage

The bill is debated, without the possibility of amendment, on the motion that it now pass.

✦ Referral to UK Parliament

Unless the Secretary of State considers that a bill contains no provision which deals with an excepted or reserved matter other than by way of an ancillary provision dealing with transferred matters (or in a case of urgency), the bill must be referred by the Secretary of State before Royal Assent to the UK Parliament, where a motion that the bill should not be submitted for Royal Assent may be tabled in either House within a period of 20 days.

✦ Royal Assent

Bills are required to be submitted for Royal Assent by the Secretary of State rather than the Assembly. Royal Assent is given by Letters Patent under the Great Seal of Northern Ireland signed by the Sovereign.

8.13 Subordinate Legislation

8.13.1 Procedural Scrutiny

All rules and draft rules laid before the Assembly are to be referred to the appropriate statutory committee to consider whether they impose a charge on public revenues and certain procedural aspects not touching on the substance or the policy behind the rules.

Statutory committees can delegate their responsibility in relation to any rules to an officer of the Assembly to be known as the Examiner of Statutory Rules.

8.14 Finance and Taxation

8.14.1 Grants of Expenditure

As in Scotland (see 6.15.1), the Barnett formula will continue to be used to assess the block grant paid by the UK Parliament. This arrangement is not contained in the devolution legislation and it will be open to future UK Governments to change the way in which Northern Ireland spending is assessed and funded.

The block grant determined under the Barnett formula will be paid into the Consolidated Fund for Northern Ireland.

The Assembly may not pass a vote, resolution or Act imposing or increasing a charge on the Consolidated Fund or appropriating a sum out of that Fund except pursuant to a recommendation made by the Minister of Finance and Personnel or otherwise than with cross-community support.

8.14.2 *Taxation*

Whilst taxes or duties under any law applicable to the UK as a whole, stamp duty levied before the transfer of devolved powers and taxes or duties similar to either of these categories are excepted matters, subject to that extensive reservation, the Assembly may introduce new or increase existing fiscal impositions. However, the Assembly may not pass a vote, resolution or Act for this purpose except pursuant to a recommendation made by the Minister of Finance and Personnel or otherwise than with cross-community support.

8.14.3 *The Annual Programme*

The Minister of Finance and Personnel is required, before the beginning of each financial year (31st March), to lay before the Assembly a draft budget setting out the programme of expenditure proposals for that year as agreed by the Executive Committee.

Provision is also made to enable the authorised officer of the Department of Finance and Personnel to authorise payments out of the Consolidated Fund where an appropriation Act has not been passed before the end of July in any financial year or, in respect of the next financial year, at least three working days before the end of the previous financial year.

8.14.4 *Scrutiny of Public Accounts*

The Comptroller and Auditor General for Northern Ireland (CAGNI) will be responsible for auditing the accounts of the Assembly. In so far as it does not already do so, legislation is to require the preparation of accounts by Northern Ireland Departments and other recipients of sums from the Consolidated Fund, for the preparation of accounts of payments into and out of the fund by the Department of Finance and Personnel and for the CAGNI to exercise a number of functions, including examination of the accounts so prepared and carrying out investigations into the economy, efficiency and effectiveness with which the Northern

Ireland departments and others receiving sums from the Fund have discharged their functions.

In addition to scrutiny of financial matters by the Assembly as a whole, accounts and reports laid before the Assembly are to be referred to the Public Accounts Committee whilst there is also to be an Audit Committee to exercise, in place of the Department of Finance and Personnel, its functions in relation to scrutiny of the expenses of the Northern Ireland Office.

Chapter 9

The European Union

9.7 *Business*

9.8 *Public Access & Information*

9.9 *Conduct and Ethics*

9.10 *Powers and Privileges*

9.11 *Committees*

9.12 *Legislative Functions*

9.13 *Finance and Taxation*

9.1 Form and Functions

9.1.1 Overview

The European Parliament, together with the Council of Ministers, the European Commission, the European Court of Justice and the European Court of Auditors, is one of the five principal institutions of the European Community:

+ It is an elected assembly (626 members) taking its membership from the fifteen member states of the European Community.

+ It provides a democratic forum for examining and shaping developments in the European Community and European Union and, in particular, the work of the Commission whose appointment by the member states it must approve and whom it can dismiss en bloc.

+ It has powers of approval and veto over the Community budget.

+ It is consulted upon and in certain cases has powers to amend or block community legislation.

9.2 Electoral Arrangements

9.2.1 Composition

The European Parliament comprises 626 members from the 15 EC member states of which 87 are from the United Kingdom. Seats are allocated according to the size of a member state's population but there is substantial variation in the number of seats allocated which results in an over-representation of the smaller states. Thus, Luxembourg with six members has 40,000 electors per member whereas Germany with 99 members has 610,000 electors per member. In the UK the ratio is one member per 450,000 electors.

The UK is divided into 12 multi-member electoral regions, nine in England (71 members in regions which vary in representation from between four and 11 members each) and one each in Scotland (eight members), Wales (five members) and Northern Ireland (three members).

In Northern Ireland election is by the single transferable vote system of proportional representation which is used for all other elections there (see 8.2.1). In the rest of the UK election is by means of the closed list system of proportional representation under which a single vote is cast for a registered party (whose candidates are listed on the ballot paper) or an independent candidate. Under the closed list system the order in which party candidates appear on the ballot paper (and thus their likelihood of being elected) is a matter for the party to determine and a vote cannot be cast for a particular candidate on a registered party's list. The first seat is allocated to the party or independent candidate with the highest vote and all subsequent seats are allocated on a similar basis but with each party's vote being divided by the number of seats it has already gained plus one (the "d'Hondt" system).

9.2.2 Electoral Franchise

The electoral franchise is the same as for local elections in the UK. All British, other Commonwealth, Irish and other EU citizens (including peers) are entitled to be registered and may vote in one region if they are aged 18 or over and resident there except convicted prisoners in detention or unlawfully at large, detained mental patients and those convicted of corrupt or illegal practices at elections.

9.2.3 Candidacy and Election Rules

Those eligible for election will include all British, other Commonwealth, Irish and other EU citizens (including peers) aged 21 or over and resident in the UK, provided they do not hold an "incompatible" Community post or, subject to certain exceptions, would be disqualified from membership of the House of Commons (see 9.9.11). The election rules are set out in the European Parliamentary Elections Act 1978 as amended by the European Parliamentary Elections Act 1999.

9.2.4 Vacancies

Vacancies which arise on the death or resignation of a member are filled by the person who was next on the list of the party which won the seat. If no such person exists, a by-election will be held.

9.3   Community Institutions

9.3.1   *The European Commission*

The Commission brings forward proposals for Community legislation and is responsible for taking action to uphold existing laws. It comprises 20 Commissioners supported by 15,000 staff, based predominantly in Brussels. There are two Commissioners from each of France, Germany, Italy, Spain and the United Kingdom and one from each of the other member state. Once appointed, the Commissioners are obliged to be independent of their national governments and to act only in the interests of the European Union. The Commission meets formally once a week to conduct its business and operates under the principle of collective responsibility.

The President of the Commission is appointed by the governments of the member states subject to confirmation by the Parliament, which may approve or reject the appointment.

Similarly, other members of the Commission are nominated by the member states but must be confirmed by the Parliament, which has the power to approve or reject their appointment. The Parliament may also pass a motion of censure in the Commission, requiring all the Commissioners to resign and be replaced. In order to be passed a motion requires a two-thirds majority of those voting, who together represent an absolute majority of MEPs.

The Commission is organised into 23 Directorates-General, with an additional 15 or so specialised services, each of which reports to a Commissioner.

9.3.2   *The Council of the European Union*

The Council of Ministers is the body which determines whether or not a proposal for Community legislation will be enacted. The Council consists of a minister from each of the member state. The ministers attending will vary according to the subject matters being discussed. For example, the monthly General Affairs Councils are attended by the Foreign Affairs Ministers.

The Presidency of the Council rotates between the member states every six months. The Presidency arranges and presides over all meetings of the Council. It also hosts the European Council every six months, which is a summit of all the Heads of State or Government together with the President of the Commission.

The Council decides matters either by unanimity or, more frequently (and subject to the "legal base" of the matter under the EC Treaty), by a qualified-majority voting system. This system allocates weighted voting rights to the member states as follows:

France, Germany, Italy and UK	10 votes each
Spain	8 votes
Belgium, Greece, Netherlands and Portugal	5 votes each
Austria and Sweden	4 votes each
Denmark, Finland and Ireland	3 votes each
Luxembourg	2 votes
Total	*87 votes*

62 votes must be cast by at least 10 member states in favour of a proposal for it to be carried, or 62 votes in favour (regardless of the numbers voting) where the Treaty requires proposals to be adopted on a proposal from the Commission.

9.3.3   The European Court of Justice and the Court of First Instance

The Court of Justice hears cases involving points of EC law that are referred to it by the Commission, the other institutions, member states, national courts and individuals. It has jurisdiction to interpret the EC Treaty and other laws and to rule on the validity of acts of the institutions. Infraction proceedings are frequently brought by the Commission against member states for failure properly to implement a Community obligation. If such a case is proven, the Court will require the state concerned to comply with the obligation and may impose a financial penalty. It also deals with issues relating to the employees of the Community institutions. Since 1989, it has been assisted by the Court of First Instance, which has jurisdiction over actions brought by private parties against the Community institutions. Appeals from the Court of First Instance to the Court of Justice may only be made on points of law. While the Court of Justice has no direct relationship with the national courts, Community law takes precedence over the domestic law of the member states and the court is often asked by domestic courts to provide "preliminary rulings" on the interpretation of community law. The 15 Judges of the Court of Justice (usually one per member state) are appointed by agreement between the member states for six year terms. The Court sits either as two chambers of five Judges each, or as four chambers of three. There is also provision for urgent cases to be heard by the President of the Court alone, who may make a preliminary ruling. The Court is assisted by nine Advocates-General, also appointed by the member states for six year terms, who provide opinions on each of the cases before the Court. The Court of First Instance also has 15 Judges, although it does not have Advocates-General.

9.3.4 *The European Court of Auditors*

The Court of Auditors is responsible for ensuring that the European Union spends money according to its budgetary rules and regulations and for the intended purposes. It is independent of the other institutions of the Union. The Court has the power to require information and documents of these other institutions, as well as from national, regional and local institutions that administer Community funds. It has the power to carry audits whenever necessary.

The Court's annual report - together with the relevant institutions' replies - is examined by the Parliament every year before it decides whether to approve the Commission's budget.

Candidates for membership of the Court of Auditors must be approved by the responsible committee of the Parliament before they can be appointed by the Council.

9.3.5 *The Economic and Social Committee*

The Committee was set up in order to involve economic and social interest groups in the establishment of the Common Market and to brief the Commission and the Council on EU issues. It has 222 members drawn from three groups: employers, workers and various interests. Germany, France, Italy and the United Kingdom each have 24 members; Spain has 21; Belgium, Greece, the Netherlands, Portugal, Austria and Sweden each have 12; Denmark, Ireland and Finland nine and Luxembourg six.

The Committee's main task is to issue opinions on matters referred to it by the Commission and the Council. This consultation is mandatory in certain areas (such as regional and environmental policies), optional in others. The Committee also issues opinions on its own initiative and these comprise about 15% of the 170 or so advisory documents that it issues each year.

9.3.6 The Committee of the Regions

The Committee was created as a consultative body by the Treaty of European Union and has sat since 1994. Its members, which are allocated among the member states in the same proportions as the members of the Economic and Social Committee, are drawn from the ranks of regional, local and municipal government. The Treaty requires the Committee to be consulted on a number of issues relating to trans-European networks, public health, education, youth, culture and economic and social cohesion. It also reports on matters of its own initiative.

9.4 Officers

9.4.1 President and Vice-Presidents

The Parliament's activities are directed by its President and its 14 Vice-Presidents, who serve two-year terms. They have responsibility for ensuring that the proceedings of the Parliament are properly conducted and represent the Parliament in international and ceremonial matters.

9.4.2 The Bureau

The President and the Vice-Presidents form the Bureau of the Parliament, which takes financial, organisational and administrative decisions in relation to the Parliament, including decisions on the conduct and timing of business. The President has the casting vote in the Bureau.

9.4.3   *The Conference of Presidents and the Quaestors*

The Bureau is assisted by the Conference of Presidents, which comprises the President and the chairmen of each of the political groups. It draws up the draft agendas for the Parliament, and by the College of Quaestors. The five Quaestors, who are also elected for two year terms, have responsibility for administrative and financial matters directly concerning individual members.

9.5   Opening and Dissolution

9.5.1   *Duration*

The parliamentary term is for a fixed five year period and runs concurrently with the term of office of its members. Parliament meets (without requiring to be convened) on the second Tuesday in March each year and sets its own sessional calendar and adjournments.

Each month there is a part session, divided into daily sittings.

The Conference of Presidents may alter the duration of adjournments at least two weeks before the date previously fixed by Parliament for resuming the session but the date of resumption may not be postponed for more than two weeks.

Exceptionally, after consulting the Conference of Presidents, the President may convene Parliament at the request of a majority of its members or at the request of the Commission or the Council. The President may also, with the approval of the Conference of the Presidents, convene Parliament at the request of one third of its members.

9.5.2   *Opening*

At the first session of a new Parliament the oldest member takes the chair until the President, Vice-President and Bureau are elected.

9.5.3   *Dissolution*

There is no formal dissolution of the Parliament as it has a fixed five year term.

9.6   Sittings

9.6.1   Location

The Parliament meets in plenary session for one week each month (except August) in Strasbourg and meets in mini-plenary session for two days every month in Brussels. In October there is a second Strasbourg session to consider the budget.

9.6.2   Annual Programme

Before the end of each year and following a debate and vote in Parliament on the annual programme of the Commission, the Presidents of the Parliament and the Commission agree on behalf of their institutions a legislative programme for the following year. This programme establishes the priorities in the legislative field and fixes a timetable for the submission by the Commission of all the proposals and documents contained in the programme and for their examination by Parliament and the Council. Parliament designates a committee to be responsible for each proposal or document in the programme. Where there are urgent and unforeseeable circumstances, the Commission or Parliament may propose a legislative measure on its own initiative to be added to the measures proposed in the legislative programme. Where an institution is unable to comply with the timetable laid down it must notify the other institution as to the reasons for the delay and propose a new timetable. The programme may be revised at the beginning of the second half of the year.

At the end of the last part-session before elections, all Parliament's unfinished business lapses. However, at the beginning of each parliamentary term the Conference of Presidents may decide, at the request of a parliamentary committee and one of the other institutions, to resume or continue the consideration of such a matter.

9.6.3   *Sitting Times*

Sitting times for plenary sessions in Strasbourg are normally:-

Monday:	5.00am - 7.00pm
Tuesday:	9.00am - 1.00pm
	3.00pm - 7.00pm
	9.00pm - 12.00am
Wednesday:	1.00am - 1.00pm
	3.00pm - 8.00pm
Thursday:	10.00am - 1.00pm
	3.00pm - 8.00pm
Friday:	9.00am - 1.00pm

Sitting times for Brussels mini-plenary sessions are typically:

Wednesday:	3.00pm - 6.00pm
Thursday:	9.30am - 1.00pm

9.6.4   *Adjournments and Dissolutions*

The Parliament has the power to determine its own adjournments and normally these are agreed as part of the arrangements for setting the work programmes and agenda.

Adjournment of a particular debate to a specific date and time or closure of a sitting may be agreed by vote of the Parliament on a motion moved by a political group of 29 members (or, in the case of closure) the President.

9.7   Business

9.7.1   *Arrangement of Business*

Before each part-session the draft agenda is drawn up by the Conference of Presidents on the basis of recommendations by the Conference of Committee Chairmen, taking account of the annual legislative programme. The draft agenda is then adopted at the beginning of each part-session.

9.7.2   *Daily Programme*

✦ Approval of Minutes

The daily minutes of the previous day's sitting are approved unless objections are raised.

✦ Membership of Parliament

The President announces any changes in the Parliament's membership.

✦ Membership of political groups

The President announces any changes to the membership of the political groups.

✦ Membership of committees

Parliament ratifies any changes to the composition of the committees

✦ Procedural motions

For all procedural motions, the President, after having heard the mover of the motion, calls for one speaker in favour and one against. The chairman or the rapporteur of the committee responsible is also entitled to speak. Speaking time is limited to one minute.

• Points of order

A member is permitted to draw the President's attention to any failure to respect Parliament's rules of procedure. The President should make an immediate ruling on points of order; only exceptionally can the ruling be postponed (but for not more than 24 hours). No vote can be taken on the President's decision.

• Referral Back to Committee

Referral back to committee and thus curtailment of debate on the matter in question may be requested by a political group or at least 29 members when the agenda is fixed or before the start of the debate or the final vote.

• Closure of a Debate

A debate may be closed before the list of speakers has been exhausted on a proposal from the President or at the request of a political group or at least 29 members. Such a proposal or request is put to the vote immediately. If the vote is carried, only one member may speak from each political group which has not yet provided a speaker in that debate.

• Adjournment of a Debate

At the start of a debate on an item on the agenda, a political group or at least 29 members may move that the debate be adjourned to a specific date and time, and the motion is voted upon immediately. If the motion is carried, Parliament proceeds to the next item on the agenda. The adjourned debate is resumed at the specified date and time. If the motion is rejected, it may not be tabled again during that part-session.

- Suspension or Closure of the Sitting

The sitting may be suspended or closed during a debate or a vote if Parliament so decides on a proposal from the President or at the request of a political group or at least 29 members, and is voted upon immediately.

+ Written declarations

Any member may submit a written declaration of not more than 200 words on a matter falling within the sphere of activities of the European Union. Written declarations are printed in the official languages, distributed and entered in a register. Any member may add his signature to a declaration entered in the register. If a declaration is signed by at least one half of the component members of Parliament it is forwarded to the institutions named by the author together with the names of the signatories. The President announces this at the next sitting and the text of the declaration and the names of the signatories are included in the minutes of that sitting as an annex.

+ Petitions

Any citizen of the European Union, and any natural or legal person residing or having its registered office in a member state, has the right to address a petition to the Parliament on a matter which comes within the EU's fields of activity and which directly affects them. Petitions are entered in a register and forwarded by the President to the Committee on Petitions. The committee may submit motions for a resolution on petitions it has considered or request that its opinion be forwarded by the President to the Commission or the Council. The Petitions Committee prepares an annual report on its work which is submitted to the Parliament for debate in plenary, and also a short statement six months after the annual report.

+ Draft agenda

At the beginning of each part-session, Parliament takes a decision on the final draft agenda of the order of business. Amendments may be proposed by a committee, a political group or at least 29 members and must be received by the President at least one hour before the part-session begins. The President may give the floor to the mover, one speaker in favour and one speaker against. The maximum speaking time is one minute. If a procedural motion to amend the agenda is rejected, it may not be tabled again during the part-session.

✦ Topical and urgent debates

Parliament sets aside three hours per part-session for debates on topical and urgent subjects. A political group or at least 29 members may ask the President in writing for such a debate which must be linked with a motion for a resolution. The President notifies Parliament immediately of any such request and the Conference of Presidents draws up a list of subjects to be included on the agenda of the next debate on the basis of the requests submitted. The main criteria for selection of topics include the need for Parliament to express a view before a particular event has taken place, for Parliament to express a rapid opinion, or to comment on a major issue relating to the Union's powers.

✦ Debates on statements

A member of the Commission or Council may at any time ask the President for permission to make a statement. The President decides when any such statement may be made and a statement may be followed by a debate. If no debate is held, members are allowed 30 minutes in which to put brief and concise questions.

Parliament may also hold a separate debate on the Annual Report of the Court of Auditors and a debate may also be held following the presentation of the Annual Report of the European Central Bank.

✦ Committee reports on legislative proposals

✦ Agenda for next sitting

Before closing the sitting, the President announces the date, time and agenda of the next sitting.

9.7.3   Questions and Answers

✦ Questions for oral answer (with debate)

Questions may be put to the Council or the Commission by a committee, a political group or at least 29 members with a request that they be placed on the agenda of Parliament. The Conference of Presidents decides whether and in what order questions should be placed on the agenda.

Questions to the Commission must be referred to that institution at least one week before the relevant sitting and questions to the Council at least three weeks before that date. One of the questioners may move the question for five minutes and a member of the institution concerned replies. The reply is followed by a debate which may in turn be followed by the adoption of a resolution.

+ Question Time

Any member may table questions to the Commission or Council, and the President of Parliament decides on their admissibility and on the order in which they are to be taken. Answers are given during two 90 minute periods known as "question time" in each part-session. Each member may only table one question to each institution per month. The questioner may ask a supplementary question following the reply, and extra supplementaries may be taken from other members. Questions not reached are answered in writing.

9.7.4 Motions

+ Motions for a resolution

Any member may table a motion for a resolution of not more than 200 words on a matter falling within the sphere of activities of the European Union. The committee responsible decides what procedure is to be adopted - it may combine the motion for a resolution with other motions for resolutions or reports, or it may adopt an opinion, which may take the form of a letter, or it may decide to draw up a report which requires the approval of the Conference of Presidents.

+ Procedural Motions

Procedural motions include motions on:

- the inadmissibility of a matter;
- referral back to committee;
- the closure of a debate;
- the adjournment of a debate;
- the suspension or closure of a sitting.

In addition to the mover of a motion, one member may speak in favour and one against the motion, and the chairman or rapporteur of the committee responsible may also speak. Speaking time is limited to one minute.

9.7.5 **Rules of Debate**

No member may speak unless called upon to do so by the President. Members speak from their places and must address the Chair. The President can delete from the reports of debates the speeches of members who have not been called upon to speak by him or who continue to speak beyond the time allotted to them. A speaker may not be interrupted but may, by leave of the President, give way during a speech to allow another member, the Commission or the Council to put a question on a particular point in the speech.

No speaker may speak more than twice on the same subject, except by leave of the President.

The Conference of Presidents may propose to Parliament that speaking time be allocated for a particular debate. Parliament decides on this proposal without debate. Speaking time is allocated in accordance with the following criteria:

- a first fraction of speaking time is divided equally among all the political groups;
- a further fraction is divided among the political groups in proportion to the total number of their members;
- the non-attached members are allocated an overall speaking time based on the fractions allocated to each political group.

Where a total speaking time is allocated for several items on the agenda, the political groups inform the President of how the fraction of their speaking time is to be used for each individual item.

No member may speak for more than one minute on the minutes of proceedings, procedural motions, amendments to the final draft agenda or to the agenda.

9.7.6 **Voting and Decisions**

Voting times are grouped at certain fixed times. The order in which votes are taken is different for non-legislative texts and legislative texts. When a non-legislative text is put to the vote, Parliament first votes on amendments to specific parts of a resolution. It then votes on the unamended parts of a motion (but which may be taken en bloc to save time), and finally on the motion for a resolution as a whole.

Once the voting on separate amendments is concluded, an opportunity is given for explanations of vote by individual members before the final vote is taken. Explanations are limited to one minute for individual members and two minutes for an explanation on behalf of a group.

Most votes on non-legislative resolutions require simple majorities only. Unless a quorum call is made or an electronic vote taken there is no check on how many members are actually voting. Certain non-legislative votes, such as amendments to the Rules of Procedure, require a majority of the total number of members, and censure votes on the Commission require a two-thirds majority of the votes cast.

Normally Parliament votes by a show of hands. If the President decides that a result is doubtful, a fresh vote is taken using the electronic voting system or by sitting and standing. Voting can also be taken by roll call if so requested in writing by at least 29 members or a political group before voting has begun. In the case of appointments, voting is by secret ballot.

9.8   Public Access and Information

9.8.1   *Access to Sittings*

Access to the public gallery is on a first come first served basis and generally tickets are not available in advance.

9.8.2   *Access to Committees*

Tickets are available on a first come first served basis. Occasionally committees sit in private - it is best to check in advance on sitting arrangements.

9.8.3   *Tours*

The Parliament receives groups of visitors in Brussels, Strasbourg and Luxembourg (the Parliament's Secretariat) throughout the year and visits often include a video presentation or a talk given by a Parliament official. The maximum number of visitors in a group is 40, and participants should be at least 14 years old. Applications for visits to all three locations should be made via an MEP or sent in writing to the European Parliament Visits Service, 97-113 rue Belliard B-1047 Brussels.

9.8.4 *Information*

Information can be obtained in the UK from the European Parliament's representative office at 2 Queen Anne's Gate London SW1H 9AA:

Telephone: 0171 227 4300
Fax: 0171 227 4302

Information can also be obtained from the Parliament's website at http://www.europarl.eu.int

9.8.5 *Documentation*

European Parliament Sessional Documents are divided into three series:

* Series A : committee reports
* Series B : motions for resolution, questions and requests for urgent and topical debate;
* Series C : proposals for legislation issued by the Commission as COM Documents and other Community legislation documents.

A daily agenda is available during each plenary session. The Minutes of Proceedings are published in the C series of the Official Journal. A verbatim report of debates in the plenary sessions known as "the rainbow" gives speeches in the original language of the person speaking. A full translation of debates in all the Community languages appears three to four months later on in the Official Journal.

9.8.6 *Broadcasting*

Proceedings of the plenary sessions and the committees are recorded live and are available to broadcasters in the member states.

9.9 Conduct and Ethics

9.9.1 *Allegiance*

Members of the European Parliament are required to act independently and may not be bound by any instructions or other binding mandate from their member state.

9.9.2 *Language*

All of the Community languages are equally valid in the Parliament. Speeches delivered in one of the official languages are simultaneously interpreted into all of the other languages and all documents of the Parliament are drawn up in all of the official languages.

9.9.3   Forms of Address

There are no formal rules on forms of address but all members must address the Chair.

9.9.4   Dress Code

The Parliament has no formal dress code.

9.9.5   Calling of Speakers

No member is permitted to speak unless called to do so by the President. Members who wish to speak enter their name on a list of speakers and the President calls members to speak as he sees fit, ensuring as far as possible that speakers of different political views and different languages are heard in turn but priority may be given to the rapporteur of the committee responsible for any report under debate and to the chairmen of political groups who wish to speak on behalf of their group. Members of the European Commission and Council of Ministers are heard in debate on a report immediately after its presentation by the rapporteur.

9.9.6   Order in the Chamber

The President is responsible for maintaining order in the chamber and is required to call to order any member who creates a disturbance in the proceedings. If the offence is repeated the President is required to again call the member to order and record the fact in the Minutes of Proceedings. If the same member commits a further offence then the President may exclude that member from the chamber for the remainder of the sitting. In the event of serious disorder the President may give formal notice and move a censure motion to exclude the member immediately and suspend him or her for a period of two-five days. Any such motion is put to an electronic vote without debate. The President may close or suspend the sitting if it becomes necessary in order to restore order.

9.9.7   Sub judice

The Parliament has no formal sub judice rule.

9.9.8 Members' Interests

Members are required to make a personal declaration of any professional or other remunerated functions and activities and any support, whether financial or in terms of staff or material, additional to that provided by Parliament and granted to the member in connection with his political activities by third parties.

Members are required to refrain from accepting any gift or benefit in the performance of their duties and, before speaking in Parliament or in one of its bodies, a member with a direct financial interest in the subject of a debate is required to disclose it orally unless it is obvious from the registered declaration that he has already made.

9.9.9 Investigation of Conduct

There is no provision in the Parliament's rules of procedure for sanctioning a member who fails to comply with the rules relating to the declaration of members' interests.

9.9.10 Exclusion

Members may be excluded in accordance with the procedures set out under 9.9.6 above.

9.9.11 Disqualification and Resignation

A person will be disqualified from being a member if he or she occupies an "incompatible" post within the Community. Such posts include being:

+ a member of the Commission;

+ a judge, advocate general or registrar of the European Court of Justice; or

+ an official of one of the Community institutions.

A member state may impose additional disqualifications in relation to members from that state and, in the case of the United Kingdom, a person is disqualified from being a member of the European Parliament if, subject to certain exceptions, they would be disqualified from being a member of the House of Commons (see 4.9.11).

The exceptions are that a person will not be so disqualified if the only reason they would not be eligible to be a member of the Commons is that they are:

+ a peer (other than a Lord of Appeal);

+ a minister of religion; or

+ a citizen of an EU member state other than the UK or Ireland.

9.9.12 Public Disturbance

Any member of the public who refuses to remain seated or silent whilst attending any proceedings of the Parliament will be ejected by the security service of the Parliament. Generally, no further action will be taken unless the conduct of the person concerned constitutes a criminal offence. In that event they will be handed over to the police or other appropriate authority of the member state in which the Parliament is sitting.

9.10 Powers and Privileges

9.10.1 Defamation

The Protocol on Privileges and Immunities of the European Communities provides the European Parliament with a similar status to a diplomatic mission and therefore its proceedings cannot be challenged in the courts of the member states. In addition, a member of the Parliament enjoys any immunity which is accorded to a member of Parliament in the territory of his or her own state and, whilst in the territory of any other member state, immunity from any measure of detention or legal proceedings except where the member is found in the act of committing a criminal offence. The Parliament is often asked to waive a member's immunity but has generally refused to do so.

9.10.2 Witnesses and Documents

The Parliament has no self-standing powers to compel witnesses to attend or produce documents but where evidence is given to the Parliament it will be subject to the same immunities as any other Parliamentary proceedings.

9.10.3 Sanctions

The Parliament has no inherent jurisdiction to punish contemnors.

9.11   Committees

9.11.1   *Establishment, Powers and Procedures*

The Parliament has the power to establish committees under its rules of procedure. The rules themselves establish the standing committees and their remits and procedures (see 9.11.3) and set out the procedures for the establishment, remits and procedures of Conciliation Committees (9.11.2) and Committees of Inquiry (9.11.4).   Members of the committees are elected by the Parliament. Committees meet when they are convened by their chairmen; meet in private unless they decide otherwise; and may invite the Commission, Council and others to attend. For votes in committees to be valid, one quarter of the members normally have to be present.

9.11.2   *Conciliation Committee*

Where the Parliament and the Council cannot reach agreement on a legislative proposal, a Conciliation Committee is formed, consisting of an equal number of delegates from the Parliament and from the Council. This Committee deliberates in camera and attempts to reach compromises on the text of the proposals.

9.11.3   *Permanent Committees*

There are twenty standing committees of the Parliament that consider various matters, including legislative proposals, in their subject fields. The current committees cover: Foreign Affairs, Security and Defence Policy; Agriculture and Rural Development; Budgets; Economic and Monetary Affairs and Industrial Policy; Research, Technological Development and Energy; External Economic Relations; Legal Affairs and Citizens' Rights; Social Affairs and Employment; Regional Policy; Transport and Tourism; Environment, Public Health and Consumer Protection; Culture, Youth, Education and the Media; Development and Co-operation; Budgetary Control; Institutional Affairs; Fisheries; Rules of Procedure, Verification of Credentials and Immunities; Women's Rights; and Petitions.

9.11.4 Committees of Inquiry

The Parliament may also establish temporary committees to inquire into contraventions or maladministration in the application of Community law by a public body of the Community or a member state. These committees have the power to call witnesses and examine evidence but the decision of the Council, Commission and Parliament of 19th April 1995 on the Parliament's right of inquiry limits the extent to which committee officials may be required to answer questions or produce documents.

9.12 Legislative Functions

9.12.1 Types of legislation and format etc.

See generally 3.1 and 3.2 for a description of regulations and directives and their format. Parliament has no right to initiate legislation as such but is able to influence, delay and in some cases revise legislation which is proposed by the Commission and adopted by the Council. Parliament can draw up its own initiative reports or make other proposals and, since 1982, the Commission has taken up any parliamentary proposal to which it does not itself have a major objection, submitting written reports every six months as to the action which it has taken on these.

9.12.2 Legislative Procedures - an overview

Draft regulations and directives follow one of the following procedures:-

✦ Consultation procedure

This is the original procedure under which the Parliament must give its opinion on a Commission proposal before further stages are taken by the Council. In doing so, it can propose amendments which, if accepted by the Commission, can only be modified or rejected by the Council on the basis of a unanimous decision.

✦ Co-operation procedure

This is the procedure introduced for single market measures under which, following an initial opinion ("first reading") from the Parliament, the Council adopts a common position. Thereafter, the Parliament gives the proposal a "second reading" and can then adopt amendments or reject the common position with consequences described in more detail below.

✦ Co-decision procedure

This is an additional procedure introduced under the Maastricht Treaty under which the Parliament has the facility to amend or reject proposals put to it by the Council. It is described in more detail below.

✦ Assent procedure

This is the procedure used to obtain Parliament's approval to accession treaties or association agreements with third countries and also to certain other matters including arrangements for structural funds and the creation of the cohesion fund. It provides for assent to be given by the Parliament on the single reading and without the opportunity for amendments to be moved.

✦ Budget procedure

This is not strictly a legislative function and is described in more detail in 9.13. The Council and the Parliament each give the annual budget two readings with Parliament being responsible for final approval of the budget.

9.12.3 *Consultation Procedure*

The Council on receipt of a proposal from the Commission, consults the Parliament upon it. The Parliament will then ordinarily refer it to the appropriate committee which considers it and issues a report to be debated at a plenary session prior to being voted upon. To take advantage of the need for an opinion from the Parliament for the measure to progress, the vote can be postponed pending the Commission taking a position on any Parliament amendments and, where these are refused, the Parliament may refer the proposal back to committee. There is, however, no power for the Parliament to amend or veto the proposal as such.

9.12.4 *Co-operation Procedure*

Initially, the same stages are followed as under the consultation procedure but the Council then adopts a "common position", possibly only by a qualified majority. Unless the "common position" is so different from the original proposal as to warrant a repeat consultation,

Parliament then has three months in which to give the proposal a second reading and to take one of the following actions:-

(a) approve the text or fail to take action upon it, whereafter the Council adopts the proposal in accordance with its common position;

(b) propose amendments to the text by an overall majority which the Commission can then either incorporate into a revised text or reject. It is then for the Council to adopt the text accepted by the Commission by qualified majority or modify the text (including rejecting amendments supported by the Commission or accepting amendments rejected by it) unanimously;

(c) reject the text by an overall majority. The proposal will then fail unless the Council agrees unanimously within three months and with the agreement of the Commission to overrule the Parliament.

9.12.5 *Co-decision Procedure*

The same stages are followed as under the co-operation procedure up to second reading but, thereafter, further stages are added the nature of which are dependent upon the Parliament's stance at second reading. The choices are as follows:-

(a) if the Parliament approves the text or fails to take action upon it within three months, as with co-operation procedure, the Council adopts the proposal in accordance with its common position;

(b) if it amends the common position by an absolute majority, the Commission is then required to issue its opinion on the Parliament's amendments and these are submitted individually to the Council where a qualified majority is needed to approve those accepted by the Commission and unanimity is required for those rejected. If the Council does not approve the common position as amended, the text is referred to a conciliation committee, comprising an equal number of members of the Council and the Parliament. The conciliation committee has six weeks to reach agreement. Thereafter, the full Council and Parliament have six weeks to adopt the proposals by qualified majority in the Council and simple majority in the Parliament. If the conciliation committee does not reach agreement, the Council may unilaterally restate its common position (with or without some of the Parliament's amendments) and this will then become law unless, within six weeks, the Parliament rejects the text by an absolute majority (313 votes).

(c) if the Parliament announces its intention to reject the common position by an absolute majority at second reading, the text is also referred to a conciliation committee (as described in paragraph (b) above) after which the Parliament can go ahead with its rejection by absolute majority (thereby killing off the proposal) or it can propose amendments whereafter the measure proceeds in accordance with the arrangements described above following amendment of a common position by the Parliament at second reading.

9.13   Finance and Taxation

9.13.1   *Grants of Expenditure*

Expenditure by the European Union falls into two categories. The first category is "compulsory expenditure" which is expenditure required as a result of Treaty provisions or Community legislation. This includes spending on agriculture, administrative refunds to member states and expenditure resulting from agreements with third (non-EC) countries. The second category is "non-compulsory expenditure" which constitutes the remainder of Community expenditure. This includes the Regional and Social Funds, energy and research, transport, development aid, the environment, education and culture. Both types of expenditure feature in the annual budget procedures but, whereas the European Parliament has the final power over non-compulsory expenditure, the Council of Ministers has the last word on compulsory expenditure.

A maximum rate for non-compulsory expenditure is determined by the Commission, based on factors including GDP, inflation and government spending. The Council of Ministers and the Parliament are bound by this maximum unless they jointly (the Council acting by a qualified majority and the Parliament by a majority of members and three-fifths of votes cast) agree on a higher maximum.

9.13.2   *Taxation*

Until 1970 the European Economic Community was financed by contributions from member states. Since 1970 it has been financed from what are known as "own resources". These consist of customs duties and agricultural levies on imports from outside the Union, a proportion

(1.16% in 1997 falling to 1% in 1999) of VAT on goods and services throughout the Union and a "fourth resource" calculated on the basis of the gross national product of each member state. An upper limit on the revenue available to the Union is fixed by the member states and any increase requires their ratification.

9.13.3 The Annual Programme

The European Union's financial year runs from January to December. Each institution draws up its estimates of expenditure for the coming financial year and sends them to the Commission, which at the end of April produces a preliminary draft budget for the following year containing, in addition to estimates of expenditure, an estimate of revenue. The preliminary draft budget is forwarded by the Commission to the Council of Ministers which, acting by a qualified majority, adopts a draft budget, generally at the end of July. The adopted draft budget is then forwarded to the European Parliament. The Parliament's Committee on Budgets, its specialised committees, political groups and individual members then consider the draft budget and the implementation of the current year's budget. Modifications to compulsory expenditure and amendments to non-compulsory expenditure may then be proposed. The Parliament is able, by way of modifications and amendments, to increase as well as to decrease or redistribute expenditure. Amendments and modifications are considered initially by the Committee on Budgets and then, at the first reading of the budget, by the whole Parliament in plenary session. This usually takes place at the end of October. Where modifications to compulsory expenditure are proposed, these need only be supported by a majority of those voting whereas amendments to non-compulsory expenditure require the support of a majority of members of the Parliament. The draft budget as prepared by the Council of Ministers is adopted if the Parliament does not act within 45 days to amend or modify the budget or if it explicitly approves the draft budget without any changes.

The draft budget returns to the Council of Ministers for a second reading if it has been changed by the Parliament. The Council has 15 days to take a decision and, so far as compulsory expenditure is concerned, it is required to act by a qualified majority in approving any modifications increasing expenditure or in overruling any that do not increase expenditure. Once the Council of Ministers has considered the Parliament's modifications to compulsory expenditure the Parliament may not make any further changes in respect of such spending (although it may still reject the budget as a whole). The Council (again acting by a qualified majority) may modify Parliament's amendments to non-compulsory expenditure but, following any such modification by the Council, non-compulsory expenditure may be considered again by the Parliament at the second reading of the budget (generally in December). The Parliament requires a three-fifths majority (and at least an overall majority of members) to change the Council's modifications. By the same majority the Parliament may also reject the entire draft budget. If the draft budget is rejected expenditure will be frozen at the previous year's level and the whole budget procedure starts again. Once the budget procedures have been completed, the President of the Parliament signs the budget to bring it into effect.

Once the budget has come into effect the Commission is under a duty to implement it as approved. If the Commission wishes to transfer appropriations from one part of the budget to another it must seek approval. This must come from the Council of Ministers in the case of compulsory expenditure (in which case the Parliament is entitled to give an opinion) and from the Parliament in the case of non-compulsory expenditure. During the currency of the budget the Commission also provides the Parliament with monthly reports on the use of appropriations and with reports on agricultural spending.

9.13.4 *Scrutiny of Public Accounts*

The scrutiny of accounts of the European Union is the responsibility of the Court of Auditors and the European Parliament's Committee on Budgetary Control. The Court of Auditors was established in 1977 and it became an institution of the European Union following the Maastricht Agreement. As an institution of the Union the Court is now entitled to take other institutions of the Union to the European Court of Justice.

The functions of the Court of Auditors are to ensure the legality and regularity of Union income and expenditure, to ensure sound financial management by Union institutions, to provide an annual report on the Union's budget at the end of each financial year, to draft reports on its own initiative and to submit observations on specific topics in response to requests from other European Union institutions. The Court's annual report following each financial year is published in the Official Journal together with replies from the institutions upon which it reports.

The European Parliament's Committee on Budgetary Control monitors the use of public funds and the annual report of the Court of Auditors provides an important source of information for this work. The role of the Committee is particularly significant as the European Parliament has the power to discharge the European Union's budget. This involves the adoption on the recommendation of the Council of Ministers of the annual accounts and financial statement submitted by the Commission for the previous financial year. This gives the Parliament an opportunity to inquire into fraud and mismanagement in the institutions of the Union. The refusal by the Parliament in December 1998 to discharge the 1996 budget began the proceedings that led to the resignation of the Commission in 1999.

SENIOR OFFICIALS OF THE HOUSE OF COMMONS

The Speaker	*Rt Hon Betty Boothroyd MP*
Chairman of Ways and Means	*Rt Hon Sir Alan Haselhurst MP*
First Deputy Chairman of Ways and Means	*Michael J Martin MP*
Second Deputy Chairman of Ways and Means	*Michael Lord MP*

Chairmen's Panel

Irene Adams MP, Donald Anderson MP, Peter Atkinson MP, Joe Benton MP, John Butterfill MP, Dr Michael Clark MP, Frank Cook MP, Jim Cunningham MP, Gwyneth Dunwoody MP, Roger Gale MP, Jimmy Hood MP, Barry Jones MP, John McWilliam MP, Humfrey Malins MP, John Maxton MP, [Mrs] Ray Michie MP, Bill O'Brien MP, Eddie O'Hara MP, Bill Olner MP, Marion Roe MP, George Stevenson MP, Bowen Wells MP, Andrew Welsh MP, Nicholas Winterton MP.

House of Commons Commission

Rt Hon Betty Boothroyd MP (Madam Speaker), Rt Hon Margaret Beckett (Leader of the House), Archy Kirkwood MP, Rt Hon Sir Peter Lloyd MP, Dr Lewis Moonie MP, Rt Hon Sir George Young MP.

Secretary of the Commission	*M R Jack*

Public Accounts Commission

Rt Hon Robert Sheldon MP (Chairman), Roy Beggs MP, Geoffrey Clifton-Brown MP, Rt Hon David Davis MP, Austin Mitchell MP, William O'Brien MP, Rt Hon Margaret Beckett MP, Andrew Tyrie MP, Rt Hon Alan J Williams MP.

Secretary of the Commission	*Mr Patrick*

Board of Management

W R MacKay CB (Clerk of the House), P N W Jennings (Serjeant at Arms), Miss J B Tanfield (Librarian), A J Walker (Director of Finance & Administration), I D Church (Editor of the Official Report), Mrs S J Harrison (Director of Catering Services).

Secretary of the Board of Management
B A Wilson (Head of the Establishments Office)

OFFICE OF THE SPEAKER

Speaker's Secretary	*N Bevan CB*
Speaker's Chaplain	*Rev Canon A R Wright*
Speaker's Counsel	*J S Mason CB*
	J E G Vaux

****

Parliamentary Commissioner for Standards	*Ms Elizabeth Filkin*
Parliamentary Commissioner for Administration	*M S Buckley*

ALPHABETICAL LIST OF THE MEMBERS OF PARLIAMENT

ABBOTT, Diane Julie	*Hackney North & Stoke Newington*	Lab
ADAMS, Gerard (Gerry)	*Belfast West*	SF
ADAMS, Katherine (Irene)	*Paisley North*	Lab
AINGER, Nicholas (Nick)	*Carmarthen West & South Pembrokeshire*	Lab
AINSWORTH, Peter Michael	*East Surrey*	Con
AINSWORTH, Robert William (Bob)	*Coventry North East*	Lab
ALEXANDER, Douglas Garven	*Paisley South*	Lab
ALLAN, Richard Beecroft	*Sheffield Hallam*	Lib Dem
ALLEN, Graham William	*Nottingham North*	Lab
AMESS, David Anthony Andrew	*Southend West*	Con
ANCRAM, Rt Hon Michael	*Devizes*	Con
ANDERSON, Donald	*Swansea East*	Lab
ANDERSON, Janet	*Rossendale & Darwen*	Lab
ARBUTHNOT, Rt Hon James Norwich	*North East Hampshire*	Con
ARMSTRONG, Rt Hon Hilary Jane	*North West Durham*	Lab
ASHDOWN, Rt Hon Jeremy John Durham (Paddy)	*Yeovil*	Lib Dem
ASHTON, Joseph William (Joe)	*Bassetlaw*	Lab
ATHERTON, Candice Kathleen (Candy)	*Falmouth & Camborne*	Lab
ATKINS, Charlotte	*Staffordshire Moorlands*	Lab
ATKINSON, David Anthony	*Bournemouth East*	Con
ATKINSON, Peter Landreth	*Hexham*	Con
AUSTIN, John Eric	*Erith & Thamesmead*	Lab
BAKER, Norman John	*Lewes*	Lib Dem
BALDRY, Antony Brian (Tony)	*Banbury*	Con
BALLARD, Jacqueline Margaret (Jackie)	*Taunton*	Lib Dem
BANKS, Anthony Louis (Tony)	*West Ham*	Lab
BARNES, Harold (Harry)	*North East Derbyshire*	Lab
BARRON, Kevin John	*Rother Valley*	Lab
BATTLE, John Dominic	*Leeds West*	Lab
BAYLEY, Hugh	*York*	Lab
BEARD, Christopher Nigel	*Bexleyheath & Crayford*	Lab
BECKETT, Rt Hon Margaret Mary	*Derby South*	Lab
BEGG, Anne	*Aberdeen South*	Lab
BEGGS, Roy	*East Antrim*	UU
BEITH, Rt Hon Alan James	*Berwick-upon-Tweed*	Lib Dem
BELL, Martin	*Tatton*	Ind
BELL, Stuart	*Middlesbrough*	Lab
BENN, Rt Hon Anthony Neil Wedgwood (Tony)	*Chesterfield*	Lab

BENN, Hilary James	*Leeds Central*	Lab
BENNETT, Andrew Francis	*Denton & Reddish*	Lab
BENTON, Joseph Edward (Joe)	*Bootle*	Lab
BERCOW, John Simon	*Buckingham*	Con
BERESFORD, Sir Alexander Paul	*Mole Valley*	Con
BERMINGHAM, Gerald Edward (Gerry)	*St Helens South*	Lab
BERRY, Roger Leslie	*Kingswood*	Lab
BEST, Harold	*Leeds North West*	Lab
BETTS, Clive James Charles	*Sheffield Attercliffe*	Lab
BLACKMAN, Elizabeth Marion	*Erewash*	Lab
BLAIR, Rt Hon Anthony Charles Lynton (Tony)	*Sedgefield*	Lab
BLEARS, Hazel Anne	*Salford*	Lab
BLIZZARD, Robert John (Bob)	*Waveney*	Lab
BLUNKETT, Rt Hon David	*Sheffield Brightside*	Lab
BLUNT, Crispin Jeremy Rupert	*Reigate*	Con
BOATENG, Paul Yaw	*Brent South*	Lab
BODY, Sir Richard Bernard Frank Stewart	*Boston & Skegness*	Con
BOOTHROYD, Rt Hon Betty	*West Bromwich West*	Speaker
BORROW, David Stanley	*South Ribble*	Lab
BOSWELL, Timothy Eric (Tim)	*Daventry*	Con
BOTTOMLEY, Peter James	*Worthing West*	Con
BOTTOMLEY, Rt Hon Virginia H B M	*South West Surrey*	Con
BRADLEY, Keith John Charles	*Manchester Withington*	Lab
BRADLEY, Peter Charles Stephen	*The Wrekin*	Lab
BRADSHAW, Benjamin Peter James (Ben)	*Exeter*	Lab
BRADY, Graham	*Altrincham & Sale West*	Con
BRAKE, Thomas Anthony (Tom)	*Carshalton & Wallington*	Lib Dem
BRAND, Dr Peter	*Isle of Wight*	Lib Dem
BRAZIER, Julian William Hendy; TD	*Canterbury*	Con
BREED, Colin Edward	*South East Cornwall*	Lib Dem
BRINTON, Helen Rosemary	*Peterborough*	Lab
BROOKE, Rt Hon Peter L; CH	*Cities of London & Westminster*	Con
BROWN, Rt Hon James Gordon	*Dunfermline East*	Lab
BROWN, Rt Hon Nick H	*Newcastle-upon-Tyne East & Wallsend*	Lab
BROWN, Russell Leslie	*Dumfries*	Lab
BROWNE, Desmond (Des)	*Kilmarnock & Loudoun*	Lab
BROWNING, Angela Frances	*Tiverton & Honiton*	Con
BRUCE, Ian Cameron	*South Dorset*	Con
BRUCE, Malcolm Gray	*Gordon*	Lib Dem

BUCK, Karen Patricia	*Regent's Park & Kensington North*	Lab
BURDEN, Richard Haines	*Birmingham Northfield*	Lab
BURGON, Colin	*Elmet*	Lab
BURNETT, John Patrick Aubone	*Torridge & West Devon*	Lib Dem
BURNS, Simon Hugh McGuigan	*Chelmsford West*	Con
BURSTOW, Paul Kenneth	*Sutton & Cheam*	Lib Dem
BUTLER, Christine Margaret	*Castle Point*	Lab
BUTTERFILL, John Valentine	*Bournemouth West*	Con
BYERS, Rt Hon Stephen John	*North Tyneside*	Lab
CABLE, Dr John Vincent	*Twickenham*	Lib Dem
CABORN, Rt Hon Richard George	*Sheffield Central*	Lab
CAMPBELL, Alan	*Tynemouth*	Lab
CAMPBELL, Anne	*Cambridge*	Lab
CAMPBELL, Ronald (Ronnie)	*Blyth Valley*	Lab
CAMPBELL, Rt Hon Walter Menzies; CBE QC	*North East Fife*	Lib Dem
CAMPBELL-SAVOURS, Dale Norman	*Workington*	Lab
CANAVAN, Dennis Andrew; MSP	*Falkirk West*	Ind
CANN, James Charles (Jamie)	*Ipswich*	Lab
CAPLIN, Ivor Keith	*Hove*	Lab
CASALE, Roger Mark	*Wimbledon*	Lab
CASH, William Nigel Paul (Bill)	*Stone*	Con
CATON, Martin Philip	*Gower*	Lab
CAWSEY, Ian Arthur	*Brigg & Goole*	Lab
CHAPMAN, James Keith (Ben)	*Wirral South*	Lab
CHAPMAN, Sir Sydney Brookes	*Chipping Barnet*	Con
CHAYTOR, David Michael	*Bury North*	Lab
CHIDGEY, David William George	*Eastleigh*	Lib Dem
CHISHOLM, Malcolm G R; MSP	*Edinburgh North & Leith*	Lab
CHOPE, Christopher Robert	*Christchurch*	Con
CHURCH, Judith Ann	*Dagenham*	Lab
CLAPHAM, Michael	*Barnsley West & Penistone*	Lab
CLAPPISON, William James	*Hertsmere*	Con
CLARK, Rt Hon Alan Kenneth McKenzie	*Kensington & Chelsea*	Con
CLARK, Rt Hon David George	*South Shields*	Lab
CLARK, Lynda Margaret; QC	*Edinburgh Pentlands*	Lab
CLARK, Dr Michael	*Rayleigh*	Con
CLARK, Paul Gordon	*Gillingham*	Lab
CLARKE, Anthony Richard (Tony)	*Northampton South*	Lab
CLARKE, Charles Rodway	*Norwich South*	Lab

CLARKE, Eric Lionel	*Midlothian*	Lab
CLARKE, Rt Hon Kenneth Harry; QC	*Rushcliffe*	Con
CLARKE, Rt Hon Thomas (Tom); CBE	*Coatbridge & Chryston*	Lab
CLELLAND, David Gordon	*Tyne Bridge*	Lab
CLIFTON-BROWN, Geoffrey Robert	*Cotswold*	Con
CLWYD, Ann	*Cynon Valley*	Lab
COAKER, Vernon Rodney	*Gedling*	Lab
COFFEY, Ann	*Stockport*	Lab
COHEN, Harry Michael	*Leyton & Wanstead*	Lab
COLEMAN, Iain	*Hammersmith & Fulham*	Lab
COLLINS, Timothy William George; CBE	*Westmorland & Lonsdale*	Con
COLMAN, Anthony (Tony)	*Putney*	Lab
COLVIN, Michael Keith Beale	*Romsey*	Con
CONNARTY, Michael	*Falkirk East*	Lab
COOK, Francis (Frank)	*Stockton North*	Lab
COOK, Rt Hon Robert Finlayson (Robin)	*Livingston*	Lab
COOPER, Yvette	*Pontefract & Castleford*	Lab
CORBETT, Robin	*Birmingham Erdington*	Lab
CORBYN, Jeremy Bernard	*Islington North*	Lab
CORMACK, Sir Patrick Thomas	*South Staffordshire*	Con
CORSTON, Jean Ann	*Bristol East*	Lab
COTTER, Brian Joseph	*Weston-super-Mare*	Lib Dem
COUSINS, James Mackay (Jim)	*Newcastle-upon-Tyne Central*	Lab
COX, Thomas Michael (Tom)	*Tooting*	Lab
CRAN, James Douglas	*Beverley & Holderness*	Con
CRANSTON, Ross Frederick; QC	*Dudley North*	Lab
CRAUSBY, David Anthony	*Bolton North East*	Lab
CRYER, Constance Ann	*Keighley*	Lab
CRYER, John Robert	*Hornchurch*	Lab
CUMMINGS, John Scott	*Easington*	Lab
CUNLIFFE, Lawrence Francis	*Leigh*	Lab
CUNNINGHAM, James Dolan (Jim)	*Coventry South*	Lab
CUNNINGHAM, Rt Hon Dr John Anderson (Jack)	*Copeland*	Lab
CUNNINGHAM, Roseanna; MSP	*Perth*	SNP
CURRY, Rt Hon David Maurice	*Skipton & Ripon*	Con
CURTIS-THOMAS, Claire	*Crosby*	Lab
DAFIS, Cynog Glyndwr; AM	*Ceredigion*	PC
DALYELL, Tam	*Linlithgow*	Lab
DARLING, Rt Hon Alistair Maclean	*Edinburgh Central*	Lab

DARVILL, Keith Ernest	*Upminster*	Lab
DAVEY, Edward Jonathon	*Kingston & Surbiton*	Lib Dem
DAVEY, Valerie	*Bristol West*	Lab
DAVIDSON, Ian Graham	*Glasgow Pollok*	Lab
DAVIES, Rt Hon David John Denzil	*Llanelli*	Lab
DAVIES, Geraint Richard	*Croydon Central*	Lab
DAVIES, John Quentin	*Grantham & Stamford*	Con
DAVIES, Rt Hon Ronald (Ron); AM	*Caerphilly*	Lab
DAVIS, Rt Hon David Michael	*Haltemprice & Howden*	Con
DAVIS, Terence Anthony Gordon (Terry)	*Birmingham Hodge Hill*	Lab
DAWSON, Thomas Hilton	*Lancaster & Wyre*	Lab
DAY, Stephen Richard	*Cheadle*	Con
DEAN, Janet Elizabeth Ann	*Burton*	Lab
DENHAM, John Yorke	*Southampton Itchen*	Lab
DEWAR, Rt Hon Donald Campbell; MSP	*Glasgow Anniesland*	Lab
DISMORE, Andrew Hartley	*Hendon*	Lab
DOBBIN, James (Jim)	*Heywood & Middleton*	Lab
DOBSON, Rt Hon Frank Gordon	*Holborn & St Pancras*	Lab
DONALDSON, Jeffrey Mark	*Lagan Valley*	UU
DONOHOE, Brian Harold	*Cunninghame South*	Lab
DORAN, Frank	*Aberdeen Central*	Lab
DORRELL, Rt Hon Stephen James	*Charnwood*	Con
DOWD, James Patrick (Jim)	*Lewisham West*	Lab
DREW, David Elliott	*Stroud*	Lab
DROWN, Julia Kate	*Swindon South*	Lab
DUNCAN, Alan James Carter	*Rutland & Melton*	Con
DUNCAN SMITH, George Iain	*Chingford & Woodford Green*	Con
DUNWOODY, Hon Gwyneth Patricia	*Crewe & Nantwich*	Lab
EAGLE, Angela	*Wallasey*	Lab
EAGLE, Maria	*Liverpool Garston*	Lab
EDWARDS, Huw William Edmund	*Monmouth*	Lab
EFFORD, Clive Stanley	*Eltham*	Lab
ELLMAN, Louise Joyce	*Liverpool Riverside*	Lab
EMERY, Rt Hon Sir Peter Frank Hannibal	*East Devon*	Con
ENNIS, Jeffrey (Jeff)	*Barnsley East & Mexborough*	Lab
ETHERINGTON, William (Bill)	*Sunderland North*	Lab
EVANS, Nigel Martin	*Ribble Valley*	Con
EWING, Margaret Anne; MSP	*Moray*	SNP
FABER, David James Christian	*Westbury*	Con

FABRICANT, Michael Louis David	*Lichfield*	Con
FALLON, Michael Cathel	*Sevenoaks*	Con
FEARN, Ronald Cyril (Ronnie)	*Southport*	Lib Dem
FIELD, Rt Hon Frank	*Birkenhead*	Lab
FISHER, Mark	*Stoke-on-Trent Central*	Lab
FITZPATRICK, James (Jim)	*Poplar & Canning Town*	Lab
FITZSIMONS, Lorna	*Rochdale*	Lab
FLIGHT, Howard Emerson	*Arundel & South Downs*	Con
FLINT, Caroline Louise	*Don Valley*	Lab
FLYNN, Paul Phillip	*Newport West*	Lab
FOLLETT, Daphne Barbara	*Stevenage*	Lab
FORSYTHE, Clifford	*South Antrim*	UU
FORTH, Rt Hon Eric	*Bromley & Chislehurst*	Con
FOSTER, Rt Hon Derek	*Bishop Auckland*	Lab
FOSTER, Donald Michael Ellison (Don)	*Bath*	Lib Dem
FOSTER, Michael Jabez	*Hastings & Rye*	Lab
FOSTER, Michael John	*Worcester*	Lab
FOULKES, George	*Carrick, Cumnock & Doon Valley*	Lab
FOWLER, Rt Hon Sir Peter Norman	*Sutton Coldfield*	Con
FOX, Dr Liam	*Woodspring*	Con
FRASER, Christopher James	*Mid Dorset & Poole North*	Con
FYFE, Mrs Maria	*Glasgow Maryhill*	Lab
GALBRAITH, Samuel Laird (Sam); MSP	*Strathkelvin & Bearsden*	Lab
GALE, Roger James	*Thanet North*	Con
GALLOWAY, George	*Glasgow Kelvin*	Lab
GAPES, Michael John (Mike)	*Ilford South*	Lab
GARDINER, Barry Strachan	*Brent North*	Lab
GARNIER, Edward Henry; QC	*Harborough*	Con
GEORGE, Andrew Henry	*St Ives*	Lib Dem
GEORGE, Bruce Thomas	*Walsall South*	Lab
GERRARD, Neil Francis	*Walthamstow*	Lab
GIBB, Nicolas John (Nick)	*Bognor Regis & Littlehampton*	Con
GIBSON, Dr Ian	*Norwich North*	Lab
GILL, Christopher John Fred; RD	*Ludlow*	Con
GILLAN, Cheryl Elise Kendall	*Chesham & Amersham*	Con
GILROY, Linda Wade	*Plymouth Sutton*	Lab
GODMAN, Dr Norman Anthony	*Greenock & Inverclyde*	Lab
GODSIFF, Roger Duncan	*Birmingham Sparkbrook & Small Heath*	Lab
GOGGINS, Paul Gerard	*Wythenshawe & Sale East*	Lab

GOLDING, Llinos (Llin)	*Newcastle-under-Lyme*	Lab
GOODLAD, Rt Hon Sir Alastair Robertson; KCMG	*Eddisbury*	Con
GORDON, Eileen	*Romford*	Lab
GORMAN, Teresa Ellen	*Billericay*	Con
GORRIE, Donald Cameron Easterbrook; MSP	*Edinburgh West*	Lib Dem
GRAHAM, Thomas	*West Renfrewshire*	Scot Lab
GRANT, Bernard Alexander Montgomery (Bernie)	*Tottenham*	Lab
GRAY, James Whiteside	*North Wiltshire*	Con
GREEN, Damian Howard	*Ashford*	Con
GREENWAY, John Robert	*Ryedale*	Con
GRIEVE, Dominic Charles Roberts	*Beaconsfield*	Con
GRIFFITHS, Jane Patricia	*Reading East*	Lab
GRIFFITHS, Nigel	*Edinburgh South*	Lab
GRIFFITHS, Winston James (Win)	*Bridgend*	Lab
GROCOTT, Bruce Joseph	*Telford*	Lab
GROGAN, John Timothy	*Selby*	Lab
GUMMER, Rt Hon John Selwyn	*Suffolk Coastal*	Con
GUNNELL, William John	*Morley & Rothwell*	Lab
HAGUE, Rt Hon William Jefferson	*Richmond*	Con
HAIN, Peter Gerald	*Neath*	Lab
HALL, Michael Thomas (Mike)	*Weaver Vale*	Lab
HALL, Patrick	*Bedford*	Lab
HAMILTON, Rt Hon Sir Archibald Gavin	*Epsom & Ewell*	Con
HAMILTON, Fabian	*Leeds North East*	Lab
HAMMOND, Philip	*Runnymede & Weybridge*	Con
HANCOCK, Michael Thomas (Mike); CBE	*Portsmouth South*	Lib Dem
HANSON, David George	*Delyn*	Lab
HARMAN, Rt Hon Harriet Ruth	*Camberwell & Peckham*	Lab
HARRIS, Dr Evan	*Oxford West & Abingdon*	Lib Dem
HARVEY, Nicholas Barton (Nick)	*North Devon*	Lib Dem
HASELHURST, Rt Hon Sir Alan G B	*Saffron Walden*	Con
HAWKINS, Nicholas John (Nick)	*Surrey Heath*	Con
HAYES, John Henry	*South Holland & The Deepings*	Con
HEAL, Sylvia Lloyd	*Halesowen & Rowley Regis*	Lab
HEALD, Oliver	*North East Hertfordshire*	Con
HEALEY, John	*Wentworth*	Lab
HEATH, David William St John	*Somerton & Frome*	Lib Dem
HEATH, Rt Hon Sir Edward R G; KG MBE	*Old Bexley & Sidcup*	Con
HEATHCOAT-AMORY, Rt Hon David Philip	*Wells*	Con

HENDERSON, Douglas John (Doug)	*Newcastle-upon-Tyne North*	Lab
HENDERSON, Ivan John	*Harwich*	Lab
HEPBURN, Stephen	*Jarrow*	Lab
HEPPELL, John	*Nottingham East*	Lab
HESELTINE, Rt Hon Michael Ray Dibdin; CH	*Henley*	Con
HESFORD, Stephen	*Wirral West*	Lab
HEWITT, Patricia Hope	*Leicester West*	Lab
HILL, Trevor Keith	*Streatham*	Lab
HINCHLIFFE, David Martin	*Wakefield*	Lab
HODGE, Margaret Eve; MBE	*Barking*	Lab
HOEY, Katherine Letitia (Kate)	*Vauxhall*	Lab
HOGG, Rt Hon Douglas Martin; QC	*Sleaford & North Hykeham*	Con
HOME ROBERTSON, John David; MSP	*East Lothian*	Lab
HOOD, James (Jimmy)	*Clydesdale*	Lab
HOON, Geoffrey William (Geoff)	*Ashfield*	Lab
HOPE, Philip Ian	*Corby*	Lab
HOPKINS, Kelvin Peter	*Luton North*	Lab
HORAM, John Rhodes	*Orpington*	Con
HOWARD, Rt Hon Michael; QC	*Folkestone & Hythe*	Con
HOWARTH, Alan Thomas; CBE	*Newport East*	Lab
HOWARTH, George Edward	*Knowsley North & Sefton East*	Lab
HOWARTH, James Gerald Douglas	*Aldershot*	Con
HOWELLS, Dr Kim Scott	*Pontypridd*	Lab
HOYLE, Lindsay Harvey	*Chorley*	Lab
HUGHES, Beverley June	*Stretford & Urmston*	Lab
HUGHES, Kevin Michael	*Doncaster North*	Lab
HUGHES, Simon Henry Ward	*Southwark North & Bermondsey*	Lib Dem
HUMBLE, Jovanka (Joan)	*Blackpool North & Fleetwood*	Lab
HUME, John	*Foyle*	SDLP
HUNTER, Andrew Robert Frederick	*Basingstoke*	Con
HURST, Alan Arthur	*Braintree*	Lab
HUTTON, John Matthew Patrick	*Barrow & Furness*	Lab
IDDON, Brian	*Bolton South East*	Lab
ILLSLEY, Eric Evelyn	*Barnsley Central*	Lab
INGRAM, Rt Hon Adam Paterson	*East Kilbride*	Lab
JACK, Rt Hon John Michael	*Fylde*	Con
JACKSON, Glenda May; CBE	*Hampstead & Highgate*	Lab
JACKSON, Helen Margaret	*Sheffield Hillsborough*	Lab
JACKSON, Robert Victor	*Wantage*	Con

JAMIESON, David Charles	*Plymouth Devonport*	Lab
JENKIN, Hon Bernard Christison	*North Essex*	Con
JENKINS, Brian David	*Tamworth*	Lab
JOHNSON, Alan Arthur	*Hull West & Hessle*	Lab
JOHNSON, Melanie Jane	*Welwyn Hatfield*	Lab
JOHNSON SMITH, Rt Hon Sir Geoffrey; DL	*Wealden*	Con
JONES, Fiona Elizabeth Ann	*Newark*	Lab
JONES, Helen Mary	*Warrington North*	Lab
JONES, Ieuan Wyn; AM	*Ynys Môn*	PC
JONES, Jennifer Grace (Jenny)	*Wolverhampton South West*	Lab
JONES, Jon Owen	*Cardiff Central*	Lab
JONES, Dr Lynne Mary	*Birmingham Selly Oak*	Lab
JONES, Martyn David	*Clwyd South*	Lab
JONES, Nigel David	*Cheltenham*	Lib Dem
JONES, Rt Hon Stephen Barry	*Alyn & Deeside*	Lab
JOWELL, Rt Hon Tessa J H D	*Dulwich & West Norwood*	Lab
KAUFMAN, Rt Hon Gerald Bernard	*Manchester Gorton*	Lab
KEEBLE, Sally Curtis	*Northampton North*	Lab
KEEN, Ann Lloyd	*Brentford & Isleworth*	Lab
KEEN, David Alan	*Feltham & Heston*	Lab
KEETCH, Paul Stuart	*Hereford*	Lib Dem
KELLY, Ruth Maria	*Bolton West*	Lab
KEMP, Fraser	*Houghton & Washington East*	Lab
KENNEDY, Charles Peter	*Ross, Skye & Inverness West*	Lib Dem
KENNEDY, Jane Elizabeth	*Liverpool Wavertree*	Lab
KEY, Simon Robert	*Salisbury*	Con
KHABRA, Piara Singh	*Ealing Southall*	Lab
KIDNEY, David Neil	*Stafford*	Lab
KILFOYLE, Peter	*Liverpool Walton*	Lab
KING, Andrew (Andy)	*Rugby & Kenilworth*	Lab
KING, Oona Tamsyn	*Bethnal Green & Bow*	Lab
KING, Rt Hon Thomas Jeremy (Tom); CH	*Bridgwater*	Con
KINGHAM, Teresa Jane (Tess)	*Gloucester*	Lab
KIRKBRIDE, Julie	*Bromsgrove*	Con
KIRKWOOD, Archy J	*Roxburgh & Berwickshire*	Lib Dem
KUMAR, Ashok	*Middlesbrough South & East Cleveland*	Lab
LADYMAN, Stephen John	*Thanet South*	Lab
LAING, Eleanor Fulton	*Epping Forest*	Con
LAIT, Jacqueline Anne Harkness (Jacqui)	*Beckenham*	Con

LANSLEY, Andrew David	*South Cambridgeshire*	Con
LAWRENCE, Jacqueline Rita (Jackie)	*Preseli Pembrokeshire*	Lab
LAXTON, Robert (Bob)	*Derby North*	Lab
LEIGH, Edward Julian Egerton	*Gainsborough*	Con
LEPPER, David	*Brighton Pavilion*	Lab
LESLIE, Christopher Michael	*Shipley*	Lab
LETWIN, Oliver	*West Dorset*	Con
LEVITT, Thomas (Tom)	*High Peak*	Lab
LEWIS, Ivan	*Bury South*	Lab
LEWIS, Dr Julian Murray	*New Forest East*	Con
LEWIS, Terence (Terry)	*Worsley*	Lab
LIDDELL, Rt Hon Helen Lawrie	*Airdrie & Shotts*	Lab
LIDINGTON, David Roy	*Aylesbury*	Con
LILLEY, Rt Hon Peter Bruce	*Hitchin & Harpenden*	Con
LINTON, John Martin	*Battersea*	Lab
LIVINGSTONE, Kenneth Robert (Ken)	*Brent East*	Lab
LIVSEY, Richard Arthur Lloyd	*Brecon & Radnorshire*	Lib Dem
LLOYD, Anthony Joseph (Tony)	*Manchester Central*	Lab
LLOYD, Rt Hon Sir Peter Robert Cable	*Fareham*	Con
LLWYD, Elfyn	*Meirionnydd Nant Conwy*	PC
LOCK, David Anthony	*Wyre Forest*	Lab
LORD, Michael Nicholson	*Central Suffolk & Ipswich North*	Con
LOUGHTON, Timothy Paul (Tim)	*Worthing East & Shoreham*	Con
LOVE, Andrew (Andy)	*Edmonton*	Lab
LUFF, Peter James	*Mid Worcestershire*	Con
LYELL, Rt Hon Sir Nicholas Walter; QC	*North East Bedfordshire*	Con
McALLION, John; MSP	*Dundee East*	Lab
McAVOY, Thomas McLaughlin	*Glasgow Rutherglen*	Lab
McCABE, Stephen James	*Birmingham Hall Green*	Lab
McCAFFERTY, Christine	*Calder Valley*	Lab
McCARTNEY, Rt Hon Ian	*Makerfield*	Lab
McCARTNEY, Robert Law; QC	*North Down*	UK Un'ist
McDONAGH, Siobhain Ann	*Mitcham & Morden*	Lab
MACDONALD, Calum Alasdair	*Western Isles*	Lab
McDONNELL, John Martin	*Hayes & Harlington*	Lab
McFALL, John	*Dumbarton*	Lab
McGRADY, Edward Kevin (Eddie)	*South Down*	SDLP
MacGREGOR, Rt Hon John Roddick Russell; OBE	*South Norfolk*	Con
McGUINNESS, Martin	*Mid Ulster*	SF

McGUIRE, Anne	*Stirling*	Lab
McINTOSH, Anne Caroline Ballingall	*Vale of York*	Con
McISAAC, Shona	*Cleethorpes*	Lab
MACKAY, Rt Hon Andrew James	*Bracknell*	Con
McKENNA, Rosemary	*Cumbernauld & Kilsyth*	Lab
MACKINLAY, Andrew Stuart	*Thurrock*	Lab
MACLEAN, Rt Hon David John	*Penrith & The Border*	Con
McLEISH, Henry Baird; MSP	*Fife Central*	Lab
MACLENNAN, Rt Hon Robert	*Caithness, Sutherland & Easter Ross*	Lib Dem
McLOUGHLIN, Patrick Allen	*West Derbyshire*	Con
McNAMARA, Joseph Kevin	*Hull North*	Lab
McNULTY, Anthony James (Tony)	*Harrow East*	Lab
MacSHANE, Denis	*Rotherham*	Lab
MACTAGGART, Fiona Margaret	*Slough*	Lab
McWALTER, Anthony (Tony)	*Hemel Hempstead*	Lab
McWILLIAM, John David	*Blaydon*	Lab
MADEL, Sir William David	*South West Bedfordshire*	Con
MAGINNIS, Kenneth (Ken)	*Fermanagh & South Tyrone*	UU
MAHON, Alice	*Halifax*	Lab
MAJOR, Rt Hon John; CH	*Huntingdon*	Con
MALINS, Humfrey Jonathon	*Woking*	Con
MALLABER, Clare Judith (Judy)	*Amber Valley*	Lab
MALLON, Seamus	*Newry & Armagh*	SDLP
MANDELSON, Rt Hon Peter Benjamin	*Hartlepool*	Lab
MAPLES, John Cradock	*Stratford-on-Avon*	Con
MAREK, Dr John; AM	*Wrexham*	Lab
MARSDEN, Gordon	*Blackpool South*	Lab
MARSDEN, Paul William Barry	*Shrewsbury & Atcham*	Lab
MARSHALL, David	*Glasgow Shettleston*	Lab
MARSHALL, James (Jim)	*Leicester South*	Lab
MARSHALL-ANDREWS, Robert Graham	*Medway*	Lab
MARTIN, Michael John	*Glasgow Springburn*	Lab
MARTLEW, Eric Anthony	*Carlisle*	Lab
MATES, Michael John	*East Hampshire*	Con
MAUDE, Rt Hon Francis Anthony Aylmer	*Horsham*	Con
MAWHINNEY, Rt Hon Dr Sir Brian S	*North West Cambridgeshire*	Con
MAXTON, John Alston	*Glasgow Cathcart*	Lab
MAY, Theresa Mary	*Maidenhead*	Con
MEACHER, Rt Hon Michael Hugh	*Oldham West & Royton*	Lab

MEALE, Joseph Alan	*Mansfield*	Lab
MERRON, Gillian Joanna	*Lincoln*	Lab
MICHAEL, Rt Hon Alun Edward; AM	*Cardiff South & Penarth*	Lab
MICHIE, Janet Ray	*Argyll & Bute*	Lib Dem
MICHIE, William (Bill)	*Sheffield Heeley*	Lab
MILBURN, Rt Hon Alan	*Darlington*	Lab
MILLER, Andrew Peter	*Ellesmere Port & Neston*	Lab
MITCHELL, Austin Vernon	*Great Grimsby*	Lab
MOFFAT, Laura Jean	*Crawley*	Lab
MOONIE, Dr Lewis George	*Kirkcaldy*	Lab
MOORE, Michael Kevin	*Tweeddale, Ettrick & Lauderdale*	Lib Dem
MORAN, Margaret	*Luton South*	Lab
MORGAN, Alasdair Neil; MSP	*Galloway & Upper Nithsdale*	SNP
MORGAN, Julie	*Cardiff North*	Lab
MORGAN, Hywel Rhodri; AM	*Cardiff West*	Lab
MORLEY, Elliot Anthony	*Scunthorpe*	Lab
MORRIS, Estelle	*Birmingham Yardley*	Lab
MORRIS, Rt Hon John; QC	*Aberavon*	Lab
MOSS, Malcolm Douglas	*North East Cambridgeshire*	Con
MOUNTFORD, Kali Carol Jean	*Colne Valley*	Lab
MOWLAM, Rt Hon Dr Marjorie (Mo)	*Redcar*	Lab
MUDIE, George Edward	*Leeds East*	Lab
MULLIN, Christopher John (Chris)	*Sunderland South*	Lab
MURPHY, Denis	*Wansbeck*	Lab
MURPHY, James (Jim)	*Eastwood*	Lab
MURPHY, Rt Hon Paul Peter	*Torfaen*	Lab
NAYSMITH, Dr John Douglas (Doug)	*Bristol North West*	Lab
NICHOLLS, Patrick Charles Martyn	*Teignbridge*	Con
NORMAN, Archibald John (Archie)	*Tunbridge Wells*	Con
NORRIS, Dan	*Wansdyke*	Lab
OATEN, Mark	*Winchester*	Lib Dem
O'BRIEN, Michael (Mike)	*North Warwickshire*	Lab
O'BRIEN, William (Bill)	*Normanton*	Lab
O'HARA, Edward (Eddie)	*Knowsley South*	Lab
OLNER, William John (Bill)	*Nuneaton*	Lab
O'NEILL, Martin John	*Ochil*	Lab
ÖPIK, Lembit	*Montgomeryshire*	Lib Dem
ORGAN, Diana Mary	*Forest of Dean*	Lab
OSBORNE, Sandra Currie	*Ayr*	Lab

OTTAWAY, Richard Geoffrey James	*Croydon South*	Con
PAGE, Richard Lewis	*South West Hertfordshire*	Con
PAICE, James Edward Thornton (Jim)	*South East Cambridgeshire*	Con
PAISLEY, Rev Ian Richard Kyle	*Antrim North*	DUP
PALMER, Nicholas Douglas	*Broxtowe*	Lab
PATERSON, Owen William	*North Shropshire*	Con
PEARSON, Ian Phares	*Dudley South*	Lab
PENDRY, Thomas (Tom)	*Stalybridge & Hyde*	Lab
PERHAM, Linda	*Ilford North*	Lab
PICKLES, Eric Jack	*Brentwood & Ongar*	Con
PICKTHALL, Colin	*West Lancashire*	Lab
PIKE, Peter Leslie	*Burnley*	Lab
PLASKITT, James Andrew	*Warwick & Leamington*	Lab
POLLARD, Kerry Patrick	*St Albans*	Lab
POND, Christopher Richard (Chris)	*Gravesham*	Lab
POPE, Gregory James (Greg)	*Hyndburn*	Lab
POUND, Stephen Pelham	*Ealing North*	Lab
POWELL, Sir Raymond (Ray)	*Ogmore*	Lab
PRENTICE, Bridget Theresa	*Lewisham East*	Lab
PRENTICE, Gordon	*Pendle*	Lab
PRESCOTT, Rt Hon John Leslie	*Hull East*	Lab
PRIMAROLO, Dawn	*Bristol South*	Lab
PRIOR, Hon David Gifford Leathes	*North Norfolk*	Con
PROSSER, Gwynfor Mathews (Gwyn)	*Dover*	Lab
PURCHASE, Kenneth (Ken)	*Wolverhampton North East*	Lab
QUIN, Rt Hon Joyce Gwendolen	*Gateshead East & Washington West*	Lab
QUINN, Lawrence William (Lawrie)	*Scarborough & Whitby*	Lab
RADICE, Rt Hon Giles Heneage	*North Durham*	Lab
RAMMELL, William Ernest (Bill)	*Harlow*	Lab
RANDALL, Alexander John	*Uxbridge*	Con
RAPSON, Sydney Norman John (Syd)	*Portsmouth North*	Lab
RAYNSFORD, Wyvill Richard Nicolls (Nick)	*Greenwich & Woolwich*	Lab
REDWOOD, Rt Hon John Alan	*Wokingham*	Con
REED, Andrew John	*Loughborough*	Lab
REID, Rt Hon Dr John	*Hamilton North & Bellshill*	Lab
RENDEL, David Digby	*Newbury*	Lib Dem
ROBATHAN, Andrew Robert George	*Blaby*	Con
ROBERTSON, Rt Hon George Islay Macneill	*Hamilton South*	Lab
ROBERTSON, Laurence Anthony	*Tewkesbury*	Con

ROBINSON, Geoffrey	*Coventry North West*	Lab
ROBINSON, Peter David	*Belfast East*	DUP
ROCHE, Barbara Maureen	*Hornsey & Wood Green*	Lab
ROE, Marion Audrey	*Broxbourne*	Con
ROGERS, Allan Ralph	*Rhondda*	Lab
ROOKER, Jeffrey William (Jeff)	*Birmingham Perry Barr*	Lab
ROONEY, Terence Henry (Terry)	*Bradford North*	Lab
ROSS, Ernest (Ernie)	*Dundee West*	Lab
ROSS, William	*Londonderry East*	UU
ROWE, Andrew John Bernard	*Faversham & Mid Kent*	Con
ROWLANDS, Edward (Ted)	*Merthyr Tydfil & Rhymney*	Lab
ROY, Frank	*Motherwell & Wishaw*	Lab
RUANE, Christopher Shaun (Chris)	*Vale of Clwyd*	Lab
RUDDOCK, Joan Mary	*Lewisham Deptford*	Lab
RUFFLEY, David Laurie	*Bury St Edmunds*	Con
RUSSELL, Christine Margaret	*City of Chester*	Lab
RUSSELL, Robert Edward (Bob)	*Colchester*	Lib Dem
RYAN, Joan Marie	*Enfield North*	Lab
ST AUBYN, Nicholas Francis (Nick)	*Guildford*	Con
SALMOND, Alex(ander) Elliott Anderson; MSP	*Banff & Buchan*	SNP
SALTER, Martin John	*Reading West*	Lab
SANDERS, Adrian	*Torbay*	Lib Dem
SARWAR, Mohammad	*Glasgow Govan*	Lab
SAVIDGE, Malcolm Kemp	*Aberdeen North*	Lab
SAWFORD, Philip Andrew	*Kettering*	Lab
SAYEED, Jonathan	*Mid Bedfordshire*	Con
SEDGEMORE, Brian Charles John	*Hackney South & Shoreditch*	Lab
SHAW, Jonathan Rowland	*Chatham & Aylesford*	Lab
SHEERMAN, Barry John	*Huddersfield*	Lab
SHELDON, Rt Hon Robert Edward	*Ashton-under-Lyne*	Lab
SHEPHARD, Rt Hon Gillian Patricia	*South West Norfolk*	Con
SHEPHERD, Richard Charles Scrimgeour	*Aldridge-Brownhills*	Con
SHIPLEY, Debra Ann	*Stourbridge*	Lab
SHORT, Rt Hon Clare	*Birmingham Ladywood*	Lab
SIMPSON, Alan John	*Nottingham South*	Lab
SIMPSON, Keith Robert	*Mid Norfolk*	Con
SINGH, Marsha	*Bradford West*	Lab
SKINNER, Dennis Edward	*Bolsover*	Lab
SMITH, Rt Hon Andrew David	*Oxford East*	Lab

SMITH, Angela Evans	*Basildon*	Lab
SMITH, Rt Hon Chris R	*Islington South & Finsbury*	Lab
SMITH, Geraldine	*Morecambe & Lunesdale*	Lab
SMITH, Jacqueline Jill (Jacqui)	*Redditch*	Lab
SMITH, John William Patrick	*Vale of Glamorgan*	Lab
SMITH, Llewellyn Thomas (Llew)	*Blaenau Gwent*	Lab
SMITH, Sir Robert Hill; Bt	*West Aberdeenshire & Kincardine*	Lib Dem
SMYTH, Rev William Martin	*Belfast South*	UU
SNAPE, Peter Charles	*West Bromwich East*	Lab
SOAMES, Hon Arthur Nicholas Winston	*Mid Sussex*	Con
SOLEY, Clive Stafford	*Ealing, Acton & Shepherd's Bush*	Lab
SOUTHWORTH, Helen Mary	*Warrington South*	Lab
SPELLAR, John Francis	*Warley*	Lab
SPELMAN, Caroline Alice	*Meriden*	Con
SPICER, Sir William Michael Hardy	*West Worcestershire*	Con
SPRING, Richard John Grenville	*West Suffolk*	Con
SQUIRE, Rachel Anne	*Dunfermline West*	Lab
STANLEY, Rt Hon Sir John Paul	*Tonbridge & Malling*	Con
STARKEY, Phyllis Margaret	*Milton Keynes South West*	Lab
STEEN, Anthony David	*Totnes*	Con
STEINBERG, Gerald Neil (Gerry)	*City of Durham*	Lab
STEVENSON, George William	*Stoke-on-Trent South*	Lab
STEWART, David John	*Inverness East, Nairn & Lochaber*	Lab
STEWART, Ian	*Eccles*	Lab
STINCHCOMBE, Paul David	*Wellingborough*	Lab
STOATE, Howard Geoffrey Alvin	*Dartford*	Lab
STOTT, Roger; CBE	*Wigan*	Lab
STRANG, Rt Hon Dr Gavin Steel	*Edinburgh East & Musselburgh*	Lab
STRAW, Rt Hon John Whitaker (Jack)	*Blackburn*	Lab
STREETER, Gary Nicholas	*South West Devon*	Con
STRINGER, Graham Eric	*Manchester Blackley*	Lab
STUART, Gisela Gschaider	*Birmingham Edgbaston*	Lab
STUNELL, Andrew	*Hazel Grove*	Lib Dem
SUTCLIFFE, Gerald (Gerry)	*Bradford South*	Lab
SWAYNE, Desmond Angus	*New Forest West*	Con
SWINNEY, John Ramsay; MSP	*Tayside North*	SNP
SYMS, Robert Andrew Raymond	*Poole*	Con
TAPSELL, Sir Peter Hannay Bailey	*Louth & Horncastle*	Con
TAYLOR, Dari Jean	*Stockton South*	Lab

TAYLOR, David Leslie	*North West Leicestershire*	Lab
TAYLOR, Sir Edward M (Teddy)	*Rochford & Southend East*	Con
TAYLOR, Ian Colin; MBE	*Esher & Walton*	Con
TAYLOR, Rt Hon John David	*Strangford*	UU
TAYLOR, John Mark	*Solihull*	Con
TAYLOR, Matthew Owen John	*Truro & St Austell*	Lib Dem
TAYLOR, Rt Hon Winifred Ann	*Dewsbury*	Lab
TEMPLE-MORRIS, Peter	*Leominster*	Lab
THOMAS, Gareth	*Clwyd West*	Lab
THOMAS, Gareth Richard	*Harrow West*	Lab
THOMPSON, William John	*West Tyrone*	UU
TIMMS, Stephen Cresswell	*East Ham*	Lab
TIPPING, Simon Patrick (Paddy)	*Sherwood*	Lab
TODD, Mark Wainwright	*South Derbyshire*	Lab
TONGE, Dr Jennifer Louise (Jenny)	*Richmond Park*	Lib Dem
TOUHIG, James Donnelly (Don)	*Islwyn*	Lab
TOWNEND, John Ernest	*East Yorkshire*	Con
TREDINNICK, David Arthur Stephen	*Bosworth*	Con
TREND, Hon Michael St.John; CBE	*Windsor*	Con
TRICKETT, Jon Hedley	*Hemsworth*	Lab
TRIMBLE, Rt Hon William David	*Upper Bann*	UU
TRUSWELL, Paul Anthony	*Pudsey*	Lab
TURNER, Dennis	*Wolverhampton South East*	Lab
TURNER, Desmond Stanley	*Brighton Kemptown*	Lab
TURNER, George	*North West Norfolk*	Lab
TWIGG, John Derek	*Halton*	Lab
TWIGG, Stephen	*Enfield Southgate*	Lab
TYLER, Paul Archer; CBE	*North Cornwall*	Lib Dem
TYRIE, Andrew Guy	*Chichester*	Con
VAZ, Nigel Keith Anthony Standish	*Leicester East*	Lab
VIGGERS, Peter John	*Gosport*	Con
VIS, Rudolf Jan (Rudi)	*Finchley & Golders Green*	Lab
WALKER, Alfred Cecil	*Belfast North*	UU
WALLACE, James Robert (Jim); MSP QC	*Orkney & Shetland*	Lib Dem
WALLEY, Joan Lorraine	*Stoke-on-Trent North*	Lab
WALTER, Robert John	*North Dorset*	Con
WARD, Claire Margaret	*Watford*	Lab
WARDLE, Charles Frederick	*Bexhill & Battle*	Con
WAREING, Robert Nelson (Bob)	*Liverpool West Derby*	Lab

WATERSON, Nigel Christopher	*Eastbourne*	Con
WATTS, David Leonard	*St Helens North*	Lab
WEBB, Steven John (Steve)	*Northavon*	Lib Dem
WELLS, Bowen	*Hertford & Stortford*	Con
WELSH, Andrew Paton; MSP	*Angus*	SNP
WHITE, Brian Arthur Robert	*Milton Keynes North East*	Lab
WHITEHEAD, Alan Patrick Vincent	*Southampton Test*	Lab
WHITNEY, Sir Raymond William (Ray); OBE	*Wycombe*	Con
WHITTINGDALE, John F L; OBE	*Maldon & Chelmsford East*	Con
WICKS, Malcolm Hunt	*Croydon North*	Lab
WIDDECOMBE, Rt Hon Ann Noreen	*Maidstone & The Weald*	Con
WIGLEY, Rt Hon Dafydd; AM	*Caernarfon*	PC
WILKINSON, John Arbuthnot Ducane	*Ruislip-Northwood*	Con
WILLETTS, David Lindsay	*Havant*	Con
WILLIAMS, Rt Hon Alan John	*Swansea West*	Lab
WILLIAMS, Dr Alan Wynne	*Carmarthen East & Dinefwr*	Lab
WILLIAMS, Betty Helena	*Conwy*	Lab
WILLIS, George Philip (Phil)	*Harrogate & Knaresborough*	Lib Dem
WILLS, Michael David	*Swindon North*	Lab
WILSHIRE, David	*Spelthorne*	Con
WILSON, Brian David Henderson	*Cunninghame North*	Lab
WINNICK, David Julian	*Walsall North*	Lab
WINTERTON, Jane Ann	*Congleton*	Con
WINTERTON, Nicholas Raymond	*Macclesfield*	Con
WINTERTON, Rosalie (Rosie)	*Doncaster Central*	Lab
WISE, Audrey	*Preston*	Lab
WOOD, Michael Roy (Mike)	*Batley & Spen*	Lab
WOODWARD, Shaun Anthony	*Witney*	Con
WOOLAS, Philip James (Phil)	*Oldham East & Saddleworth*	Lab
WORTHINGTON, Anthony (Tony)	*Clydebank & Milngavie*	Lab
WRAY, James	*Glasgow Baillieston*	Lab
WRIGHT, Anthony David (Tony)	*Great Yarmouth*	Lab
WRIGHT, Dr Anthony Wayland (Tony)	*Cannock Chase*	Lab
WYATT, Derek Murray	*Sittingbourne & Sheppey*	Lab
YEO, Timothy Stephen Kenneth (Tim)	*South Suffolk*	Con
YOUNG, Rt Hon Sir George S K; Bt	*North West Hampshire*	Con

SENIOR OFFICERS AND STAFF
OF THE HOUSE OF LORDS

Lord Chancellor	*The Rt Hon Lord Irvine of Lairg QC*
Chairman of Committees	*The Lord Boston of Faversham QC*
Principal Deputy Chairman of Committees	*The Lord Tordoff*
Clerk of the Parliaments	*J M Davies*
Clerk Assistant and Clerk of Legislation	*P D G Hayter LVO*
Reading Clerk and Principal Finance Officer	*M G Pownall*
Internal Auditor	*C H Rogers*
Staff Adviser	*D A W Dunn*
Accountant	*C Preece*

Gentleman Usher of the Black Rod & Serjeant-at-Arms
General Sir Edward Jones KCB CBE

Yeoman Usher of the Black Rod & Deputy Serjeant-at-Arms
Air Vice-Marshal D R Hawkins-Leth CB MBE DL

Administration Officer	*Brigadier A J McD Clark*
Staff Superintendent	*Major A M Charlesworth*
Senior Information Officer	*Miss M Morgan*
Establishment Office	*R H Walters, G Embleton*
Hansard Editor	*Mrs M E Villiers*
Deputy Hansard Editor	*G R Goodbarne*
Librarian	*D L Jones*
Deputy Librarian	*Dr P G Davies*
Overseas Office	*D R Beamish*
Clerk of Private Bills	*Miss F P Tudor*
Clerk of Public Bills	*E C Ollard*
Establishment Officer	*R H Walters*
Registrar of Lords' Interests	*J A Vallance White CB*

****

ROYAL COMMISSION on the REFORM of the HOUSE of LORDS
4 Central Buildings, Matthew Parker Street, London SW1H 9NL
Tel: 0171 210 0450 Fax: 0171 210 0451.
Members: Rt Hon Lord Wakeham DL (Chair), Rt Hon Gerald Kaufman MP, Rt Hon Baroness Dean of Thornton-le-Fylde, Rt Hon Lord Hurd of Westwell CH CBE, Lord Butler of Brockwell GCB CVO; Rt Rev Lord Bishop of Oxford, Sir Michael Wheeler-Booth KCB, Professor Anthony King, Bill Morris, Professor Dawn Oliver, Kenneth Munro, Ann Benyon.

ALPHABETICAL LIST OF PEERS

ABERCONWAY, Lord	H	Con
ABERCORN, Duke of; KG	H	Con
ABERDARE, Lord; PC KBE DL	H	Con
ABERDEEN and TEMAIR, Marquess of	H	C/B
ABERGAVENNY, Marquess of; KG OBE	H	C/B
ABINGER, Lord	H	Con
ACKNER, Lord; PC	Law	C/B
ACTON, Lord	H	C/B
ADDINGTON, Lord	H	Lib Dem
ADDISON, Viscount	H	Con
AHMED, Lord	L	Lab
AILESBURY, Marquess of	H	C/B
AILSA, Marquess of	H	Con
AIRLIE, Earl; Kt PC GCVO	H	C/B
ALANBROOKE, Viscount	H	C/B
ALBEMARLE, Earl of	H	C/B
ALDENHAM, Lord	H	Con
ALDERDICE, Lord	L	Lib Dem
ALDINGTON, Lord; PC KCMG CBE DSO TD DL	H	Con
ALEXANDER of Tunis, Earl	H	Con
ALEXANDER of Weedon, Lord; QC	L	Con
ALLEN of Abbeydale, Lord; GCB	L	C/B
ALLENBY of Megiddo, Lt-Col the Viscount	H	C/B
ALLENDALE, Viscount; DL	H	(Con)
ALLI, Lord	L	Lab
ALPORT, Lord; PC TD DL	L	Ind Con
ALTON of Liverpool, Lord	L	C/B
ALVINGHAM, Major General the Lord; CBE	H	(Ind)
AMHERST of Hackney, Lord	H	C/B
AMOS, Baroness	L	Lab
AMPTHILL, Lord; CBE	H	C/B
AMWELL, Lord	H	C/B
ANELAY of St Johns, Baroness; DBE	L	Con
ANGLESEY, Marquess of	H	(Ind)
ANNALY, Lord	H	Con
ANNAN, Lord; OBE	L	C/B
ANNANDALE and HARTFELL, Earl of	H	Con
ARBUTHNOTT, Viscount of; KT CBE DSC	H	C/B
ARCHER of Sandwell, Lord; PC QC	L	Lab
ARCHER of Weston-super-Mare, Lord	L	Con
ARGYLL, Duke of; VL	H	Con
ARLINGTON, Baroness	H	C/B

ARMSTRONG of Ilminster, Lord; GCB CVO	L	C/B
ARRAN, Earl of	H	Con
ASHBOURNE, Lt-Cmdr Lord	H	Con
ASHBURTON, Lord	H	C/B
ASHCOMBE, Lord	H	Ind
ASHLEY of Stoke, Lord; PC CH	L	Lab
ASHTON of Hyde, Lord; TD	H	C/B
ASTOR, Viscount	H	Con
ASTOR of Hever, Lord	H	Con
ATHOLL, Duke of	H	(Ind)
ATTENBOROUGH, Lord; Kt CBE	L	Lab
ATTLEE, Earl	H	Con
AUCKLAND, Lord	H	(Ind)
AVEBURY, Lord	H	Lib Dem
AYLESFORD, Earl of	H	(Con)
BACH, Lord	L	Lab
BADEN-POWELL, Lord	H	(Ind)
BAGOT, Lord	H	Ind
BAGRI, Lord; CBE	L	C/B
BAILLIEU, Lord	H	(Ind)
BAKER of Dorking, Lord; PC CH	L	Con
BALDWIN of Bewdley, Earl	H	C/B
BALFOUR, Earl of	H	Con
BALFOUR of Burleigh, Lord	H	C/B
BALFOUR of Inchrye, Lord	H	C/B
BANBURY of Southam, Lord	H	Con
BARBER, Lord; PC TD DL	L	Con
BARBER of Tewkesbury, Lord; Kt	L	C/B
BARNARD, Lord; TD	H	C/B
BARNETT, Lord; PC JP	L	Lab
BASING, Lord	H	(Ind)
BASSAM of Brighton, Lord	L	Lab
BATH, Marquess of	H	Lib Dem
BATH & WELLS, Bishop of	Bp	Ind
BATHURST, Earl; DL	H	Con
BAUER, Lord	L	Con
BEARSTED, Viscount	H	Con
BEATTY, Earl	H	(Ind)
BEAUFORT, Col the Duke of	H	Con
BEAUMONT of Whitley, Lord	L	Lib Dem
BEAVERBROOK, Lord	H	Ind
BEDFORD, Duke of	H	(Ind)
BELHAVEN and STENTON, Lord	H	Con

BELL, Lord; Kt	*L*	Con
BELLWIN, Lord; DL	*L*	Con
BELPER, Lord	*H*	(Ind)
BELSTEAD, Lord; PC DL	*H*	Con
BERKELEY, Lord	*H*	Lab
BERNERS, Baroness	*H*	Ind
BESSBOROUGH, Earl	*H*	(Ind)
BETHELL, Lord; MEP	*H*	Con
BICESTER, Lord	*H*	(Ind)
BIDDULPH, Lord	*H*	Con
BIFFEN, Lord; PC	*L*	Con
BINGHAM of Cornhill, Lord	*Law*	C/B
BIRDWOOD, Lord	*H*	Con
BIRKETT, Lord	*H*	C/B
BIRMINGHAM, Bishop of	*Bp*	Ind
BLACKBURN, Bishop of	*Bp*	Ind
BLACKSTONE, Baroness	*L*	Lab
BLACKWELL, Lord	*L*	Con
BLAKE, Lord	*L*	Con
BLAKENHAM, Viscount	*H*	Con
BLAKER, Lord; PC KCMG	*L*	Con
BLATCH, Baroness; PC CBE	*L*	Con
BLEASE, Lord	*L*	Lab
BLEDISLOE, Viscount; QC	*H*	C/B
BLYTH, Lord	*H*	C/B
BLYTH of Rowington, Lord	*L*	Con
BOARDMAN, Lord; MC TD DL	*L*	Con
BOLINGBROKE and St JOHN, Viscount	*H*	(Ind)
BOLTON, Lord	*H*	Con
BORRIE, Lord; Kt	*L*	Lab
BORTHWICK, Lord	*H*	Ind
BORWICK, Lord; MC	*H*	(Ind)
BOSTON, Lord	*H*	(Con)
BOSTON of Faversham, Lord; QC	*L*	C/B
BOWNESS, Lord; Kt	*L*	Con
BOYD of Merton, Viscount	*H*	(Ind)
BOYNE, Viscount; DL	*H*	C/B
BRABAZON of Tara, Lord	*H*	Con
BRABOURNE, Lord; CBE	*H*	(C/B)
BRADBURY, Lord	*H*	C/B
BRADFORD, Bishop of	*Bp*	Ind
BRADFORD, Earl of	*H*	Con
BRAGG, Lord	*L*	Lab

BRAIN, Lord	H	C/B
BRAINE of Wheatley, Lord; DL Kt PC	L	Con
BRAMALL, Field Marshal the Lord; GCB OBE MC	L	C/B
BRASSEY of Apethorpe, Lord; DL	H	(Con)
BRAYBROOKE, Lord	H	Con
BRAYE, Baroness	H	(Con)
BRENTFORD, Viscount	H	Con
BRIDGE of Harwich, Lord; Kt PC	Law	C/B
BRIDGEMAN, Viscount	H	Con
BRIDGES, Lord; GCMG	H	C/B
BRIDPORT, Viscount	H	(Ind)
BRIGGS, Lord	L	C/B
BRIGHTMAN, Lord; Kt PC	Law	C/B
BRIGSTOCKE, Baroness	L	Con
BRISTOL, Bishop of	Bp	Ind
BROADBRIDGE, Lord	H	C/B
BROCKET, Lord	H	(Con)
BROOKE and WARWICK, Earl	H	(Ind)
BROOKE of Alverthorpe, Lord	L	Lab
BROOKE of Ystradfellte, Baroness; DBE	L	(Ind)
BROOKEBOROUGH, Viscount; DL	H	Con
BROOKES, Lord	L	C/B
BROOKMAN, Lord	L	Lab
BROOKS of Tremorfa, Lord	L	Lab
BROUGHAM and VAUX, Lord	H	Con
BROUGHSHANE, Lord	H	C/B
BROWNE-WILKINSON, Lord; Kt PC	Law	C/B
BROWNLOW, Lord	H	(Ind)
BRUCE of Donington, Lord	L	Lab
BRUNTISFIELD, Lord; OBE MC	H	Con
BUCCLEUCH and QUEENSBERRY, Duke of; KT	H	Con
BUCHAN, Earl	H	C/B
BUCKINGHAMSHIRE, Earl of	H	Con
BUCKMASTER, Viscount; OBE	H	C/B
BULLOCK, Lord; Kt	L	C/B
BURDEN, Lord	H	(Ind)
BURGH, Lord	H	(Ind)
BURLISON, Lord	L	Lab
BURNHAM, Lord	H	Con
BURNS, Lord; GCB	L	C/B
BURTON, Lord	H	Con
BUSCOMBE, Baroness	L	Con
BUTE, Marquess of; KBE	H	(Ind)

BUTLER of Brockwell, Lord; GCB CVO	L	C/B
BUTTERFIELD, Lord; OBE DM FRCP	L	C/B
BUTTERWORTH, Lord; CBE DL	L	Con
BUXTON of Alsa, Lord; MC DL	L	Con
BYFORD, Baroness; DBE	L	Con
BYRON, Lord	H	Con
CADMAN, Lord	H	Con
CADOGAN, Earl	H	Ind
CAIRNS, the Earl; CBE	H	C/B
CAITHNESS, Earl of; PC ARICS	H	Con
CALDECOTE, Viscount; KBE DSC DL	H	Con
CALLAGHAN of Cardiff, Lord; KG PC	L	Lab
CALVERLEY, Lord	H	(Ind)
CAMDEN, Marquess	H	Con
CAMERON of Lochbroom, Lord; PC QC	Law	C/B
CAMOYS, Lord	H	C/B
CAMPBELL of Alloway, Lord; QC	L	Con
CAMPBELL of Croy, Lord; PC MC DL	L	Con
CANTERBURY, Archbishop of; PC	Bp	Ind
CAREW, Lord	H	C/B
CARLISLE, Bishop of	Bp	Ind
CARLISLE, Earl of	H	Lib Dem
CARLISLE of Bucklow, Lord; PC QC DL	L	Con
CARMICHAEL of Kelvingrove, Lord	L	Lab
CARNARVON, Earl of; KCVO KBE DL	H	C/B
CARNEGY of Lour, Baroness; DL	L	Con
CARNOCK, Major the Lord	H	Con
CARR of Hadley, Lord; PC	L	Con
CARRICK, Earl of	H	Con
CARRINGTON, Lord; KG GCMG CH MC PC	H	Con
CARTER, Lord; PC	L	Lab
CARVER, Field Marshal, Lord; GCB CBE DSO MC	L	C/B
CASTLE of Blackburn, Baroness; PC	L	Lab
CATTO, Lord	H	(Ind)
CAVENDISH of Furness, Lord; DL	L	Con
CAWDOR, Earl of	H	C/B
CAWLEY, Lord	H	Con
CHADLINGTON, Lord	L	Con
CHALFONT, Lord; PC OBE MC	L	C/B
CHALKER of Wallasey, Baroness; PC	L	Con
CHANDOS, Viscount	H	Lab
CHAPPLE, Lord	L	C/B
CHARTERIS of Amisfield, Lord; PC GCB GCVO	H	C/B

CHATFIELD, Lord	H	(Ind)
CHELMSFORD, Viscount	H	Con
CHESHAM, Lord	H	Con
CHETWODE, Lord	H	Ind
CHICHESTER, Bishop of	Bp	Ind
CHICHESTER, Earl of	H	(Con)
CHILSTON, Viscount	H	Con
CHILVER, Lord; Kt FRS	L	Con
CHITNIS, Lord	L	(Ind)
CHOLMONDELEY, Marquess	H	C/B
CHORLEY, Lord	H	C/B
CHRISTOPHER, Lord; CBE	L	Lab
CHURCHILL, Viscount	H	(Ind)
CHURSTON, Lord	H	Con
CLANCARTY, Earl of	H	C/B
CLANWILLIAM, Earl of	H	Con
CLARENDON, Earl of	H	(Ind)
CLARK of Kempston, Lord; Kt PC	L	Con
CLARKE of Hampstead, Lord; CBE	L	Lab
CLEDWYN of Penrhos, Lord; PC CH DL	L	Lab
CLEMENT-JONES, Lord; CBE	L	Lib Dem
CLIFFORD of Chudleigh, Lord	H	C/B
CLINTON, Lord; DL	H	Con
CLINTON-DAVIS, Lord; PC	L	Lab
CLITHEROE, Lord; DL	H	Con
CLWYD, Lord	H	C/B
CLYDE, Lord	Law	C/B
CLYDESMUIR, Lord	H	(Ind)
COBBOLD, Lord	H	Ind
COBHAM, Viscount	H	(Ind)
COCHRANE of Cults, Lord; DL	H	Con
COCKFIELD, Lord; PC Kt	L	Con
COCKS of Hartcliffe, Lord; PC	L	Lab
COGGAN, Rt Rev Lord; PC MA DD	L	C/B
COLERAINE, Lord	H	Con
COLERIDGE, Major the Lord	H	Ind
COLGRAIN, Lord	H	C/B
COLVILLE of Culross, Viscount; QC	H	C/B
COLWYN, Lord; CBE	H	Con
COLYTON, Lord	H	Ind
COMBERMERE, Viscount	H	C/B
CONGLETON, Lord	H	C/B
CONSTANTINE of Stanmore, Lord; CBE TD Kt AE DL	L	Con

CONYNGHAM, Marquess of	H	(Ind)
COOKE of Islandreagh, Lord; OBE DL	L	C/B
COOKE of Thorndon, Lord; KBE	Law	Ind
COPE of Berkeley, Lord; PC Kt	L	Con
CORK and ORRERY, Earl	H	Ind
CORNWALLIS, Lord; OBE DL	H	C/B
COTTENHAM, Earl of	H	C/B
COTTESLOE, Lord	H	C/B
COURTOWN, Earl of	H	Con
COVENTRY, Earl of	H	Con
COWDRAY, Viscount	H	Ind
COWDREY of Tonbridge, Lord; Kt CBE	L	Con
COWLEY, Earl	H	Con
COX, Baroness	L	Con
CRAIG of Radley, Lord; GCB OBE	L	C/B
CRAIGAVON, Viscount	H	C/B
CRAIGMYLE, Lord	H	C/B
CRANBORNE, Viscount (Lord Cecil of Essenden); PC	H	Con
CRANBROOK, Earl of; DL	H	Con
CRANWORTH, Lord	H	Con
CRATHORNE, Lord; DL	H	Con
CRAVEN, Earl of	H	(Ind)
CRAWFORD and BALCARRES, Earl of; KT PC	H	Con
CRAWLEY, Baroness	L	Lab
CRAWSHAW, Lord	H	Ind
CRICKHOWELL, Lord; PC	L	Con
CROHAM, Lord; GCB	L	C/B
CROMARTIE, Earl	H	C/B
CROMER, Earl	H	Con
CROMWELL, Lord	H	C/B
CROOK, Lord	H	C/B
CROSS, Viscount	H	Con
CUCKNEY, Lord	L	Ind
CULLEN of Ashbourne, Lord; MBE	H	Con
CUMBERLEGE, Baroness; CBE	L	Con
CUNLIFFE, Lord	H	C/B
CURRIE of Marylebone, Lord	L	Lab
DACRE, Baroness	H	C/B
DACRE of Glanton, Lord	L	Con
DAHRENDORF, Lord; KBE	L	Lib Dem
DALHOUSIE, Earl of; Kt GCVO GBE MC DL	H	(Ind)
DARCY de KNAYTH, Baroness; DBE	H	C/B
DARESBURY, Lord	H	Con

DARLING, Major the Lord; DL	H	(Ind)
DARNLEY, Earl of	H	Con
DARTMOUTH, Earl of	H	Con
DARWEN, Lord	H	(Ind)
DAVENTRY, Viscount	H	(Con)
DAVID, Baroness	L	Lab
DAVIDSON, Viscount	H	Con
DAVIES, Lord	H	Lib Dem
DAVIES of Coity, Lord; CBE	L	Lab
DAVIES of Oldham, Lord	L	Lab
DEAN of Beswick, Lord	L	Lab
DEAN of Harptree, Lord; Kt PC	L	Con
DEAN of Thornton-le-Fylde, Baroness	L	Lab
DEARING, Lord	L	C/B
DE CLIFFORD, Lord	H	(Ind)
DE L'ISLE, Viscount; MBE	H	Con
DEEDES, Lord; KBE PC MC DL	L	Con
DE FREYNE, Lord	H	Con
DELACOURT-SMITH of Alteryn, Baroness	L	Lab
DELAMERE, Lord	H	(Ind)
DE LA WARR, Earl	H	Con
DE MAULEY, Lord	H	(Ind)
DENBIGH, Earl of	H	Con
DENHAM, Lord; PC KBE	H	Con
DENMAN, Lord	H	Con
DENTON of Wakefield, Baroness; CBE	L	Con
DERAMORE, Lord	H	(Ind)
DE RAMSEY, Lord; KBE TD DL	H	Con
DE ROS, Lord	H	(Ind)
DERBY, Earl of	H	C/B
DERWENT, Lord; LVO DL	H	Con
DESAI, Lord	L	Lab
DE SAUMAREZ, Lord	H	Con
DE VILLIERS, Lord	H	(Ind)
DEVON, Earl	H	Ind
DEVONPORT, Viscount	H	C/B
DEVONSHIRE, Duke of; PC MC	H	C/B
DHOLAKIA, Lord; OBE	L	Lib Dem
DIAMOND, Lord; PC	L	Lab
DICKINSON, Lord	H	C/B
DIGBY, Lord	H	Con
DILHORNE, Viscount	H	Con
DINEVOR, Lord	H	(Ind)

DIXON, Lord; PC DL	*L*	Lab
DIXON-SMITH, Lord; DL	*L*	Con
DONALDSON of Lymington, Lord; Kt PC	*Law*	C/B
DONEGALL, Marquess of; LVO	*H*	Con
DONOUGHMORE, Earl of	*H*	Con
DONOUGHUE, Lord	*L*	Lab
DORMAND of Easington, Lord	*L*	Lab
DORMER, Lord	*H*	(Ind)
DOWDING, Lord	*H*	C/B
DOWNE, Viscount; DL	*H*	Con
DOWNSHIRE, Marquess of	*H*	Ind
DROGHEDA, Earl	*H*	C/B
DUBS, Lord	*L*	Lab
DUCIE, Earl of	*H*	(Ind)
DUDLEY, Earl of	*H*	Con
DUDLEY, Baroness	*H*	(Ind)
DULVERTON, Lord	*H*	Ind
DUNDEE, Earl of	*H*	Con
DUNDONALD, Earl of	*H*	Con
DUNLEATH, Lord	*H*	C/B
DUNMORE, Earl of	*H*	Ind
DUNN, Baroness; DBE	*L*	C/B
DUNROSSIL, Viscount; CMG DL	*H*	C/B
DURHAM, Bishop of	*Bp*	Ind
DYSART, Countess of	*H*	(Ind)
EAMES, Lord	*L*	C/B
EATWELL, Lord	*L*	Lab
EBURY, Lord	*H*	(Ind)
ECCLES, Viscount	*H*	(Ind)
ECCLES of Moulton, Baroness	*L*	Con
EDEN of Winton, Lord; PC	*L*	Con
EDINBURGH, HRH Duke of; KG KT OM GBE PC	*R*	(C/B)
EFFINGHAM, Earl of	*H*	(C/B)
EGLINTON, Earl of	*H*	Ind
EGMONT, Earl of	*H*	(Ind)
ELDON, Earl of	*H*	(C/B)
ELGIN and KINCARDINE, Earl of; KT	*H*	Con
ELIBANK, Lord	*H*	Con
ELIS-THOMAS, Lord; AM	*L*	C/B
ELLENBOROUGH, Lord	*H*	Con
ELLES, Baroness	*L*	Con
ELLIOTT of Morpeth, Lord; DL	*L*	Con
ELPHINSTONE, Lord	*H*	(Ind)

ELTON, Lord; TD	*H*	Con
ELY, Bishop of	*Bp*	Ind
ELY, Marquess of	*H*	Ind
ELYSTAN-MORGAN, Lord	*L*	(Ind)
EMERTON, Baroness; DBE	*L*	C/B
EMSLIE, Lord ; PC MBE	*Law*	C/B
ENNISKILLEN, Earl of; MBE	*H*	C/B
ERNE, Earl of	*H*	Con
ERROLL, Earl of	*H*	C/B
ERROLL of Hale, Lord; PC	*H*	Con
ESHER, Viscount; CBE	*H*	Lib Dem
ESSEX, Earl of	*H*	C/B
EVANS of Parkside, Lord	*L*	Lab
EVANS of Watford, Lord	*L*	Lab
EWING of Kirkford, Lord	*L*	Lab
EXETER, Bishop of	*Bp*	Ind
EXETER, Marquess	*H*	C/B
EXMOUTH, Viscount	*H*	Ind
EZRA, Lord; Kt MBE	*L*	Lib Dem
FAIRFAX of Cameron, Lord	*H*	Con
FAIRHAVEN, Lord	*H*	Con
FALCONER of Thoroton, Lord; QC	*L*	Lab
FALKENDER, Baroness; CBE	*L*	Lab
FALKLAND, Viscount	*H*	Lib Dem
FALMOUTH, Viscount	*H*	Con
FANSHAWE of Richmond, Lord; KCMG	*L*	Con
FARINGDON, Lord	*H*	C/B
FARRINGTON of Ribbleton, Baroness	*L*	Lab
FELDMAN, Lord; Kt	*L*	Con
FERRERS, Earl; PC DL	*H*	Con
FEVERSHAM, Lord	*H*	C/B
FIFE, Duke of	*H*	Ind
FISHER, Lord; DSC	*H*	(Con)
FISHER of Rednal, Baroness	*L*	Lab
FITT, Lord	*L*	Ind Soc
FITZWALTER, Lord	*H*	(Ind)
FLATHER, Baroness	*L*	C/B
FLOWERS, Lord; Kt FRS	*L*	C/B
FOLEY, Lord	*H*	Ind
FOOKES, Baroness; DBE	*L*	Con
FOOT, Lord	*L*	Lib Dem
FORBES, Lord; KBE DL	*H*	Con
FORESTER, Lord	*H*	Con

FORRES, Lord	*H*	(C/B)
FORTE, Lord; Kt	*L*	Con
FORTESCUE, Earl	*H*	Ind
FORTEVIOT, Lord	*H*	Con
FRASER of Carmyllie, Lord; PC QC	*L*	Con
FREEMAN, Lord; PC	*L*	Con
FREYBERG, Lord	*H*	C/B
GAGE, Lord	*H*	C/B
GAINFORD, Lord	*H*	Con
GAINSBOROUGH, Earl of	*H*	C/B
GALLACHER, Lord	*L*	Lab
GALLOWAY, Earl of	*H*	(Con)
GARDNER of Parkes, Baroness	*L*	Con
GAREL-JONES, Lord; PC	*L*	Con
GEDDES, Lord	*H*	Con
GERAINT, Lord	*L*	Lib Dem
GERARD, Lord	*H*	C/B
GIBSON, Lord	*L*	C/B
GIBSON-WATT, Lord; PC MC DL	*L*	Con
GIFFORD, Lord; QC	*H*	Lab
GILBERT, Lord; PC	*L*	Lab
GILMOUR of Craigmillar, Lord; PC Bt	*L*	Con
GISBOROUGH, Col Lord	*H*	Con
GLADWIN of Clee, Lord; CBE	*L*	Lab
GLADWYN, Lord	*H*	C/B
GLANUSK, Lord	*H*	C/B
GLASGOW, Earl of	*H*	Lib Dem
GLENAMARA, Lord; CH PC	*L*	Lab
GLENARTHUR, Lord; DL	*H*	Con
GLENCONNER, Lord	*H*	Lib Dem
GLENDEVON, Lord	*H*	(Ind)
GLENDYNE, Lord	*H*	Con
GLENTORAN, Lord	*H*	Con
GLOUCESTER, Bishop of	*Bp*	C/B
GLOUCESTER, HRH Duke of; GCVO ARIBA KStJ	*H*	C/B
GOFF of Chieveley, Lord; Kt PC	*Law*	C/B
GOODHART, Lord; Kt QC	*L*	Lib Dem
GORDON of Strathblane, Lord; CBE	*L*	Lab
GORELL, Lord	*H*	C/B
GORMANSTON, Viscount	*H*	Con
GOSCHEN, Viscount	*H*	Con
GOSFORD, Earl of	*H*	(C/B)
GOUDIE, Baroness	*L*	Lab

GOUGH, Viscount	H	(C/B)
GOULD of Potternewton, Baroness	L	Lab
GOWRIE, Earl of; PC	H	C/B
GRAFTON, Duke of; KG DL	H	Con
GRAHAM of Edmonton, Lord	L	Lab
GRANARD, Earl of	H	Con
GRANTCHESTER, Lord	H	Lab
GRANTLEY, Lord	H	Ind
GRANVILLE, Earl; MC	H	(Ind)
GRAY, Lord	H	Con
GRAY of Contin, Lord; PC DL	L	Con
GREENE of Harrow Weald, Lord; Kt CBE	L	Lab
GREENHILL, Lord; OBE	H	(C/B)
GREENHILL of Harrow, Lord; GCMG OBE	L	C/B
GREENWAY, Lord	H	C/B
GREENWOOD, Viscount	H	(Ind)
GREGSON, Lord; DL	L	Lab
GRENFELL, Lord	H	Lab
GRETTON, Lord	H	Ind
GREY, Earl	H	Lib Dem
GREY of Codnor, Lord	H	Ind
GREY of Naunton, Lord; GCMG GCVO OBE	L	C/B
GRIDLEY, Lord	H	Ind
GRIFFITHS, Lord; PC MC	Law	C/B
GRIFFITHS of Fforestfach, Lord	L	Con
GRIMSTON of Westbury, Lord	H	Con
GRIMTHORPE, Brigadier the Lord; OBE DL	H	Con
HABGOOD, Lord	L	C/B
HACKING, Lord	H	Lab
HADDINGTON, Earl of	H	Con
HADEN-GUEST, Lord	H	Ind
HAIG, Major the Earl; OBE DL	H	Con
HAILSHAM of St Marylebone, Lord; KG PC CH FRS	L	Con
HALIFAX, Earl of; DL	H	Con
HALSBURY, Earl of; FRS	H	C/B
HAMBLEDEN, Viscount	H	Con
HAMBRO, Lord	L	Con
HAMILTON of Dalzell, Lord	H	Con
HAMILTON and BRANDON, Duke of	H	(C/B)
HAMLYN, Lord	L	Lab
HAMPDEN, Viscount; DL	H	C/B
HAMPTON, Lord	H	Lib Dem
HAMWEE, Baroness	L	Lib Dem

HANKEY, Lord	H	C/B
HANNINGFIELD, Lord	L	Con
HANSON, Lord; Kt	L	Con
HANWORTH, Viscount	H	Lab
HARDIE, Lord: PC QC	L	Lab
HARDING of Petherton, Lord	H	Con
HARDINGE, Viscount	H	C/B
HARDINGE of Penshurst, Lord	L	C/B
HARDWICKE, Earl of	H	Con
HARDY of Wath, Lord	L	Lab
HAREWOOD, Earl of; KBE	H	(Ind)
HARLECH, Lord	H	Con
HARMAR-NICHOLLS, Lord	L	Con
HARMSWORTH, Lord	H	Con
HARRINGTON, Earl of	H	(Ind)
HARRIS, Lord	H	(Ind)
HARRIS of Greenwich, Lord; PC	L	Lib Dem
HARRIS of Haringey, Lord	L	Lab
HARRIS of High Cross, Lord	L	C/B
HARRIS of Peckham, Lord; Kt	L	Con
HARROWBY, Earl of; TD	H	Con
HARTWELL, Lord; MBE TD	L	C/B
HARVEY of Tasburgh, Lord	H	(Con)
HASKEL, Lord	L	Lab
HASKINS, Lord	L	Lab
HASLAM, Lord; Kt	L	Con
HASTINGS, Lord	H	Con
HATHERTON, Lord	H	(Ind)
HATTERSLEY, Lord; PC	L	Lab
HAWKE, Lord	H	(Con)
HAYHOE, Lord; Kt PC	L	Con
HAYMAN, Baroness	L	Lab
HAYTER, Lord; KCVO CBE	H	C/B
HAZLERIGG, Lord; MC TD	H	(Ind)
HEAD, Viscount	H	C/B
HEADFORT, Marquess of	H	C/B
HEALEY, Lord; PC CH MBE	L	Lab
HEMINGFORD, Lord	H	C/B
HEMPHILL, Lord	H	Con
HENDERSON of Brompton, Lord; KCB	L	C/B
HENLEY, Lord	H	Con
HENNIKER, Lord; KCMG CVO MC DL	H	C/B
HEREFORD, Bishop of	Bp	Ind

HEREFORD, Viscount	*H*	(Ind)
HERRIES, The Lady	*H*	(Ind)
HERSCHELL, Lord	*H*	(Ind)
HERTFORD, Marquess	*H*	(Ind)
HESKETH, Lord; PC KBE	*H*	Con
HEYTESBURY, Lord	*H*	(Ind)
HIGGINS, Lord; PC KBE DL	*L*	Con
HILL, Viscount	*H*	(Ind)
HILL-NORTON, Adm of the Fleet, Lord; GCB	*L*	C/B
HILTON of Eggardon, Baroness; QPM	*L*	Lab
HINDLIP, Lord	*H*	C/B
HIVES, Lord	*H*	Ind
HOBHOUSE of Woodborough, Lord; PC Kt	*Law*	C/B
HOFFMAN, Lord	*Law*	C/B
HOGG of Cumbernauld, Lord	*L*	Lab
HOGG of Kettlethorpe, Baroness	*L*	Con
HOLDERNESS, Lord; PC DL	*L*	Con
HOLLICK, Lord	*L*	Lab
HOLLIS of Heigham, Baroness; PC	*L*	Lab
HOLME of Cheltenham, Lord; CBE	*L*	Lib Dem
HOLMPATRICK, Lord	*H*	Con
HOME, Earl of	*H*	Con
HOOD, Viscount	*H*	Con
HOOPER, Baroness	*L*	Con
HOOSON, Lord; QC	*L*	Lib Dem
HOPE of Craighead, Lord	*Law*	Ind
HOTHFIELD, Lord	*H*	Con
HOWARD de WALDEN, Lord; TD	*H*	(Ind)
HOWARD of Penrith, Lord; DL	*H*	(Ind)
HOWE, Earl	*H*	Con
HOWE of Aberavon, Lord; CH Kt PC QC	*L*	Con
HOWELL of Guildford, Lord; PC	*L*	Con
HOWICK of Glendale, Lord	*H*	(Ind)
HOWIE of Troon, Lord	*L*	Lab
HOYLE, Lord	*L*	Lab
HUGHES of Hawkhill, Lord; PC CBE DL	*L*	Lab
HUGHES of Woodside, Lord	*L*	Lab
HUNT of Kings Heath, Lord; OBE	*L*	Lab
HUNT of Tanworth, Lord; GCB	*L*	C/B
HUNT of Wirral, Lord; PC MBE	*L*	Con
HUNTINGDON, Earl of	*H*	C/B
HUNTLY, Marquess of	*H*	Con
HURD of Westwell, Lord; PC CH CBE	*L*	Con

HUSSEY of North Bradley, Lord	*L*	Ind
HUTCHINSON of Lullington, Lord; QC	*L*	Lib Dem
HUTTON, Lord; PC	*Law*	Ind
HYLTON, Lord	*H*	C/B
HYLTON-FOSTER, Baroness; DBE	*L*	C/B
IDDESLEIGH, Earl of; DL	*H*	C/B
ILCHESTER, Earl of	*H*	C/B
ILIFFE, Lord	*H*	Con
IMBERT, Lord	*L*	C/B
INCHCAPE, Earl of	*H*	Con
INCHRYA, Lord	*H*	C/B
INGE, Field Marshal the Lord; GCB	*L*	C/B
INGLEBY, Viscount	*H*	C/B
INGLEWOOD, Lord; TD MEP	*H*	Con
INGROW, Lord; Kt OBE TD	*L*	(Con)
INVERFORTH, Lord	*H*	(Ind)
IRONSIDE, Lord	*H*	Con
IRVINE of Lairg, Lord; PC QC	*L*	Lab
ISLWYN, Lord; DL	*L*	Lab
IVEAGH, Earl of	*H*	C/B
JACOBS, Lord; Kt	*L*	Lib Dem
JAKOBOVITS, Lord; Kt	*L*	C/B
JAMES of Holland Park, Baroness; OBE	*L*	Con
JANNER of Braunstone, Lord; QC	*L*	Lab
JAUNCEY of Tullichettle, Lord; PC	*Law*	C/B
JAY of Paddington, Baroness; PC	*L*	Lab
JEFFREYS, Lord	*H*	Con
JEGER, Baroness	*L*	Lab
JELLICOE, Earl; PC KBE DSO MC FRS	*H*	Con
JENKIN of Roding, Lord; PC	*L*	Con
JENKINS of Hillhead, Lord; PC OM	*L*	Lib Dem
JENKINS of Putney, Lord	*L*	Ind
JERSEY, Earl of	*H*	Ind
JOHNSTON of Rockport, Lord; TD	*L*	Con
JOICEY, Lord	*H*	C/B
JOPLING, Lord; PC	*L*	Con
JUDD, Lord	*L*	Lab
KEITH of Castleacre, Lord; Kt	*L*	Con
KEITH of Kinkel, Lord; PC GBE	*Law*	C/B
KELVEDON, Lord; PC	*L*	Con
KENILWORTH, Lord	*H*	Con
KENNEDY of The Shaws, Baroness; QC	*L*	Lab
KENNET, Lord	*H*	Lab

KENSINGTON, Lord	*H*	**(Ind)**
KENSWOOD, Lord	*H*	**(Ind)**
KENT, HRH Duke of; KG GCMG GCVO	*R*	**C/B**
KENYON, Lord	*H*	**Con**
KERSHAW, Lord	*H*	**(Ind)**
KEYES, Lord	*H*	**Con**
KILBRACKEN, Lord; DSC	*H*	**Lab**
KILLEARN, Lord	*H*	**C/B**
KILMARNOCK, Lord	*H*	**C/B**
KILPATRICK of Kincraig, Lord; Kt	*L*	**C/B**
KIMBALL, Lord; DL	*L*	**Con**
KIMBERLEY, Earl of	*H*	**Con**
KINDERSLEY, Lord; DL	*H*	**Con**
KING of Wartnaby, Lord; Kt	*L*	**Con**
KINGSDOWN, Lord; KG PC	*L*	**C/B**
KINGSLAND, Lord; PC TD QC	*L*	**Con**
KINLOSS, The Lady	*H*	**C/B**
KINNOULL, Earl	*H*	**Con**
KINROSS, Lord	*H*	**(Ind)**
KINTORE, Earl	*H*	**C/B**
KIRKHILL, Lord; JP	*L*	**Lab**
KIRKWOOD, Lord	*H*	**Lib Dem**
KITCHENER of Khartoum, Earl; TD DL	*H*	**Con**
KNIGHT of Collingtree, Baroness; DBE	*L*	**Con**
KNIGHTS, Lord; CBE DL	*L*	**C/B**
KNOLLYS, Viscount	*H*	**Con**
KNUTSFORD, Viscount; DL	*H*	**Con**
LAING of Dunphail, Lord; Kt	*L*	**Con**
LAMBERT, Viscount; TD	*H*	**(Ind)**
LAMING, Lord; CBE Kt	*L*	**C/B**
LAMONT of Lerwick, Lord; PC	*L*	**Con**
LANE of Horsell, Lord; Kt JP FCA	*L*	**Con**
LANE of St Ippollitts, Lord; Kt PC AFC	*Law*	**C/B**
LANG of Monkton, Lord; PC	*L*	**Con**
LANSDOWNE, Marquess of; PC	*H*	**Ind**
LATHAM, Lord	*H*	**(Ind)**
LATYMER, Lord	*H*	**(Ind)**
LAUDERDALE, Earl	*H*	**Con**
LAWRENCE, Lord	*H*	**C/B**
LAWSON of Blaby, Lord; PC	*L*	**Con**
LAYTON, Lord	*H*	**Con**
LEATHERS, Viscount	*H*	**C/B**
LECONFIELD and EGREMONT, Lord	*H*	**Con**

LEICESTER, Earl of	*H*	(Ind)
LEIGH, Lord	*H*	Con
LEIGHTON of Saint Mellons, Lord	*H*	(Ind)
LEINSTER, Duke of	*H*	(Ind)
LESTER of Herne Hill, Lord; QC	*L*	Lib Dem
LEVEN and MELVILLE, Earl of	*H*	(Ind)
LEVENE of Portsoken, Lord; KBE	*L*	C/B
LEVERHULME, Viscount; KG TD	*H*	Con
LEVY, Lord	*L*	Lab
LEWIS of Newnham, Lord; Kt FRS	*L*	C/B
LICHFIELD, Bishop of	*Bp*	Ind
LICHFIELD, Earl of	*H*	(Con)
LILFORD, Lord	*H*	(Ind)
LIMERICK, Earl of; KBE	*H*	Con
LINCOLN, Bishop of	*Bp*	Ind
LINCOLN, Earl of	*H*	(Ind)
LINDSAY, Earl of	*H*	Con
LINDSAY of Birker, Lord	*H*	C/B
LINDSEY and ABINGDON, Earl of	*H*	Con
LINKLATER of Butterstone, Baroness	*L*	Lib Dem
LINLITHGOW, Marquess of	*H*	Con
LISTOWEL, Earl	*H*	Ind
LIVERPOOL, Earl of	*H*	Con
LLOYD of Berwick, Lord	*Law*	C/B
LLOYD of Highbury, Baroness; DBE	*L*	Ind
LLOYD-GEORGE of Dwyfor, Earl	*H*	C/B
LLOYD-WEBBER, Lord; Kt	*L*	Con
LOCKWOOD, Baroness; DL	*L*	Lab
LOFTHOUSE of Pontefract, Lord; Kt	*L*	Lab
LONDESBOROUGH, Lord	*H*	(Ind)
LONDON, Bishop of; PC	*Bp*	Ind
LONDONDERRY, Marquess of	*H*	(Ind)
LONG, Viscount; CBE	*H*	Con
LONGFORD, Earl of; KG PC	*H*	Lab
LONSDALE, Earl of	*H*	Con
LOTHIAN, Marquess of; KCVO DL	*H*	Con
LOUDOUN, Countess of	*H*	C/B
LOVAT, Lord	*H*	Ind
LOVELACE, Earl of	*H*	Ind
LOVELL-DAVIS, Lord	*L*	Lab
LUCAN, Earl of	*H*	(Ind)
LUCAS of Chilworth, Lord	*H*	Con
LUCAS of Crudwell, Lord	*H*	Con

LUDFORD, Baroness	*L*	**Lib Dem**
LUKE, Lord	*H*	**Con**
LYELL, Lord	*H*	**Con**
LYTTON, Earl of	*H*	**C/B**
LYVEDEN, Lord	*H*	**(Ind)**
McALPINE of West Green, Lord	*L*	**Ind**
MacANDREW, Lord	*H*	**Con**
McCARTHY, Lord	*L*	**Lab**
MACAULAY of Bragar, Lord; QC	*L*	**Lab**
MACCLESFIELD, Earl of	*H*	**C/B**
McCLUSKEY, Lord	*Law*	**C/B**
McCOLL of Dulwich, Lord; CBE	*L*	**Con**
McCONNELL, Lord; PC	*L*	**C/B**
MACDONALD of Gwaenysgor, Lord	*H*	**(Ind)**
MACDONALD of Tradeston, Lord	*L*	**Lab**
MACFARLANE of Bearsden, Lord; KT	*L*	**Con**
McFARLANE of Llandaff, Baroness	*L*	**C/B**
McGOWAN, Lord	*H*	**Con**
McINTOSH of Haringey, Lord	*L*	**Lab**
MACKAY of Ardbrecknish, Lord; PC	*L*	**Con**
MACKAY of Clashfern, Lord; PC	*Law*	**Con**
MACKAY of Drumadoon, Lord; QC PC	*L*	**Con**
MACKENZIE of Framwellgate, Lord; OBE	*L*	**Lab**
MACKENZIE-STUART, Lord; QC	*Law*	**C/B**
MACKIE of Benshie, Lord; CBE DSO DFC LLD	*L*	**Lib Dem**
MACKINTOSH of Halifax, Viscount	*H*	**Con**
MACLAURIN OF Knebworth, Lord; Kt	*L*	**Con**
MACLAY, Lord; DL	*H*	**(Ind)**
MACLEHOSE of Beoch, Lord; GBE KCMG KCVO DL	*L*	**C/B**
MACLEOD of Borve, Baroness; DL	*L*	**Con**
McNAIR, Lord	*H*	**Lib Dem**
McNALLY, Lord	*L*	**Lib Dem**
MACPHERSON of Drumochter, Lord	*H*	**Con**
MADDOCK, Baroness	*L*	**Lib Dem**
MALLALIEU, Baroness; QC	*L*	**Lab**
MALMESBURY, Earl of; TD DL	*H*	**Con**
MALVERN, Viscount	*H*	**(Ind)**
MANCHESTER, Bishop of	*Bp*	**Ind**
MANCHESTER, Duke of	*H*	**(C/B)**
MANCROFT, Lord	*H*	**Con**
MANNERS, Lord; DL	*H*	**(C/B)**
MANSFIELD, Earl of; DL	*H*	**Con**
MANTON, Lord; DL	*H*	**Con**

MAR, Countess of	H	C/B
MAR and KELLIE, Earl of	H	Lib Dem
MARCHAMLEY, Lord	H	(Ind)
MARCHWOOD, Viscount	H	Con
MARGADALE, Lord	H	(Ind)
MARGESSON, Viscount	H	(Ind)
MARLBOROUGH, Duke of; DL	H	Con
MARLESFORD, Lord; DL	L	Con
MARSH, Lord; Kt PC	L	C/B
MARSHALL of Knightsbridge, Lord; Kt	L	Ind
MARTONMERE, Lord; PC GBE KCMG	H	C/B
MASHAM of Ilton, Baroness; DL	L	C/B
MASON of Barnsley, Lord; PC	L	Lab
MASSEREENE and FERRARD, Viscount	H	Con
MAY, Lord	H	Con
MAYHEW of Twysden, Lord; PC Kt QC	L	Con
MEATH, Earl of	H	(Ind)
MELCHETT, Lord	H	(Lab)
MELVILLE,Viscount	H	Con
MERLYN-REES, Lord; PC	L	Lab
MERRIVALE, Lord	H	Con
MERSEY,Viscount	H	Con
MESTON, Lord; QC	H	Lib Dem
METHUEN, Lord	H	Lib Dem
MIDDLETON, Lord; MC DL	H	Con
MIDLETON, Viscount	H	C/B
MILFORD, Lord	H	(Ind)
MILFORD HAVEN, Marquess of	H	(C/B)
MILLER of Chilthorne Domer, Baroness	L	Lib Dem
MILLER of Hendon, Baroness; MBE	L	Con
MILLETT, Lord; PC	Law	C/B
MILLS, Viscount	H	Con
MILNE, Lord; TD	H	Ind
MILNER of Leeds, Lord; AE	H	Lab
MILVERTON, The Rev Lord	H	Con
MINTO, Earl of; OBE DL	H	C/B
MISHCON, Lord; QC	L	Lab
MOLLOY, Lord; TD	L	Lab
MOLYNEAUX of Killead, Lord; Kt PC	L	C/B
MONCK,Viscount	H	(Ind)
MONCKTON of Brenchley, Viscount; CB OBE MC DL	H	C/B
MONCRIEFF, Lord	H	(Ind)
MONK BRETTON, Lord; DL	H	Con

MONKSWELL, Lord	H	Lab
MONRO of Langholm, Lord; PC Kt AE	L	Con
MONSON, Lord	H	C/B
MONTAGU of Beaulieu, Lord	H	Con
MONTAGUE of Oxford, Lord; CBE	L	Lab
MONTEAGLE of Brandon, Lord	H	Con
MONTGOMERY of Alamein, Viscount; CBE	H	Con
MONTROSE, Duke of	H	Con
MOORE of Lower Marsh, Lord; PC	L	Con
MOORE of Wolvercote, Lord; PC GCB GCVO CMG	L	C/B
MORAN, Lord; KCMG	H	C/B
MORAY, Earl of	H	Ind
MORLEY, Lt-Col the Earl of	H	(Con)
MORRIS, Lord	H	(Con)
MORRIS of Castle Morris, Lord	L	Lab
MORRIS of Kenwood, Lord	H	C/B
MORRIS of Manchester, Lord; PC	L	Lab
MORTON, Earl of	H	C/B
MOSTYN, Lord; MC	H	(Con)
MOTTISTONE, Capt the Lord; RN CBE	H	Con
MOUNTBATTEN of Burma, Countess; CBE DL DStJ	H	(C/B)
MOUNT EDGCUMBE, Earl of	H	Ind
MOUNTEVANS, Lord	H	Con
MOUNTGARRET, Viscount	H	Con
MOWBRAY and STOURTON, Lord; CBE	H	Con
MOYNE, Lord	H	C/B
MOYNIHAN, Lord	H	Con
MOYOLA, Lord; PC DL	L	(Con)
MUNSTER, Earl of	H	Con
MURRAY of Epping Forest, Lord; PC OBE	L	Lab
MURTON of Lindisfarne, Lord; PC OBE TD	L	Con
MUSTILL, Lord; Kt PC	Law	C/B
NAPIER and ETTRICK, Major the Lord; KCVO DL	H	C/B
NAPIER of Magdala, Lord	H	C/B
NASEBY, Lord; PC	L	Con
NATHAN, Lord	H	C/B
NEILL of Bladen, Lord; QC	Law	Ind
NELSON, Earl	H	C/B
NELSON of Stafford, Lord	H	C/B
NETHERTHORPE, Lord	H	C/B
NEWALL, Lord	H	Con
NEWBY, Lord; CBE	L	Lib Dem
NEWTON, Lord	H	(Ind)

NEWTON of Braintree, Lord PC OBE	*L*	Con
NICHOLLS of Birkenhead, Lord	*Law*	C/B
NICHOLSON of Winterbourne, Baroness	*L*	Lib Dem
NICKSON, Lord; KBE	*L*	Con
NICOL, Baroness	*L*	Lab
NOEL-BUXTON, Lord	*H*	Con
NOLAN, Lord	*Law*	Ind
NORFOLK, Duke of; KG GCVO CB MC CBE DL	*H*	Con
NORMANBY, Marquess of	*H*	Ind
NORMANTON, Earl of	*H*	(Ind)
NORRIE, Lord	*H*	C/B
NORTHAMPTON, Marquess of; DL	*H*	(Ind)
NORTHBOURNE, Lord	*H*	C/B
NORTHBROOK, Lord	*H*	Con
NORTHESK, Earl of	*H*	Con
NORTHFIELD, Lord	*L*	Lab
NORTHUMBERLAND, Duke of	*H*	Con
NORTON, Lord	*H*	C/B
NORTON of Louth, Lord	*L*	Con
NORWICH, Bishop of	*Bp*	Ind
NORWICH, Viscount; CVO	*H*	(Ind)
NUNBURNHOLME, Lord	*H*	Ind
O'CATHAIN, Baroness; OBE	*L*	Con
OGMORE, Lord	*H*	Lib Dem
O'HAGAN, Lord	*H*	Con
OLIVER of Aylmerton, Lord; Kt PC	*Law*	C/B
O'NEILL, Col the Lord; TD DL	*H*	(Ind)
O'NEILL of Bengarve, Baroness; CBE	*L*	C/B
ONSLOW, Earl of	*H*	Con
ONSLOW of Woking, Lord; PC KCMG	*L*	Con
OPPENHEIM-BARNES, Baroness; PC	*L*	Con
ORAM, Lord	*L*	(Lab)
ORANMORE and BROWNE, Lord	*H*	(Ind)
ORKNEY, Earl of	*H*	(Ind)
ORME, Lord: PC	*L*	Lab
ORR-EWING, Lord; OBE	*L*	Con
OWEN, Lord; PC CH	*L*	C/B
OXFORD and ASQUITH, Earl of; KCMG	*H*	C/B
OXFORD, Bishop of	*Bp*	Ind
OXFUIRD, Viscount of; CBE	*H*	Con
PALMER, Lord	*H*	C/B
PALUMBO, Lord	*L*	C/B
PARK of Monmouth, Baroness; CMG OBE	*L*	Con

PARKINSON of Carnforth, Lord; PC	L	Con
PARMOOR, Lord	H	Ind
PARRY, Lord	L	Lab
PATEL, Lord; Kt	L	C/B
PATTEN of Wincanton, Lord; PC	L	Con
PAUL, Lord	L	Lab
PEARSON of Rannoch, Lord	L	Con
PEEL, Earl	H	Con
PEMBROKE and MONTGOMERY, Earl of	H	Con
PENDER, Lord	H	Con
PENRHYN, Lord; DSO MBE	H	Con
PERRY of Southwark, Baroness	L	Con
PERRY of Walton, Lord; Kt FRS OBE	L	Lib Dem
PERTH, Earl of; PC	H	C/B
PESTON, Lord	L	Lab
PETRE, Lord; DL	H	(C/B)
PEYTON of Yeovil, Lord; PC	L	Con
PHILLIMORE, Lord	H	Ind
PHILLIPS of Sudbury, Lord; OBE	L	Lab
PHILLIPS of Worth Matravers, Lord; Kt PC	Law	C/B
PIERCY, Lord	H	(Ind)
PIKE, Baroness; DBE	L	Con
PILKINGTON of Oxenford, Rev the Lord	L	Con
PITKEATHLEY, Baroness; OBE	L	Lab
PLANT of Highfield, Lord	L	Lab
PLATT of Writtle, Baroness; CBE DL	L	Con
PLOWDEN, Lord; GBE KCB	L	C/B
PLUMB, Lord; Kt DL	L	Con
PLUMMER of St Marylebone, Lord; Kt TD DL	L	Con
PLUNKET, Lord	H	Con
PLYMOUTH, Earl of; DL	H	(Ind)
POLTIMORE, Lord	H	Con
POLWARTH, Lord; TD DL	H	C/B
PONSONBY of Shulbrede, Lord	H	Lab
POOLE, Lord	H	C/B
PORTER of Luddenham, Lord: Kt FRS FRSC OM	L	C/B
PORTLAND, Earl of	H	C/B
PORTSMOUTH, Earl of	H	Con
POWERSCOURT, Viscount	H	(Ind)
POWIS, Earl of	H	C/B
PRENTICE, Lord; Kt PC	L	Con
PRIOR, Lord; PC	L	Con
PRYS-DAVIES, Lord	L	Lab

PUTTNAM, Lord; Kt CBE	L	Lab
PYM, Lord; PC MC DL	L	Con
QUEENSBERRY, Marquess of	H	(Lib Dem)
QUINTON, Lord	L	Con
QUIRK, Lord; Kt	L	C/B
RADNOR, Earl of	H	Con
RAGLAN, Lord	H	C/B
RAMSAY of Cartvale, Baroness	L	Lab
RANDALL of St Budeaux, Lord	L	Lab
RANFURLY, Earl of	H	C/B
RANKEILLOUR, Lord	H	Con
RATHCAVAN, Lord	H	C/B
RATHCREEDAN, Lord	H	C/B
RAVENSDALE, Lord; MC	H	C/B
RAVENSWORTH, Lord	H	(Ind)
RAWLINGS, Baroness	L	Con
RAWLINSON of Ewell, Lord; Kt PC QC	L	Con
RAYLEIGH, Lord	H	Con
RAYNE, Lord	L	C/B
RAZZALL, Lord; CBE	L	Lib Dem
REA, Lord	H	Lab
READING, Marquess of	H	Con
REAY, Lord	H	Con
REDESDALE, Lord	H	Lib Dem
REES, Lord; PC QC	L	Con
REES-MOGG, Lord; Kt	L	C/B
REMNANT, Lord; CVO	H	Con
RENDELL of Babergh, Baroness; CBE	L	Lab
RENFREW of Kaimsthorn, Lord	L	Con
RENNELL, Lord	H	Con
RENTON, Lord; PC KBE TD QC DL	L	Con
RENTON of Mount Harry, Lord; PC	L	Con
RENWICK, Lord	H	Con
RENWICK of Clifton, Lord; KCMG	L	Lab
REVELSTOKE, Lord	H	(Ind)
RICHARD, Lord; PC QC	L	Lab
RICHARDSON, Lord; Kt LVO ND FRCF	L	C/B
RICHARDSON of Calow, Rev the Baroness; OBE	L	Lab
RICHARDSON of Duntisbourne, Lord; KG PC MBE TD DL	L	C/B
RICHMOND, LENNOX and GORDON, Duke of	H	(C/B)
RIDLEY, Viscount; GCVO KG TD	H	C/B
RIPON, Bishop of	Bp	Ind
RITCHIE of Dundee, Lord	H	Lib Dem

RIX, Lord; Kt CBE	L	C/B
ROBENS of Woldingham, Lord; PC	L	(Ind)
ROBERTS of Conwy, Lord; PC Kt	L	Con
ROBERTSON of Oakridge, Lord	H	C/B
ROBOROUGH, Lord	H	Ind
ROCHDALE, Viscount	H	(Ind)
ROCHESTER, Lord; DL	H	Lib Dem
ROCKLEY, Lord	H	C/B
RODGER of Earlsferry, Lord; PC QC	Law	Con
RODGERS of Quarry Bank, Lord PC	L	Lib Dem
RODNEY, Lord	H	Con
ROGERS of Riverside, Lord	L	Lab
ROLL of Ipsden, Lord; KCMG CB	L	C/B
ROLLO, Lord	H	(Ind)
ROMNEY, Earl	H	Con
ROOTES, Lord	H	(Ind)
ROSEBERY, Earl of; DL	H	(Ind)
ROSSLYN, Earl of	H	C/B
ROSSMORE, Lord	H	(Ind)
ROTHERMERE, Viscount	H	C/B
ROTHERWICK, Viscount	H	Ind
ROTHES, Earl of	H	(Ind)
ROTHSCHILD, Lord; GBE	H	C/B
ROWALLAN, Lord	H	Ind
ROXBURGHE, Duke of	H	Con
RUGBY, Lord	H	C/B
RUNCIE, Lord; PC MC	L	C/B
RUNCIMAN, Viscount; CBE FBA	H	C/B
RUSSELL, Earl	H	Lib Dem
RUSSELL of Liverpool, Lord	H	C/B
RUSSELL-JOHNSTON, Lord; Kt	L	Lib Dem
RYDER of Eaton Hastings, Lord; Kt	L	(C/B)
RYDER of Warsaw, Baroness; CMG OBE	L	C/B
RYDER of Wensum, Lord; PC OBE	L	Con
SAATCHI, Lord	L	Con
SACKVILLE, Lord	H	Con
SAINSBURY of Preston Candover, Lord; KG Kt	L	Con
SAINSBURY of Turville, Lord	L	Lab
St ALBANS, Duke of	H	Con
St ALDWYN, Earl	H	Con
St DAVIDS, Viscount	H	Con
St GERMANS, Earl of	H	Con
St HELENS, Lord	H	Ind

St JOHN of Bletso, Lord	H	C/B
St JOHN of Fawsley, Lord; PC	L	Con
St LEVAN, Lord; DSC	H	Con
St OSWALD, Lord	H	C/B
St VINCENT, Viscount	H	(Ind)
SALISBURY, Bishop of	Bp	Ind
SALISBURY, Marquess of; DL	H	(Con)
SALTOUN of Abernethy, The Lady	H	C/B
SAMUEL, Viscount	H	C/B
SANDBERG, Lord; CBE Kt	L	Lib Dem
SANDERSON of Bowden, Lord; Kt DL	L	Con
SANDFORD, The Rev Lord; DSC	H	Con
SANDHURST, Lord; DVC	H	C/B
SANDWICH, Earl of	H	C/B
SANDYS, Lord; DL	H	Con
SAVILE, Lord; CStJ JP DL	H	Con ·
SAVILLE of Newdigate, Lord; PC Kt	Law	C/B
SAWYER, Lord	L	Lab
SAYE and SELE, Lord; DL	H	(Ind)
SCANLON, Lord	L	Lab
SCARBOROUGH, Earl of	H	(Ind)
SCARMAN, Lord; Kt PC OBE	Law	C/B
SCARSDALE, Viscount	H	Ind
SCOTLAND of Asthal, Baroness; QC	L	Lab
SEAFIELD, Earl of	H	Con
SECCOMBE, Baroness; DBE	L	Con
SEFTON of Garston, Lord	L	Lab
SELBORNE, Earl of; KBE FRS DL	H	Con
SELKIRK of Douglas, Lord; PC QC MSP	L	Con
SELSDON, Lord	H	Con
SEMPILL, Lord	H	Con
SEROTA, Baroness; DBE JP	L	Lab
SEWEL, Lord	L	Lab
SHAFTESBURY, Earl of	H	(Con)
SHANNON, Earl of	H	C/B
SHARP of Guildford, Baroness	L	Lib Dem
SHARPLES, Baroness	L	Con
SHAUGHNESSY, Lord	H	C/B
SHAW of Northstead, Lord; DL	L	Con
SHAWCROSS, Lord; PC GBE QC	L	(C/B)
SHEPHERD, Lord; PC	H	Lab
SHEPPARD of Didgemere, Lord	L	Con
SHEPPARD of Liverpool, Rt Rev the Lord	L	Lab

SHERFIELD, Lord	H	(Ind)
SHORE of Stepney, Lord; PC	L	Lab
SHREWSBURY and WATERFORD, Earl of	H	C/B
SHUTTLEWORTH, Lord; DL	H	Con
SIDMOUTH, Viscount	H	C/B
SIEFF of Brimpton, Lord; Kt OBE	L	(C/B)
SILSOE, Lord; QC	H	(Ind)
SIMON, Viscount	H	C/B
SIMON of Glaisdale, Lord; Kt PC DL	Law	C/B
SIMON of Highbury, Lord; Kt CBE	L	Lab
SIMON of Wythenshawe, Lord	H	(Ind)
SIMPSON of Dunkeld, Lord	L	Lab
SINCLAIR, Lord; CVO	H	(Ind)
SINCLAIR of Cleeve, Lord	H	(Ind)
SKELMERSDALE, Lord	H	Con
SKIDELSKY, Lord	L	Con
SLIGO, Marquess of	H	(Ind)
SLIM, Viscount; OBE DL	H	C/B
SLYNN of Hadley, Lord; Kt PC	Law	C/B
SMITH of Clifton, Lord; Kt	L	Lib Dem
SMITH of Gilmorehill, Baroness	L	Lab
SNOWDON, Earl of; GCVO	H	(C/B)
SOMERLEYTON, Lord; DL	H	C/B
SOMERS, Lord	H	(C/B)
SOMERSET, Duke of	H	C/B
SOULBURY, Viscount	H	(C/B)
SOULSBY of Swaffham Prior, Lord	L	Con
SOUTHAMPTON, Lord	H	Con
SOUTHWARK, Bishop of	Bp	Ind
SOUTHWELL, Bishop of	Bp	Ind
SPENCER, Earl	H	(C/B)
SPENS, Lord	H	C/B
STAFFORD, Lord	H	Con
STAIR, Earl of	H	Ind
STALLARD, Lord	L	Lab
STAMP, Lord	H	C/B
STANLEY of Alderley, Lord; DL	H	Con
STEEL of Aikwood, Lord; PC KBE MSP	L	Lib Dem
STERLING of Plaistow, Lord; Kt CBE	L	Con
STEVENS of Ludgate, Lord	L	Con
STEWARTBY, Lord; Kt PC RD FBA	L	Con
STEYN, Lord	Law	Ind
STOCKTON, Earl of; MEP	H	Con

STODART of Leaston, Lord; PC	L	Con
STODDART of Swindon, Lord	L	Lab
STOKES, Lord; TD DL	L	C/B
STONE of Blackheath, Lord	L	Lab
STRABOLGI, Lord	H	Lab
STRADBROKE, Earl of	H	(Ind)
STRAFFORD, Earl of	H	C/B
STRANG, Lord	H	(Ind)
STRANGE, Baroness	H	C/B
STRATHALMOND, Lord	H	C/B
STRATHCARRON, Lord	H	Con
STRATHCLYDE, Lord; PC	H	Con
STRATHCONA and MOUNT ROYAL, Lord	H	Con
STRATHEDEN and CAMPBELL, Lord	H	(Ind)
STRATHMORE and KINGHORNE, Earl of	H	Con
STRATHSPEY, Lord	H	(Ind)
STUART of Findhorn, Viscount	H	(Ind)
SUDELEY, Lord	H	Con
SUFFIELD, Lord; MC	H	Con
SUFFOLK and BERKSHIRE, Earl of	H	C/B
SUTHERLAND, Countess of	H	(Ind)
SUTHERLAND, Duke of; TD DL	H	(Ind)
SWANSEA, Lord; DL	H	C/B
SWAYTHLING, Lord	H	C/B
SWINFEN, Lord	H	Con
SWINTON, Earl of; DL	H	Con
SYMONS of Vernham Dean, Baroness	L	Lab
SYSONBY, Lord	H	(Ind)
TANKERVILLE, Earl of	H	(Ind)
TANLAW, Lord	L	C/B
TAVERNE, Lord; QC	L	Lib Dem
TAYLOR of Blackburn, Lord; CBE	L	Lab
TAYLOR of Gryfe, Lord; DL	L	Lab
TAYLOR of Warwick, Lord	L	Con
TEBBIT, Lord; PC CH	L	Con
TEDDER, Lord	H	(Ind)
TEMPLE of Stowe, Earl	H	C/B
TEMPLEMAN, Lord; PC MBE	Law	C/B
TENBY, Viscount	H	C/B
TENNYSON, Lord; DSC	H	(Ind)
TEVIOT, Lord	H	Con
TEYNHAM, Lord	H	Con
THATCHER, Baroness PC OM FRS LG	L	Con

THOMAS of Gresford, Lord; OBE QC	L	Lib Dem
THOMAS of Gwydir, Lord; PC QC	L	Con
THOMAS of Macclesfield, Lord; CBE	L	Lab
THOMAS of Swynnerton, Lord	L	Lib Dem
THOMAS of Walliswood, Baroness	L	Lib Dem
THOMSON of Fleet, Lord	H	(Ind)
THOMSON of Monifieth, Lord; KT PC	L	Lib Dem
THORNTON, Baroness	L	Lab
THURLOW, Lord; KCMG	H	C/B
THURSO, Viscount	H	Lib Dem
TOLLEMACHE, Lord; DL	H	Con
TOMBS, Lord; Kt	L	C/B
TOMLINSON, Lord	L	Lab
TOPE, Lord; CBE	L	Lib Dem
TORDOFF, Lord	L	Lib Dem
TORPICHEN, Lord	H	Con
TORRINGTON, Viscount	H	Con
TOWNSHEND, Marquess	H	(Con)
TREFGARNE, Lord; PC	H	Con
TRENCHARD, Viscount	H	Con
TREVETHIN and OAKSEY, Lord; OBE	H	(Con)
TREVOR, Lord	H	Ind
TROTMAN, Lord; Kt	L	C/B
TRUMPINGTON, Baroness; PC	L	Con
TRYON, Lord; DL	H	C/B
TUGENDHAT, Lord; Kt	L	Con
TURNER of Camden, Baroness	L	Lab
TWEEDDALE, Marquess of	H	C/B
TWEEDSMUIR, Lord	H	Ind
UDDIN, Baroness	L	Lab
ULLSWATER, Viscount; PC	H	Con
VARLEY, Lord; PC DL	L	Lab
VAUX of Harrowden, Lord	H	(Con)
VERNON, Lord	H	(Ind)
VERULAM, Earl of	H	Ind
VESTEY, Lord; DL	H	Ind
VINCENT of Coleshill, Lord; GBE KCB DSO	L	C/B
VINSON, Lord; LVO DL	L	Con
VIVIAN, Lord	H	Con
WADDINGTON, Lord; PC QC DL	L	Con
WADE of Chorlton, Lord; Kt	L	Con
WAKEFIELD, Bishop of	Bp	Ind
WAKEHAM, Lord; PC FCA	L	Con

WAKEHURST, Lord	H	C/B
WALDEGRAVE, Earl	H	Con
WALES, HRH Prince of, KG KT GCB PC AK QSO	R	(C/B)
WALKER of Doncaster, Lord; PC Kt	L	Lab
WALKER of Worcester, Lord; PC MBE	L	Con
WALLACE of Coslany, Lord	L	Lab
WALLACE of Saltaire, Lord	L	Lib Dem
WALPOLE, Lord	H	C/B
WALSINGHAM, Lt-Col the Lord; MC	H	(Ind)
WALTON of Detchant, Lord; Kt TD	L	C/B
WARDINGTON, Lord	H	Con
WARNER, Lord	L	Lab
WARNOCK, Baroness; DBE	L	C/B
WATERFORD, Marquess of	H	Con
WATSON of Invergowrie, Lord; MSP	L	Lab
WAVERLEY, Viscount	H	C/B
WEATHERILL, Lord; PC DL	L	C/B
WEDDERBURN of Charlton, Lord; QC	L	Lab
WEDGWOOD, Lord	H	Con
WEIDENFELD, Lord; Kt	L	C/B
WEINSTOCK, Lord; Kt	L	C/B
WEIR, Viscount	H	Con
WELLINGTON, Duke of; KG LVO OBE MC DL	H	C/B
WEMYSS and MARCH, Earl of; KT	H	Con
WESTBURY, Lord; MC DL	H	Con
WESTMINSTER, Duke of; DL OBE	H	(Ind)
WESTMORLAND, Earl of	H	C/B
WESTWOOD, Lord	H	(Ind)
WHADDON, Lord	L	Lab
WHARNCLIFFE, Earl	H	(Ind)
WHARTON, Baroness	H	C/B
WHITE, Baroness	L	Lab
WHITELAW, Viscount; KT CH PC MC DL	LH	Con
WHITTY, Lord	L	Lab
WIGODER, Lord; QC	L	Lib Dem
WIGRAM, Lord; MC DL	H	Con
WILBERFORCE, Lord; PC CMG OBE	L	C/B
WILCOX, Baroness	L	Con
WILLIAMS of Crosby, Baroness; PC	L	Lib Dem
WILLIAMS of Elvel, Lord; CBE	L	Lab
WILLIAMS of Mostyn, Lord; PC QC	L	Lab
WILLIAMSON of Horton, Lord; GCMG CB	L	C/B
WILLOUGHBY de BROKE, Lord	H	Con

WILLOUGHBY de ERESBY, Baroness	H	(C/B)
WILSON, Lord	H	(Ind)
WILSON of Tillyorn, Lord; Kt GCMG	L	C/B
WILTON, Earl of	H	Ind
WIMBORNE, Viscount	H	(Ind)
WINCHESTER, Bishop of	Bp	Ind
WINCHESTER, Marquess of	H	(Ind)
WINCHILSEA and NOTTINGHAM, Earl of	H	Lib Dem
WINDLESHAM, Lord; PC CVO	H	Con
WINSTON, Prof the Lord	L	Lab
WISE, Lord	H	Con
WOLFSON, Lord; Kt	L	Con
WOLFSON of Sunningdale, Lord; Kt	L	Con
WOLVERTON, Lord	H	(C/B)
WOOLF, Lord; Kt PC	Law	C/B
WOOLTON, Earl of	H	Ind
WRAXALL, Lord; DL	H	(Ind)
WRENBURY, Lord	H	C/B
WRIGHT of Richmond, Lord; GCMG	L	C/B
WROTTESLEY, Lord	H	Con
WYFOLD, Lord	H	(Ind)
WYNFORD, Lt-Col the Lord; MBE DL	H	Con
YARBOROUGH, Earl	H	Con
YORK, HRH Duke of; CVO	R	(C/B)
YORK, Archbishop of; PC	Bp	Ind
YOUNG, Baroness; PC DL	L	Con
YOUNG of Dartington, Lord	L	Lab
YOUNG of Graffham, Lord; PC	L	Con
YOUNG of Old Scone, Baroness	L	Lab
YOUNGER of Leckie, Viscount; PC TD KCVO	L/H	Con
ZETLAND, Marquess	H	Con
ZOUCHE of Haryngworth, Lord	H	Con

NEW PEERS

The following new Life Peers were appointed in the Birthday Honours List :-

Rt Hon Sir Robert FELLOWES GCB GCVO QSO	ex Private Sec to Queen.
Sir Norman FOSTER OM	Architect.
Sir Ernest Ronald OXBURGH KBE	Rector, Imperial College of Science.
Usha Kumari PRASHAR CBE	Chair, Parole Board.
Vivien Helen STERN CBE	Secretary General, Penal Reform International.
Sir Dennis STEVENSON CBE	Chairman, Pearson plc.

The following new "working" Life Peers have also been appointed and will take up their seats in due course:-

Catherine ASHTON	Chair East & North Herts HA
Elizabeth Jean BARKER	Lib Dem, Field Officer, Age Concern
May BLOOD MBE	Member, N Ireland Women's Coalition
Prof W P BRADSHAW	Senior Visiting Research Fellow, Wolfson Coll, Oxford
William Henry BRETT	ex General Secretary, IPMS
Alexander Charles CARLILE QC	ex Lib Dem MP for Montgomery
Murray ELDER	Special Adviser, Scottish Office
Richard Oliver FAULKNER	First Deputy Chair, Football Trust
David Geoffrey Nigel FILKIN CBE	Policy Analyst and Writer
Rt Hon Sir Michael Bruce FORSYTH	ex Conservative MP for Stirling
Anita GALE	Gen Sec, Wales Labour Party
Robert GAVRON CBE	Chair, Folio Society Ltd; Guardian Media Group
Peter Henry GOLDSMITH QC	Barrister
Anthony Stephen GRABINER QC	a Recorder
Joan Brownlow HANHAM CBE JP	Con Leader, Kensington & Chelsea LBC
Angela Felicity HARRIS	Lib Dem, N Yorks CC
Lyndon Henry Arthur HARRISON	ex Lab MEP for Cheshire W & Wirral
Rosalind Patricia-Anne HOWELLS OBE	ex equal opportunities worker
Tarsem KING	Managing Director, Sandwell Polybags Ltd
Sir Graham KIRKHAM	Executive Chairman, DFS Furniture
John LAIRD	Chairman, John Laird Group of Communication Companies
David Edward LEA OBE	Assistant General Secretary, TUC
David Lawrence LIPSEY	Public Policy Editor, The Economist
Hector Uisdean MACKENSIE	Associate General Secretary, UNISON
Doreen Elizabeth MASSEY	Health education consultant
Genista McINTOSH	Artistic Director, National Theatre
Christopher John RENNARD MBE	Director of Campaigns, Lib Dems
Dennis Robert David ROGAN	Chairman, Ulster Unionist Party
Colin Morven SHARMAN OBE	Chairman, KPMG International
Peter SMITH	Lab Leader, Wigan Borough Council
Rt Hon William Arthur WALDEGRAVE	ex Conservative MP for Bristol West
Diana WARWICK	Chief Executive, CVCP
Prof Alan John WATSON CBE	Chair, Burson Marsteller UK
Janet WHITAKER	Consultant, Commission for Racial Equality
Rosalie Catherine WILKINS	Officer, National Centre for Independent Living
Kenneth John WOOLMER	Chairman, Leeds University Business School

SENIOR OFFICIALS OF THE
SCOTTISH PARLIAMENT

Presiding Officer	*Sir David Steel MSP*
Deputy Presiding Officers	*Patricia Ferguson MSP, George Reid MSP*
Corporate Body (appointed members)	*Robert Brown MSP, Des McNulty MSP*
	Andrew Welsh MSP, John Young MSP
Interim Clerk/Chief Executive	*Paul Grice*
Secretary to Scottish Parliamentary Corporate Body/	*Huw Williams*
Private Secretary to Presiding Officer	
Legal Adviser	*Ann Nelson*
Director of Clerking Services	*Carol McCracken*
Head of Chamber Office	*Bill Thomson*
Director of Corporate Services	*Stewart Gilfillan*
Head of Personnel	*Ian Macnicol*
Head of Finance	*Robin Andrews*
Head of Purchasing	*Lynn Garvie*
Head of Broadcasting	*Alan Smart*
Head of Security	*Bill Anderson*
Facilities Manager	*Charlie Fisher*
Director of Communications	*Lesley Beddie*
Head of Research and Information Service	*Janet Seaton*
Editor (Official Report)	*Henrietta Hales*
Deputy Editor	*Stephen Hutchinson*
Head of Information Technology	*Cathy Watkins*
Head of Information Systems	*Bethan Hubbard*
Holyrood Project Team Director	*Barbara Doig*
Audit Adviser	*Dave Ferguson*
Head of Committee Office	*Elizabeth Watson*
Clerk to European Committee	*Stephen Imrie*
Clerk to Equal Opportunities Committee	*Martin Verity*
Clerk to Finance Committee	*Sarah Davidson*
Clerk to Audit Committee	*Gillian Baxendine*
Clerk to Procedures Committee	*John Patterson*
Clerk to Standards Committee	*Vanessa Glyn*
Clerk to Public Petitions Committee	*Steve Farrell*
Clerk to Subordinate Legislation Committee	*Alasdair Rankin*
Clerk to Justice & Home Affairs Committee	*Andrew Mylne*
Clerk to Education, Culture & Sport Committee	*Gillian Baxendine*
Clerk to Social Inclusion, Housing & the Voluntary Sector Committee	
	Martin Verity
Clerk to Enterprise and Lifelong Learning Committee	*Simon Watkins*
Clerk to Health & Community Care Committee	*Jennifer Smart*
Clerk to Transport & the Environment Committee	*Lynn Tullis*
Clerk to Rural Affairs Committee	*Richard Davies*
Clerk to Local Government Committee	*Lynn Tullis*

ALPHABETICAL LIST OF
THE MEMBERS OF THE SCOTTISH PARLIAMENT

ADAM, Brian James	*North East Scotland region*	SNP
AITKEN, William Mackie	*Glasgow region*	Con
ALEXANDER, Wendy	*Paisley North*	Lab
BAILLIE, Jaqueline Marie (Jackie)	*Dumbarton*	Lab
BARRIE, Thomas Scott	*Dunfermline West*	Lab
BOYACK, Sarah	*Edinburgh Central*	Lab
BRANKIN, Rhona Margaret	*Midlothian*	Lab
BROWN, Robert Edward	*Glasgow region*	Lib Dem
CAMPBELL, Colin MacIver	*West of Scotland region*	SNP
CANAVAN, Dennis	*Falkirk West*	Ind
CHISHOLM, Malcolm George Richardson	*Edinburgh North & Leith*	Lab
CRAIGIE, Catherine (Cathy)	*Cumbernauld & Kilsyth*	Lab
CRAWFORD, Robert Hardie Bruce	*Mid Scotland & Fife*	SNP
CUNNINGHAM, Roseanna	*Perth*	SNP
CURRAN, Margaret Patricia	*Glasgow Baillieston*	Lab
DAVIDSON, David	*North East Scotland region*	Con
DEACON, Susan Catherine	*Edinburgh East & Musselburgh*	Lab
DEWAR, Donald Campbell	*Glasgow Anniesland*	Lab
DOUGLAS-HAMILTON, James Alexander	*Lothians region*	Con
EADIE, Helen Stirling	*Dunfermline East*	Lab
ELDER, Dorothy-Grace Douglas	*Glasgow region*	SNP
EWING, Fergus Stewart	*Inverness East, Nairn & Lochaber*	SNP
EWING, Margaret Anne	*Moray*	SNP
EWING, Winifred Margaret (Winnie)	*Highlands & Islands region*	SNP
FABIANI, Linda	*Central Scotland region*	SNP
FERGUSON, Patricia Josephine	*Glasgow Maryhill*	Lab
FERGUSSON, Alexander Charles Onslow	*South of Scotland region*	Con
FINNIE, James Ross	*West of Scotland region*	Lib Dem
GALBRAITH, Samuel Laird (Sam)	*Strathkelvin & Bearsden*	Lab
GALLIE, Philip Roy (Phil)	*South of Scotland region*	Con
GIBSON, Kenneth James	*Glasgow region*	SNP
GILLON, Karen Macdonald	*Clydesdale*	Lab
GODMAN, Patricia	*West Renfrewshire*	Lab

GOLDIE, Annabel MacNicoll	*West of Scotland region*	Con
GORRIE, Donald Cameron Easterbrook	*Central Scotland region*	Lib Dem
GRAHAME, Christine	*South of Scotland region*	SNP
GRANT, Rhoda	*Highlands & Islands region*	Lab
GRAY, Iain Cumming	*Edinburgh Pentlands*	Lab
HAMILTON, Duncan Graeme	*Highlands & Islands region*	SNP
HARDING, Keith	*Mid Scotland & Fife region*	Con
HARPER, Robin Charles Moreton	*Lothians region*	Green
HENRY, Hugh	*Paisley South*	Lab
HOME ROBERTSON, John	*East Lothian*	Lab
HUGHES, Janis	*Glasgow Rutherglen*	Lab
HYSLOP, Fiona Jane	*Lothians region*	SNP
INGRAM, Adam Hamilton	*South of Scotland region*	SNP
JACKSON, Sylvia	*Stirling*	Lab
JACKSON, William Gordon	*Glasgow Govan*	Lab
JAMIESON, Catherine Mary (Cathy)	*Carrick, Cumnock & Doon Valley*	Lab
JAMIESON, Margaret Nelson	*Kilmarnock & Loudoun*	Lab
JENKINS, Archibald Ian	*Tweeddale, Ettrick & Lauderdale*	Lib Dem
JOHNSTON, Paul Nicholas (Nick)	*Mid Scotland & Fife region*	Con
JOHNSTONE, Alexander (Alex)	*North East Scotland region*	Con
KERR, Andrew Palmer (Andy)	*East Kilbride*	Lab
LAMONT, Johann MacDougall	*Glasgow Pollok*	Lab
LIVINGSTON, Marilyn Margaret	*Kirkcaldy*	Lab
LOCHHEAD, Richard Neilson	*North East Scotland region*	SNP
LYON, George	*Argyll & Bute*	Lib Dem
McALLION, John	*Dundee East*	Lab
MacASKILL, Kenneth Wright (Kenny)	*Lothians region*	SNP
McAVEETY, Francis (Frank)	*Glasgow Shettleston*	Lab
McCABE, Thomas (Tom)	*Hamilton South*	Lab
McCONNELL, Jack Wilson	*Motherwell & Wishaw*	Lab
MacDONALD, Lewis Roderick	*Aberdeen Central*	Lab
MacDONALD, Margo	*Lothians region*	SNP
McGRIGOR, James Angus Roderick Neil (Jamie)	*Highlands & Islands region*	Con
McGUGAN, Irene Margaret	*North East Scotland region*	SNP
McINTOSH, Kenneth Donald (Ken)	*Eastwood*	Lab

McINTOSH, Lyndsay June	*Central Scotland region*	Con
MACKAY, Angus John	*Edinburgh South*	Lab
MacLEAN, Kathleen (Kate)	*Dundee West*	Lab
McLEISH, Henry Baird	*Fife Central*	Lab
McLEOD, Fiona Grace	*West of Scotland region*	SNP
McLETCHIE, David William	*Lothians region*	Con
McMAHON, Michael Joseph	*Hamilton North & Bellshill*	Lab
McMILLAN, Maureen Mary	*Highlands & Islands region*	Lab
MacNEIL, Duncan	*Greenock & Inverclyde*	Lab
McNEILL, Pauline Mary	*Glasgow Kelvin*	Lab
McNULTY, Desmond (Des)	*Clydebank & Milngavie*	Lab
MARTIN, Paul	*Glasgow Springburn*	Lab
MARWICK, Tricia	*Mid Scotland & Fife region*	SNP
MATHESON, Michael Stephen	*Central Scotland region*	SNP
MONTEITH, Brian	*Mid Scotland & Fife region*	Con
MORGAN, Alasdair Neil	*Galloway & Upper Nithsdale*	SNP
MORRISON, Alasdair Angus	*Western Isles*	Lab
MULDOON, Bristow Cook	*Livingston*	Lab
MULLIGAN, Margaret Mary	*Linlithgow*	Lab
MUNDELL, David Gordon	*South of Scotland region*	Con
MUNRO, John Farquhar	*Ross, Skye & Inverness West*	Lib Dem
MURRAY, Elaine Kildare	*Dumfries*	Lab
NEIL, Alexander (Alex)	*Central Scotland region*	SNP
OLDFATHER, Irene	*Cunninghame South*	Lab
PATERSON, Gil Martin	*Central Scotland region*	SNP
PEACOCK, Peter James	*Highlands & Islands region*	Lab
PEATTIE, Catherine Campbell (Cathy)	*Falkirk East*	Lab
QUINAN, Lloyd John	*West of Scotland region*	SNP
RADCLIFFE, Nora	*Gordon*	Lib Dem
RAFFAN, Keith William Twort	*Mid Scotland & Fife region*	Lib Dem
REID, George Newlands	*Mid Scotland & Fife region*	SNP
ROBISON, Shona	*North East Scotland region*	SNP
ROBSON, Euan Macfarlane	*Roxburgh & Berwickshire*	Lib Dem
RUMBLES, Michael John (Mike)	*West Aberdeenshire & Kincardine*	Lib Dem
RUSSELL, Michael William	*South of Scotland region*	SNP

SALMOND, Alexander Elliot Anderson (Alex)	*Banff & Buchan*	SNP
SCANLON, Mary Elizabeth	*Highlands & Islands region*	Con
SCOTT, Tavish Hamilton	*Shetland*	Lib Dem
SHERIDAN, Tommy	*Glasgow region*	SSP
SIMPSON, Richard John	*Ochil*	Lab
SMITH, Elaine Agnes	*Coatbridge & Chryston*	Lab
SMITH, Iain William	*North East Fife*	Lib Dem
SMITH, Margaret Joy	*Edinburgh West*	Lib Dem
STEEL, Sir David Martin Scott	*Lothians region*	Lib Dem
STEPHEN, Nicol Ross	*Aberdeen South*	Lib Dem
STONE, Jamie Hume	*Caithness, Sutherland & Easter Ross*	Lib Dem
STURGEON, Nicola	*Glasgow region*	SNP
SWINNEY, John Ramsay	*North Tayside*	SNP
THOMSON, Elaine Margaret	*Aberdeen North*	Lab
TOSH, Neil Murray	*South of Scotland region*	Con
ULLRICH, Catherine Morrison (Kay)	*West of Scotland region*	SNP
WALLACE, Robert Ben Lobban (Ben)	*North East Scotland region*	Con
WALLACE, James Robert (Jim)	*Orkney*	Lib Dem
WATSON, Michael Goodall (Mike)	*Glasgow Cathcart*	Lab
WELSH, Andrew Paton	*Angus*	SNP
WELSH, Ian Mcwilliam	*Ayr*	Lab
WHITE, Sandra	*Glasgow region*	SNP
WHITEFIELD, Karen	*Airdrie & Shotts*	Lab
WILSON, Allan	*Cunninghame North*	Lab
WILSON, Andrew John	*Central Scotland region*	SNP
YOUNG, John Henderson	*West of Scotland region*	Con

SENIOR OFFICIALS OF THE
NATIONAL ASSEMBLY FOR WALES

Presiding Officer	*Lord Dafydd Elis-Thomas AM*
Deputy Presiding Officer	*Jane Davidson AM*
Clerk of the Assembly	*John Lloyd*
Deputy Clerk of the Assmebly	*Bryan Mitchell*
Head of Assembly Communication Services	*Dr Manon Williams*
Head Librarian	*Caren Fullerton*
Deputy Head Librarian (Cardiff Bay)	*Debra Carter*
Senior Librarian (Cathays Park)	*David Allum*
Librarian (Cathays Park)	*Simon Speight*
Chamber Secretariat / Business Committee	*Sherry Rees*
Table Office Register of Interests / Assembly Standards	*Julie Grant*
Head of Translation Services	*Meinir Pritchard*
Deputy Heads of Translation Services	*Mair Parry Jones* *David Bullock*
Public Information and Education	*Gwen Parry*
Record of Proceedings (Editor)	*John Emyr*
Assistant Editors	*Rhian Watcyn Jones* *Meinir Evans*
Head of Committee Secretariat	*Marie Knox*
Clerk to Local Government & Environment Committee / SE Wales Committee	*Martin Stevenson*
Clerk to Economic Development Committee	*Helen Usher*
Clerk to Health Committee / SW Wales Committee	*Jane Westlake*
Clerk to Under-16 Education Committee	*Julia Annand*
Clerk to Agriculture Committee / N Wales Committee	*Vacant*
Clerk to Post-16 Education and Training Committee	*Delyth Thomas*
Clerk to Audit, Equal Opportunities and	*Andrew George*

ALPHABETICAL LIST OF THE MEMBERS OF
THE NATIONAL ASSEMBLY FOR WALES

BARRETT, Lorraine	*Cardiff South & Penarth/De Caerdydd a Phenarth*	Lab
BATES, Mick	*Montgomeryshire/Maldwyn*	Lib Dem
BLACK, Peter	*South Wales West/De Gorllewin Cymru list*	Lib Dem
BOURNE, Prof Nicholas	*Mid & West Wales/Canolbarth a Gorllewin Cymru list*	Con
BUTLER, Rosemary	*Newport West/Gorllewin Casnewydd*	Lab
CAIRNS, Alun	*South Wales West/De Gorllewin Cymru list*	Con
CHAPMAN, Christine	*Cynon Valley/Cwm Cynon*	Lab
DAFIS, Cynog	*Mid & West Wales/Canolbarth a Gorllewin Cymru list*	PC
DAVIDSON, Jane	*Pontypridd*	Lab
DAVIES, Andrew	*Swansea West/Gorllewin Abertawe*	Lab
DAVIES, David	*Monmouth/Mynwy*	Con
DAVIES, Geraint	*Rhondda*	PC
DAVIES, Glyn	*Mid & West Wales/Canolbarth a Gorllewin Cymru list*	Con
DAVIES, Janet	*South Wales West/De Gorllewin Cymru list*	PC
DAVIES, Jocelyn	*South Wales East/De Dwyrain Cymru list*	PC
DAVIES, Ron	*Caerphilly/Caerffili*	Lab
EDWARDS, Dr Richard	*Preseli Pembrokeshire/Preseli Penfro*	Lab
ELIS-THOMAS, Dafydd	*Meirionydd Nant Conwy*	PC
ESSEX, Sue	*Cardiff North/Gogledd Caerdydd*	Lab
FELD, Val	*Swansea East/Dwyrain Abertawe*	Lab
GERMAN, Michael	*South Wales East/De Dwyrain Cymru list*	Lib Dem
GIBBONS, Brian	*Aberavon/Afan*	Lab
GRAHAM, William	*South Wales East/De Dwyrain Cymru list*	Con
GREGORY, Janice	*Ogmore/Ogwr*	Lab
GRIFFITHS, John	*Newport East/Dwyrain Casnewydd*	Lab
GWYTHER, Christine	*Carmarthen W & S Pembroke/Gorllewin Caerfyrddin a De Penfro*	Lab
HALFORD, Alison	*Delyn*	Lab
HANCOCK, Brian	*Islwyn*	PC
HART, Edwina	*Gower/Gwyr*	Lab
HUMPHREYS, Christine	*North Wales/Gogledd Cymru list*	Lib Dem

HUTT, Jane	*Vale of Glamorgan/Bro Morgannwg*	Lab
JARMAN, Pauline	*South Wales Central/Canol De Cymru list*	PC
JONES, Ann	*Vale of Clwyd/Dyffryn Clwyd*	Lab
JONES, Carwyn	*Bridgend/Pen-y-Bont ar Ogwr*	Lab
JONES, Elin	*Ceredigion*	PC
JONES, Gareth	*Conwy*	PC
JONES, Helen Mary	*Llanelli*	PC
JONES Ieuan Wyn	*Ynys Môn*	PC
LAW, Peter	*Blaenau Gwent*	Lab
LEWIS, Huw	*Merthyr Tydfil & Rhymney*	Lab
LLOYD, Dr Dai	*South Wales West/De Gorllewin Cymru list*	PC
MAREK, Dr John	*Wrexham/Wrecsam*	Lab
MELDING, David	*South Wales Central/Canol De Cymru list*	Con
MICHAEL, Alun	*Mid & West Wales/Canolbarth a Gorllewin Cymru list*	Lab
MIDDLEHURST, Tom	*Alyn & Deeside/Alyn Dyfrdwy*	Lab
MORGAN, Jonathan	*South Wales Central/Canol De Cymru list*	Con
MORGAN, Rhodri	*Cardiff West/Gorllewin Caerdydd*	Lab
NEAGLE, Lynne	*Torfaen*	Lab
PUGH, Alun	*Clwyd West/Gorllewin Clwyd*	Lab
RANDERSON, Jenny	*Cardiff Central/Canol Caerdydd*	Lib Dem
RICHARDS, Rod	*North Wales/Gogledd Cymru list*	Con
ROGERS, Peter	*North Wales/Gogledd Cymru list*	Con
RYDER, Janet	*North Wales/Gogledd Cymru list*	
SINCLAIR, Karen	*Clwyd South/De Clwyd*	Lab
THOMAS, Gwenda	*Neath/Nedd*	Lab
THOMAS, Owen John	*South Wales Central/Canol De Cymru list*	PC
THOMAS, Rhodri	*Carmarthen East & Dinefwr/Dwyrain Caerfyrddin a Dinefwr*	PC
WIGLEY, Dafydd	*Caernarfon*	PC
WILLIAMS, Kirsty	*Brecon & Radnorshire/Brychoiniog a Maesyfed*	Lib Dem
WILLIAMS, Dr Phil	*South Wales East/De Dwyrain Cymru list*	PC

ALPHABETICAL LIST OF THE MEMBERS OF THE NORTHERN IRELAND ASSEMBLY

ADAMS, Gerry; MP	*Belfast West*	SF
ADAMSON, Dr Ian	*Belfast East*	UU
AGNEW, Fraser	*Belfast North*	United U
ALDERDICE, Lord	*Belfast East*	Alliance
ARMITAGE, Pauline	*East Londonderry*	UU
ARMSTRONG, Billy	*Mid-Ulster*	UU
ATTWOOD, Alex	*Belfast West*	SDLP
BEGGS, Roy; MP	*East Antrim*	UU
BELL, Eileen	*North Down*	Alliance
BELL, William B.	*Lagan Valley*	UU
BENSON, Thomas	*Strangford*	UU
BERRY, Paul	*Newry and Armagh*	DUP
BIRNIE, Esmond	*Belfast South*	UU
BOYD, Norman	*South Antrim*	NIUP
BRADLEY, Peadar J.	*South Down*	SDLP
BYRNE, Joe	*West Tyrone*	SDLP
CAMPBELL, Gregory	*East Londonderry*	DUP
CARRICK, Mervyn	*Upper Bann*	DUP
CARSON, Joan	*Fermanagh and South Tyrone*	UU
CLOSE, Seamus; OBE	*Lagan Valley*	Alliance
CLYDE, Wilson	*South Antrim*	DUP
COBAIN, Fred	*Belfast North*	UU
COULTER, Rev Robert	*North Antrim*	UU
DALLAT, John	*East Londonderry*	SDLP
DAVIS, Ivan	*Lagan Valley*	UU
DE BRUN, Bairbre	*Belfast West*	SF
DODDS, Nigel	*Belfast North*	DUP
DOHERTY, Arthur	*East Londonderry*	SDLP
DOHERTY, Pat	*West Tyrone*	SF
DOUGLAS, Boyd	*East Londonderry*	United U
DURKAN, Mark	*Foyle*	SDLP
EMPEY, Sir Reg	*Belfast East*	UU
ERVINE, David	*Belfast East*	PUP
FARREN, Sean	*North Antrim*	SDLP
FEE, John	*Newry and Armagh*	SDLP

FORD, David	*South Antrim*	Alliance
FOSTER, Sam	*Fermanagh and South Tyrone*	UU
GALLAGHER, Tommy	*Fermanagh and South Tyrone*	SDLP
GIBSON, Oliver	*West Tyrone*	DUP
GILDERNEW, Michelle	*Fermanagh and South Tyrone*	SF
GORMAN, Sir John; CVO CBE MC DL	*North Down*	UU
HANNA, Carmel	*Belfast South*	SDLP
HAUGHEY, Dennis	*Mid-Ulster*	SDLP
HAY, William	*Foyle*	DUP
HENDRON, Dr Joe	*Belfast West*	SDLP
HILDITCH, David	*East Antrim*	DUP
HUME, John; MEP MP	*Foyle*	SDLP
HUSSEY, Derek	*West Tyrone*	UU
HUTCHINSON, Billy	*Belfast North*	PUP
HUTCHINSON, Roger	*East Antrim*	NIUP
KANE, Gardiner	*North Antrim*	DUP
KELLY, Gerry	*Belfast North*	SF
KELLY, John	*Mid-Ulster*	SF
KENNEDY, Danny	*Newry and Armagh*	UU
LESLIE, James	*North Antrim*	UU
LEWSLEY, Patricia	*Lagan Valley*	SDLP
MAGINNESS, Alban	*Belfast North*	SDLP
MALLON, Seamus; MP	*Newry and Armagh*	SDLP
MASKEY, Alex	*Belfast West*	SF
McCARTHY, Kieran; JP	*Strangford*	Alliance
McCARTNEY, Robert; MP	*North Down*	UKUP
McCLARTY, David	*East Londonderry*	UU
McCLELLAND, Donovan	*South Antrim*	SDLP
McCREA, Rev Dr William	*Mid-Ulster*	DUP
McDONNELL, Dr Alasdair	*Belfast South*	SDLP
McELDUFF, Barry	*West Tyrone*	SF
McFARLAND, Alan	*North Down*	UU
McGIMPSEY, Michael	*Belfast South*	UU
McGRADY, Eddie; MP	*South Down*	SDLP
McGUINNESS, Martin; MP	*Mid-Ulster*	SF
McHUGH, Gerry	*Fermanagh and South Tyrone*	SF
McLAUGHLIN, Mitchel	*Foyle*	SF

McMENAMIN, Eugene	*West Tyrone*	SDLP
McNAMEE, Pat	*Newry and Armagh*	SF
McWILLIAMS, Prof Monica	*Belfast South*	NI Women
MOLLOY, Francis	*Mid-Ulster*	SF
MORRICE, Jane	*North Down*	NI Women
MORROW, Maurice	*Fermanagh and South Tyrone*	DUP
MURPHY, Conor	*Newry and Armagh*	SF
MURPHY, Mick	*South Down*	SF
NEESON, Sean	*East Antrim*	Alliance
NELIS, Mary	*Foyle*	SF
NESBITT, Dermot	*South Down*	UU
O'CONNOR, Danny	*East Antrim*	SDLP
O'HAGAN, Dara	*Upper Bann*	SF
O'NEILL, Eamonn	*South Down*	SDLP
PAISLEY Jnr, Ian	*North Antrim*	DUP
PAISLEY, Rev Ian; MEP MP	*North Antrim*	DUP
POOTS, Edwin	*Lagan Valley*	DUP
RAMSEY, Sue	*Belfast West*	SF
ROBINSON, Iris	*Strangford*	DUP
ROBINSON, Ken	*East Antrim*	UU
ROBINSON, Mark	*Belfast South*	DUP
ROBINSON, Peter; MP	*Belfast East*	DUP
ROCHE, Patrick	*Lagan Valley*	NIUP
RODGERS, Brid	*Upper Bann*	SDLP
SAVAGE, George	*Upper Bann*	UU
SHANNON, Jim	*Strangford*	DUP
SHIPLEY-DALTON, Duncan	*South Antrim*	UU
TAYLOR, Rt Hon John D; MP	*Strangford*	UU
TIERNEY, John	*Foyle*	SDLP
TRIMBLE, Rt Hon David; MP	*Upper Bann*	UU
WATSON, Denis	*Upper Bann*	United U
WEIR, Peter	*North Down*	UU
WELLS, Jim	*South Down*	DUP
WILSON, Cedric	*Strangford*	NIUP
WILSON, Jim	*South Antrim*	UU
WILSON, Sammy	*Belfast East*	DUP

THE EUROPEAN COMMISSION

The following is a list of the new European Commission with responsibilities:-

Romano PRODI (Italy)	*President*
Neil KINNOCK (UK)	*Vice-president: Administrative Reform*
Loyola de PALACIO (Spain)	
	Vice-president: Relations with the EP, Transport & Energy
Mario MONTI (Italy)	*Competition*
Franz FISCHLER (Austria)	*Agriculture & Fisheries*
Erkki LIIKANEN (Finland)	*Enterprise & Information Society*
Frits BOLKESTEIN (Netherlands)	*Internal Market*
Philippe BUSQUIN (Belgium)	*Research*
Pedro SOLBES MIRA (Spain)	*Economic & Monetary Affairs*
Poul NIELSON (Denmark)	*Development & Humanitarian Aid*
Gunter VERHEUGEN (Germany)	*Enlargement*
Chris PATTEN (UK)	*External Relations*
Pascal LAMY (France)	*Trade*
David BYRNE (Ireland)	*Health & Consumer Protection*
Michel BARNIER (France)	*Regional Policy & Cohesion*
Viviane REDING (Luxembourg)	*Education & Culture*
Michaele SCHREYER (Germany)	*Budget*
Margot WALLSTRÖM (Sweden)	*Environment*
Antonio VITORINO (Portugal)	*Justice & Home Affairs*
Anna DIAMANTOPOULOU (Greece)	*Employment & Social Affairs*

**The vote in the European Parliament to approve the new Commission
is expected to take place on 15th September.**

ALPHABETICAL LIST OF
UNITED KINGDOM MEPs

ATKINS, Sir Robert	*North West*	Con
ATTWOOLL, Elspeth	*Scotland*	Lib Dem
BALFE, Richard	*London*	Lab
BEAZLEY, Christopher	*Eastern*	Con
BETHELL, Lord	*London*	Con
BOWE, David	*Yorkshire & the Humber*	Lab
BOWIS, John	*London*	Con
BRADBOURN, Philip	*West Midlands*	Con
BUSHILL-MATTHEWS, Philip	*West Midlands*	Con
CALLANAN, Martin	*North East*	Con
CASHMAN, Michael	*West Midlands*	Lab
CHICHESTER, Giles	*South West*	Con
CLEGG, Nick	*East Midlands*	Lib Dem
CORBETT, Richard	*Yorkshire & the Humber*	Lab
CORRIE, John	*West Midlands*	Con
DAVIES, Chris	*North West*	Lib Dem
DEVA, Nirj	*South East*	Con
DONNELLY, Alan	*North East*	Lab
DOVER, Den	*North West*	Con
DUFF, Andrew	*Eastern*	Lib Dem
ELLES, James	*South East*	Con
EVANS, Jill	*Wales*	PC
EVANS, Jonathan	*Wales*	Con
EVANS, Robert	*London*	Lab
FARAGE, Nigel	*South East*	UKIP
FORD, Glyn	*South West*	Lab
FOSTER, Jacqui	*North West*	Con
GILL, Neena	*West Midlands*	Lab
GOODWILL, Robert	*Yorkshire & the Humber*	Con
GREEN, Pauline	*London*	Lab

HANNAN, Dan	*South East*	Con
HARBOUR, Malcolm	*West Midlands*	Con
HEATON-HARRIS, Chris	*East Midlands*	Con
HELMER, Roger	*East Midlands*	Con
HOLMES, Michael	*South West*	UKIP
HOWITT, Richard	*Eastern*	Lab
HUDGHTON, Ian	*Scotland*	SNP
HUGHES, Stephen	*North East*	Lab
HUHNE, Chris	*South East*	Lib Dem
HUME, John	*N Ireland*	SDLP
INGLEWOOD, [Lord] Richard	*North West*	Con
JACKSON, Caroline	*South West*	Con
KHANBHAI, Bashir	*Eastern*	Con
KINNOCK,Glenys	*Wales*	Lab
KIRKHOPE, Timothy	*Yorkshire & the Humber*	Con
LAMBERT, Jean	*London*	Green
LUCAS, Dr Caroline	*South East*	Green
LUDFORD, Sarah	*London*	Lib Dem
LYNNE, Liz	*West Midlands*	Lib Dem
MacCORMICK, Ian	*Scotland*	SNP
McAVAN, Linda	*Yorkshire & the Humber*	Lab
McCARTHY, Arlene	*North West*	Lab
McMILLAN-SCOTT, Edward	*Yorkshire & the Humber*	Con
McNALLY, Eryl	*Eastern*	Lab
MARTIN, David	*Scotland*	Lab
MILLER, Bill	*Scotland*	Lab
MORAES, Claude	*London*	Lab
MORGAN, Eluned	*Wales*	Lab
MURPHY, Simon	*West Midlands*	Lab
NEWTON DUNN, Bill	*East Midlands*	Con
NICHOLSON, Emma	*South East*	Lib Dem
NICHOLSON, Jim	*N Ireland*	UU

O'TOOLE, Mo	*North East*	Lab
PAISLEY, Rev Ian	*N Ireland*	DUP
PARRISH, Neil	*South West*	Con
PERRY, Roy	*South East*	Con
PROVAN, James	*South East*	Con
PURVIS, John	*Scotland*	Con
READ, Imelda (Mel)	*East Midlands*	Lab
SIMPSON, Brian	*North West*	Lab
SKINNER, Peter	*South East*	Lab
STEVENSON, Struan	*Scotland*	Con
STOCKTON, Alexander [Earl of]	*South West*	Con
STURDY, Robert	*Eastern*	Con
SUMBERG, David	*North West*	Con
TANNOCK, Charles	*London*	Con
TAYLOR, Catherine	*Scotland*	Lab
TITFORD, Jeffrey	*Eastern*	UKIP
TITLEY, Gary	*North West*	Lab
VAN ORDEN, Geoffrey	*Eastern*	Con
VILLIERS, Theresa	*London*	Con
WALLIS, Diana	*Yorkshire & the Humber*	Lib Dem
WATSON, Graham	*South West*	Lib Dem
WATTS, Mark	*South East*	Lab
WHITEHEAD, Philip	*East Midlands*	Lab
WYN, Eurig	*Wales*	PC
WYNN, Terry	*North West*	Lab